D0945291

THE REAL CHEKHOV

Chekhov in Melikhovo 1897

THE REAL CHEKHOV

An Introduction to Chekhov's Last Plays

by

David Magarshack

LONDON

GEORGE ALLEN & UNWIN LTD

RUSKIN HOUSE   MUSEUM STREET

© *George Allen & Unwin Ltd 1972*

ISBN 0 04 891044 9

*Printed in Great Britain
in 11 point Fournier type
by Cox & Wyman Ltd,
London, Fakenham and Reading*

52655

CONTENTS

INTRODUCTION

The stage is a scaffold on which the
playwright is executed.
Chekhov (Letters)

Chekhov's chief executioners both in Russia and England (not to mention the United States) have been the directors, who quite consistently disregard Chekhov's intention in writing his plays, inevitably producing a crude distortion of their characters and a travesty of their themes. 'It is highly necessary', Mr Basil Ashton declared in a letter to the *New Statesman* (11 September 1970)

> for anyone who really cares about the classics to insist on the theatre providing a few directors who respect their author, rather than seeking, solely, to air their egos. . . . It is only by the *writings* of dramatists that the theatre survives, and directors should consider this fact as strongly as modern conductors seem able to consider the importance of the composer. As I happen to be a director myself, I cannot be accused of self-interest when I repeat that a director is only of any use when he serves the dramatist and allows the public to see and understand what the dramatist intended.

Chekhov himself had no delusions about the 'egos' of the directors. 'Chuck the theatre,' he advised a fellow-writer. 'With a few exceptions it is nothing but an asylum for megalomaniacs.' It is not a director's 'ego', however, that is the chief culprit in the 'execution' of Chekhov on the stage and screen. What makes him so consistently ignore Chekhov's intention is his complete ignorance of the background of Chekhov's plays as well as of his personal life, of his views of the literary and political problems of his day, and of the circumstances relating to the genesis of his plays. It is the total incomprehension of the central themes of Chekhov's plays that explains why directors are so prone to indulge in wild fantasies. Their ignorance of Chekhov's personal life all too often results in grotesque inventions, which have led some well-known actors to make up to look like Chekhov in the part of Trigorin in *The Seagull*.

It was ignorance of Chekhov's attitude to the literary and political problems of his day that led Stanislavsky to describe Chekhov's comedies as 'great tragedies of Russian life'. This cardinal misconception gave rise to the sadness-cum-despair syndrome which became such a characteristic feature of most Chekhov productions.

This was already manifest in Stanislavsky's production of *The Seagull* at the close of the first season of the Moscow Art Theatre in December 1898. It was the last play of the season. The theatre had scored a moderate success with its first play, a mediocre historical drama by Count Alexey Tolstoy, but the other five plays in its repertoire had been dismal failures. The whole future of the Moscow Art Theatre depended on the success or failure of *The Seagull*. It was a resounding success and the theatre was saved. At the time this success was attributed to the 'mood' of the play and the *mises en scène*. Stanislavsky was responsible for both. The 'mood', which was to become so generally accepted as the most characteristic feature of Chekhov's plays, may have corresponded with the despondent mood of the Russian educated classes before the revolutions of 1905 and 1917, but it had nothing whatever to do with Chekhov's play. As for the *mises en scène*, they were made up entirely of the inventions and gimmicks Stanislavsky had used so successfully in his amateur productions: the nocturnal countryside noises of croaking frogs, the crake of the land-rail, the chirrings of the crickets, the ominous reddish light hovering over the darkness, and the slow tolling of a distant church bell which, Stanislavsky explains in his 'score' of *The Seagull*, 'help the audience to get the feel of the sad monotonous life of the characters'. Here we have the birth of the sadness-cum-despair syndrome, which threw Chekhov into a fit of blind fury when the play was performed for him later. Indeed, Chekhov was so furious with Stanislavsky's misinterpretation of his comedy that, unable to demand Stanislavsky's dismissal from his own theatre, he kept insisting on the instant dismissal of the young actress who played Nina and whose 'sad and monotonous' mood and bursts of loud sobbing (neither she nor Stanislavsky had the faintest idea of the real meaning of the last scene of the play), Chekhov declared had ruined his play. He was to say the same thing about Stanislavsky's production of *The Cherry Orchard*.

The two never got on. Chekhov treated Stanislavsky with half-amused contempt. Stanislavsky, as he was to admit many years later in his reminiscences, thought Chekhov to be 'supercilious and insincere'. But the reason for their disagreement lay much deeper than mere personal antipathy, and it also explains why Stanislavsky so persistently misunderstood and misinterpreted Chekhov's plays. To Chekhov, the son of an impoverished former serf, the sale of the Gayev estate and its unproductive cherry orchard was, as he makes Trofimov explain to Anya at the end of Act II, merely the inevitable consequence of the life of people who for centuries had lived at the expense of those whom they did not admit 'further than their entrance hall'. They were not tragic figures at all, but characters in a comedy. To Stanislavsky, the son and heir of a rich factory owner, they were, on the contrary, characters of 'a great tragedy', as indeed he would have regarded the failure of his father's lucrative business as 'a great tragedy'.

The most extraordinary thing in the whole history of European drama is the contemptuous dismissal by directors of Chekhov's own description of *The Seagull* and *The Cherry Orchard* as comedies. They are quick enough to acknowledge Chekhov as one of the greatest dramatists of his age, but they do not seem to take him seriously when he claims his two plays to be comedies. Do they really believe that Chekhov did not know the difference between a comedy and a tragedy? The main reason for this almost unanimous disregard of Chekhov's intention in writing the two plays is, of course, that both plays seem to end unhappily for some of their chief characters. In *The Seagull*, Konstantin's suicide is generally interpreted as being due to an unhappy love affair. B. N. Livanov, director of the Moscow Art Theatre's first revival of *The Seagull* after over sixty years, did not hesitate to distort Chekhov's intention by the insertion of new dialogue and to mutilate the play by completely ignoring Chekhov's stage directions. According to Livanov, Konstantin commits suicide because he is 'disillusioned by Nina's rejection of him'. This is what Stanislavsky and countless other directors took to be the reason for Konstantin's suicide. When, towards the end of the last act, Konstantin asks Nina where she is going, and she replies simply enough that she is going back to the town, Stanislavsky interpolates the melodramatic note: 'This is where he really dies'. But, surely, if disappointed love made him commit suicide, he should have 'died' earlier at the time when Nina had told him that she was still in love with Trigorin.

Konstantin's suicide does not make *The Seagull* into a tragedy, in the dramatic meaning of the word, any more than does Uncle Vanya's suicide at the end of the third act of *The Wood Demon* – the first Tolstoyan version of *Uncle Vanya* – which Chekhov also described as a comedy and provided with a happy ending strictly in accordance with the Tolstoyan notion (made abundantly plain in Tolstoy's famous story 'The Devil') that a man who lusts after a married woman ought to put a bullet through his head. Konstantin's suicide has a much deeper significance. It concerns Konstantin's realisation that his uncritical acceptance of the ideas of the *avant-garde* symbolist movement had resulted in his failure as a writer, a theme which has wider implications and is as pertinent today as it was in Chekhov's day.

Chekhov strongly objected to being labelled a 'realist'. To him labels like 'realism' or 'naturalism' were just, as he expressed it through the mouth of Uncle Vanya, 'nothing but a lot of nonsense'. Indeed, what makes *The Seagull* and *The Cherry Orchard* comedies in the strict meaning of the word is that both plays are based on the principle that characterises both low and high comedy, namely, the incongruity between reality and delusion. The clash between things as they are and things as they are believed to be by the characters of a comedy is also one of the most characteristic aspects of a Chekhov play. When Mrs Ranevsky is told that her estate and the unproductive, though aesthetically beautiful, cherry orchard are quite certain to be sold at a public auction, she refuses to believe it, while her brother Gayev, a confirmed escapist, takes refuge in his obsession with billiards (a situation that would have appeared more credible to English and American audiences if his obsession had been with golf). When the slow-witted country schoolmaster Medvedenko declares at the very beginning of the first act of *The Seagull* that Nina and Konstantin are in love and that in Konstantin's play 'their souls will unite in an endeavour to give expression to one and the same artistic ideas', the preciosity of such an utterance should immediately arouse the suspicions of a perceptive audience and prepare it for the following scene between Nina and Konstantin, which far from being a love scene, as it is usually played, shows the first serious rift in the boy-and-girl romance of the two chief characters of the comedy.

The Moscow Art Theatre's last production of *The Seagull* shows all too clearly how easy it is for a director to destroy and mutilate a great play by totally ignoring the playwright's intention. Stanislavsky at least was very careful not to interfere with Chekhov's text, which cannot be said of Livanov who had no compunction at all in amending, cutting, rewriting and, generally, mangling Chekhov's text to satisfy his own philistine ideas of how the play should have been written. English and American directors have it much easier. It is the translator who does most of the mangling for them.

Chekhov burst upon the English stage at a time when Stanislavsky and his Moscow Art Theatre were at the height of their fame in the West. It was natural, therefore, that Stanislavsky's idea of Chekhov's plays as 'tragedies of Russian life' should have been accepted without question. It was also at the same time – that is, in the early twenties – that the only widely recognised translator from the Russian was Constance Garnett, whose admirable zeal and indefatigable perseverance was only equalled by her inadequate knowledge of Russian which never rose above the dictionary level. It was Constance Garnett who for a long time monopolised the presentation of Chekhov plays on the English stage, leaving a ghastly legacy of misconceptions and mis-representations that made them synonymous in the mind of the English spectator with sadness, gloom and despair.

The frequent mistranslations of Russian colloquial expressions and idioms necessarily introduce an element of quaintness which is totally absent from the original text. This element of quaintness is intensified by the attempt, so beloved by directors who have no idea of their author's intention, to convey the 'Russian' atmosphere, either by the introduction of Russian words into the dialogue or by insisting that the actors should use Russian names and patronymics which are usually mispronounced so horribly that no Russian would be able to recognise them. Why insist on patronymics when they not only con-fuse the audience but also interfere with the rhythm of English speech, and when the slightest Russian variation of them, such as Potapych instead of Potapovich in the *Three Sisters*, is quite meaningless to an English or American ear? The same is true of the Russian diminutives which are also invariably mispronounced and whose infinite variations convey different meanings beyond the comprehension of an English-speaking audience. Why insist on making the actors pronounce

Petya or Alexandr when all it means is 'darling Peter' and 'Alexander'? What actually happens, therefore, is that what the director takes to be the 'Russian atmosphere' is not Russian at all. It is nothing but a fraud perpetrated upon an audience to cover up a director's ignorance.

This failure to see the hidden meaning of a word or a name is also true of American translators of Chekhov's plays. Korney Chukovsky, the well-known Russian critic, translator and poet, has this to say about Miss Marian Fell's translations of Chekhov plays in his recently-published book on *Translation as a High Art Form*:

> Marian Fell excelled herself in her translations of Chekhov plays. She has made up a hundredfold for all the howlers and mistakes ever made by her Russian colleagues. The Russian scholar and art critic Batyushkov, mentioned in *Uncle Vanya*, becomes a Greek Orthodox priest, for she seems to have confused the surname Batyushkov for *batyushka*, the Russian word for a priest. In another play she has transformed the radical critic Dobrolyubov into St Francis of Assisi by translating his name literally as 'a lover of goodness' and jumping to the conclusion that Chekhov must have meant St Francis. In *Ivanov* Count Shabelsky says that he has spent twenty thousand roubles on all sorts of cures. She translates it: 'In the course of my life I have nursed several thousand sick people.' Indeed, the whole character of Count Shabelsky has been smashed to smithereens by her translation of a short sentence. Chekhov wrote: '*Tebya, brat, zayela sreda*', which means, 'You, my dear fellow, are the victim of your environment.' Miss Fell, mistaking *sreda* for the Russian word for Wednesday, translates it: 'You have got out of your bed on the wrong side.' She describes Gogol as a Russian fabulist. Every page of Miss Fell's translation of Chekhov's plays is teeming with blunders which completely distort Chekhov's text. But let us suppose for a moment that, overcome with shame, Miss Fell eliminated all her howlers and mistakes, that *batyushka* became, as in Chekhov, Batyushkov, that St Francis became Dobrolyubov, that, in short, her translations became a faithful translinear rendering of the Russian text, even then it would have been of no use at all, for it would have lacked the most important quality of the original, its style, without which Chekhov is not Chekhov.

But, style apart, it is the ignorance of the background of the plays that more often results in the total misconception of their author's intention. A good example of this is Constance Garnett's substitution of Chekhov's Hamlet quotation in the first act of *The Seagull* by another quotation from the same play. When Chekhov first submitted his play to the censor prior to its performance at the Alexandrinsky Theatre in Petersburg, the censor objected to several passages at the beginning of the first act in which Konstantin referred in scathing terms to his mother's relationship with Trigorin. For a son to speak so disrespectfully of his mother was considered to be quite inadmissible in a public performance of a play. Chekhov was told that unless he deleted those passages he would obtain no permission for the performance of his play on the stage of what at the time was not a private but a state theatre. He, therefore, decided to make Konstantin recite Hamlet's lines to Gertrude, 'Nay, but to live in the rank sweat of an enseamed bed', etc., so as to reveal Konstantin's disapproval of Arkadina's relations with Trigorin and, at the same time, make it quite impossible for the censor to object to it. To introduce the lines and to heighten their dramatic effect, he had to give Arkadina Gertrude's preceding lines, as a cue for her son's violent outburst. Constance Garnett totally failed to grasp the relevance of the Hamlet quotation. She therefore substituted two lines Hamlet uses for the introduction of his own play: 'And let me wring your heart, for so I shall / If it be made of penetrable stuff', an utterly inappropriate quotation, for it was not Konstantin's intention to wring anybody's heart, but merely to give a dramatic form to the cosmic conflict between the two primary super-human figures of the World Soul and Satan as conceived by the poet and mystic Vladimir Solovyov, one of the leading figures of the Russian Symbolist Movement, of which Konstantin was an ardent adherent. Needless to say, Constance Garnett completely misses the meaning of the seagull theme (as, indeed, do most of the directors and actors of the play) by the mistranslation of a single word in Nina's speech in the last act by making Nina say, 'What matters is not fame... but knowing how to be patient', instead of 'knowing how to endure'.

The mistranslation of a single word may sometimes be enough to ruin a Chekhov play by reducing one of its chief characters to a state of utter idiocy. There was the case of a well-known director who used a 'new' translation of *The Cherry Orchard* (directors are very keen on using 'new' translations without bothering to find out whether the translator has the qualifications for it) in which Trofimov's advice to Lopakhin not to throw his arms about is translated: 'Don't flap your hands'. Lopakhin in this production kept flapping his hands all through the play. He would do so even in the middle of a speech, pausing to flap his hands whenever he wished to emphasise a point. It was no use explaining to the director in question the utter senselessness of Lopakhin's hand-flapping. He seemed quite convinced that the flapping had some deep meaning, some mystic revelation of the 'Russian soul', some Dostoevskian streak of submissiveness and suffering in the far from submissive or suffering Lopakhin.

Quite often a translator will deliberately mistranslate a single word to justify a generally accepted perversion of a Chekhov character. Elisaveta Fen, the translator of the Penguin edition of Chekhov's plays, does just that in translating the second line of Chebutykin's version of 'Tarara-boom-di-ay' as 'I'm sitting on a toomb-di-ay', as a final confirmation of the Chekhovian sadness-cum-despair syndrome. Miss Fen, of course, knows very well that the Russian word *toomba* does not mean a tomb but a round stone post at the corner of a street in a Russian town. The intention of the second line is simply to put the finishing touch to the man who describes himself as 'not a human being at all', whose creed is that 'nothing matters', and who does nothing to save his favourite Irene's husband-to-be from being shot dead in a duel at which he as doctor is present. Miss Fen has become the victim of the general lunacy which is so characteristic a feature of the Chekhov cult.

Another feature of this cult is boredom. 'In *Uncle Vanya*', an English critic wrote in a recent issue of a well-known Sunday paper, 'the whole theme is the boredom of comfortable provincial life'![1] The view of a lunatic? Not at all. It simply is one more proof of the well-known phenomenon, namely that once somebody or something becomes the object of a cult then even the craziest idea can be accepted without questioning. That is the explanation of why an English director does not hesitate to sit down with several translations of a Chekhov play and proceed to write his own 'version', for he is convinced that he *knows* what Chekhov *ought to have written*, and he manipulates his or

[1] *Sunday Times*, 15 November 1970.

somebody else's version of the play accordingly: gloom, despondency, a dialogue that makes no sense, a few Russian words scattered here and there, a general atmosphere of gloom and despair, and scenery that is the work of some celebrated stage designer and that by itself is sufficient to kill the play stone dead. There is, furthermore, the strong itch felt by some ignorant, fashionable directors to introduce a 'new slant' into a Chekhov play. In one production of *The Cherry Orchard* Mrs Ranevsky, it is made apparent, was about to have, or is having, an affair with Yasha of all people, for does not Gayev declare that his sister is an immoral woman? It is true that such idiocies are rare, though not so rare as an attempt to raise a laugh in the audience by making Arkadina destroy the whole meaning of the first scene of the second act of *The Seagull* by sagging and holding her side after trying to convince everybody how young she still is.

Stanislavsky was fully aware of the uncontrollable impulses of actors and directors to contrive something 'new', to give full scope to some new trend, some passing whim, some gimmick that might provide publicity and help to furbish their reputations. His remedy can be summed up in one word: *subtext* – undertext, which does not mean reading between the lines of the text, but an attempt to reconstruct the life of the characters from the sometimes insufficient data of the text. Unfortunately, the *subtext* does not prevent a director who is ignorant of the background or the genesis of the play or of the dramatist's intention in writing it, from superimposing his own ideas on it and in this way distorting both its meaning and the motives of its characters. Chekhov himself was loath to discuss his plays with the actors. But he did say something to them that sounds so simple that very few people have paid any attention to it. 'Why don't you *read* my play? It is all there!' In fact, *it is all there*. The trouble is that in reading a Chekhov play, directors and actors seem to be bereft of all commonsense by the nonsense that has been written and accepted by critics, academics and directors for the past seventy years. When urged that new movements in drama justified a new approach to his plays, Chekhov's reply was that no conditions justified a lie.

The aim of this new volume of introductions to Chekhov's last four plays is that it should act as a complimentary volume to my earlier volume, *Chekhov the Dramatist*, and should be an attempt to *read* the plays in accordance with Chekhov's advice, in the hope that it might give directors and actors a clearer idea of Chekhov's own conception of them and make it possible for the audience to understand what the dramatist intended. In this way the fusion of Chekhov's and the actor's idea of a character could result, as Chekhov declared, 'in the creation of a work of art'.

THE SEAGULL

Introduction

In *The Seagull* Chekhov deals with the problem of the nature of creative art. It was a problem that had become particularly acute at the time with the emergence of the Symbolist movement which, like every other art movement at its inception, was extremely intolerant, fanatical and militant in its demands for new forms and the abolition of all literary and dramatic traditions. The Symbolists were convinced that 'the inner meaning of the theatre' did not differ from 'the primitive Dionysian orgies', and they regarded the greatest task of the stage to be the elimination of all consciousness of everyday life and the concentration on subconscious mystical experience. In all Symbolist plays a realistic situation is treated merely as a point of departure for mysticism. The general tendency of Symbolist drama was to show fleeting happenings and the capricious play of the imagination, that is to say, a transcendental, reality. They used stage directions to assert their right to a subjective and idealistic conception of the dramatist's intention. The function o dramatic dialogue was not, according to them, the advancement of the dramatic action by a clash of wills, for they thought of the characters on the stage not as living people, but as hieroglyphics behind which a different kind of world must be felt. Despairing of the ability of the actor to embody their drama on the stage, they turned to the marionette. They believed that by the automatic copying of human actions the marionette could be used as a tool for switching the action over from the real world of cause and effect into a world of purely arbitrary causality, for in the ideal world of symbols only arbitrary causality was possible.

Chekhov dismissed the 'decadents', as the Symbolists were called, as 'frauds'. Talking to a young Russian writer about two years after the publication of *The Seagull*, he declared:

As for the decadents, they're frauds and not decadents, the lot of them. They're selling shoddy goods. Religion, mysticism and all that sort of thing . . . They made it all up. Don't believe them. And their legs are not 'pale'[1] at all, as one of their poets claims. They are hairy like the legs of other men.

Chekhov never took part in a public debate on any literary problems. He usually discussed them through the mouths of his characters. He preferred to attack the Symbolist movement in an indirect way by making Konstantin Treplyov, one of the chief characters of *The Seagull*, write a play based on the ideas of Vladimir Solovyov, poet, mystic and philosopher, a close friend of Fyodor Dostoevsky, and one of the leading lights of the Russian Symbolist movement. In his play Konstantin does his best to give a dramatic form to Solovyov's conception of the World Soul as, to quote Solovyov, 'a living being, the first of all living beings, *materia prima*, and the substratum of the created world.' Solovyov considered it 'the future potential mother of the world, existing outside God, corresponding as an ideal addition to the eternally actual Father of the three-in-one God'. As for the Fallen Angel (who also appears in Konstantin's play), Solovyov claimed that he had 'his sphere of action in the World Soul, a principle of a dual nature, placed as it is between God and the principle hostile to Him.' It was apparently Konstantin's intention to dramatise this cosmic conflict between the World Soul and the Fallen Angel. But his mother, provoked by Konstantin's furious attack on her for 'living openly with that novelist' (as he expressed it in a censored passage of the play), did her best to put an abrupt end to his play by her taunting remark about its being a 'decadent' play, her objection to the smell of sulphur, and the derision with which she declared that Dr Dorn had taken off his hat to the Devil, the Father of all Evil.

Chekhov expressed his objections to Symbolist art and abstract art in general through Dr Dorn, a romantic sympathetic to the new trends in literature. Dr Dorn finds Konstantin's attempt to take his subject from the realm of abstract ideas fully justified, but he deplores the fact that the expression of this idea was not sufficiently 'clear and definite'. A dramatist – or indeed any other creative writer – Chekhov insists, must have a clear idea why he is writing his play or novel, for otherwise, as Dr Dorn puts it, 'he is bound to lose his way and his talent will be

---

[1] White or pale was one of the 'mystic' adjectives of the Symbolist movement. Indeed, one prominent Symbolist writer, Boris Bugaev, even changed his name to Andrey Bely (Andrey the White).

his ruin'. This is the central theme of Chekhov's play and Chekhov goes on to develop it to its inevitable end.

The other theme of the play, the 'seagull' theme, appears only towards the end of the second act, though a vague hint of its existence appears in the first act in Nina's remark that she is drawn to the lake 'like a seagull'. The 'seagull' theme reaches its climax at the end of the play, where both themes coalesce in the last scene between Konstantin and Nina.

Act One

There is no trace of the 'experimental' theatre advocated by Konstantin in Chekhov's meagre but quite sufficient descriptions of the interior of the stage. On the contrary, Chekhov was not in the least worried by the conventional stage, which suited his purpose very well and which is so much part of his art that any attempt to make it conform to any 'modern' trend in stage design or construction must have a most damaging effect on the play as a whole. The same is true of Chekhov's stage directions, which can only be tampered with, altered or ignored, at the risk of destroying his play. For the slightest 'new slant' given even to a seemingly unimportant situation is bound to leave an ugly scar on the action of the play, and often lead to a distortion of its meaning. Chekhov's stage direction *'through tears'*, which occurs so often in his plays, merely means 'deeply moved'. In a letter to Nemirovich-Danchenko, the co-director of the Moscow Art Theatre, Chekhov wrote on 23 October 1903: 'You will often find the stage direction "through tears" in my plays, but that only indicates the mood of the characters, not tears.' Again, the stage direction *'a pause'* does not mean an injunction for everybody on the stage to lapse into a state of torpid inaction, which is supposed to be expressive of some meaningful, though obscure, 'Chekhovian' mood. What it means is simply that every character on the stage has to express his own individual attitude to the dramatic situation that is implicit in the pause.

Sc. 1: Masha and Medvedenko

Masha belongs to the brilliant gallery of women-predators in Chekhov's plays. All of them are in their different ways 'birds of prey' and 'destroyers', as Dr Astrov calls Helen in *Uncle Vanya*. They all shun productive work. In *The Seagull* Masha, in a sentence struck out by Chekhov for fear of the censor's objections, declares that her mother had brought her up 'like a fairy princess in a flower' and she gives that as the reason why she 'can't do anything'. In *Uncle Vanya* Sonia tells Helen that 'there is plenty to do if you really wanted to'. But Helen is too 'indolent' to do anything. In *The Three Sisters* Natasha, the most

Satanic predator of them all, makes her husband and her lover do all
the work of looking after their children. All her energies are con-
centrated on destroying the three sisters.

All three of the 'predators' seem to be eaten up with the desire to
draw attention to themselves. In Helen's case it is her beauty that
adequately fulfils this function. In the third act of *The Three Sisters*
Natasha walks across the stage in silence with a lighted candle in her
hand, provoking the comment from one of the sisters that she walks as
if she had herself set fire to the town: but it is not to the town, but to the
home of the three sisters that she has set fire. However, it is Masha in
The Seagull who is the greatest exhibitionist of them all. Her 'disgusting
habit' of taking snuff is only the outward manifestation of this com-
pulsive desire to draw attention to herself. Her constant protestations
of unhappiness are a much more reliable key to her true character. She
cherishes so much not her unhappy love for Konstantin, who, she knows
very well, despises her as a 'confounded nuisance' [literally: 'an insufferable creature'], but the opportunity this affords her of wearing
her broken heart on her sleeve. She enjoys telling Medvedenko at the
opening of the play that she is wearing black because she is in mourning
for her life, while at the same time concealing from him the real reason
for her over-dramatised statement, except by vague hints which the
slow-witted Medvedenko, whom she had already decided to marry, is
certainly the last person to make sense of. It is not a question of money,
she assures him after his objection that his own circumstances were
worse than hers, for 'even a pauper can be happy ... I'd rather a
hundred times go about in rags and beg than ...' Than what? Than to
be treated with contempt by Konstantin? She is touched by his love
and is sorry she cannot reciprocate it. 'That's all ...' Not all, surely, for
only a few days later she tells Trigorin that she is going to marry the
schoolmaster in spite of his poverty and his mother and the large family
he has to support on his beggarly salary. She goes on telling all and
sundry that she intends to tear her love by the roots from her heart,
or that she is trailing her life like an endless train behind her, or that she
does not wish to go on living; but all that does not prevent her from
enjoying a drink, marrying Medvedenko, having a child by him and
revealing by every word she utters the absence of any sense of responsibility towards her family or anybody else for that matter. To take her
protestations seriously, let alone interpret them as characteristic of 'the

gloom and despondency' of Chekhov's characters in general is not only silly: it shows how fixed this preposterous idea has become in the minds of those who pretend to admire Chekhov's genius. Can anyone really take Masha seriously when, chatting with Trigorin over a drink at the beginning of the third act after Konstantin's attempted suicide, she tells him that if Konstantin had been gravely wounded, she would not have lived 'for another minute'? Could anyone believe for a moment that after Konstantin's suicide at the end of the play, she would also have committed suicide? Would she not be more likely to find another good reason for telling people that she was about to tear something or other from her heart 'by the roots'? Masha shows her true character when Sorin asks her to tell her father about the barking of the dogs at night. Her reply is terse and to the point: she does not care a damn about the old man or his sister being kept awake by the barking of the dogs. She was not going to say anything to her father: 'Leave me out of it!'

Medvedenko is the type of foolish, good-natured and decent fellow who is the right sort of man to be exploited by a predator like Masha. He has a great reverence for learning but unfortunately does not possess the brains to make any use of it. 'You read Buckle and Spencer', Dr Dorn tells him in an excised passage, 'but you have no more knowledge than the nightwatchman. As far as you know the earth may be held up by whales.' But Medvedenko retorts rather diffidently that he knows that the earth is round and, hurt by Dr Dorn's scepticism, goes on complaining about his poor circumstances which make it a matter of indifference to him whether the earth is round or square. Medvedenko's *alter ego* is Yepikhodov in *The Cherry Orchard*, except that Yepikhodov is a character in a farce rather than in a comedy.

Sc. 2: Konstantin and Sorin

Sorin is a retired high court judge who has reached the highest rank in the civil service, that of a Regular State Councillor, which entitles him to be addressed as Your Excellency, a title that cannot possibly be translated literally, since it is reserved for people of ambassadorial rank in English. He is a typical townsman who hates country life and is quite incapable of running a country estate.

He is one of the least complicated characters in the play. In this he is quite unlike his nephew Konstantin, in whom Chekhov portrayed the revolutionary Symbolist dramatist of his day, whose cocksureness, intolerance and fanaticism is so familiar a phenomenon of the theatrical scene in England and America today that it makes *The Seagull* one of the most 'modern' plays of the entire Chekhov dramatic canon.

Konstantin is convinced that his play will revolutionise the art of the theatre:

> The curtain, the first wing, the second and beyond that open space. No scenery. You just look across towards the lake and the horizon. The curtain goes up at exactly [!] half past eight, just when the moon rises. If Nina's late, then of course [!] the whole effect will be ruined.

But it surely must have occurred to Konstantin, who was far from being a fool, that if the effect of his play depended on its being performed on his uncle's country estate with the open space provided by a lake and on the *exact* time of the rising of the moon, then its success could hardly be relied on to produce the world-shattering revolution on which he counted. That is where the real reason for his conflict with his mother must be sought. His mother was a famous actress and to convert her would be just the thing to ensure the triumph of his ideas. To persuade her to be present at the performance of his play he had to tell her the lie that it was 'just a joke'. Having given her consent, she seemed to be 'in a bad temper'. Why? Konstantin put his finger on the weakest spot of his mother's character: she was jealous of Nina! She was forty-three, Trigorin was in his mid-thirties. In his mother's circle of literary and stage 'celebrities', in which Konstantin felt that everybody regarded him as a 'nonentity', Trigorin, as Konstantin put it in the last act, managed 'to make the best of both worlds', that is to say, keep his liaison with the famous actress while having an occasional affair with someone else in their permissive circle. But it was quite a different thing if Trigorin took it into his head to have a serious affair with a young, innocent, ecstatic girl like Nina. 'Already', Konstantin tells Sorin, 'she is against my play because she fears that her novelist might fancy Nina'. It is true Chekhov had to change this line at the insistence of the censor to 'because Nina is acting in it and not she', a highly improbable reason for his mother's objection to his play. No, Konstantin, who had made a most thorough study of his mother's character, knew perfectly well the real cause of his mother's jealousy. Not that it worried him at the moment: he was so much in love with Nina that it never occurred to him that Nina's feelings for him were certainly not those of a girl in love. Indeed, for a girl in love Nina seems to be peculiarly insensitive to Konstantin's extravagant claim to have written a masterpiece that would put an end to the conventional theatre. She is, on the contrary, quite contemptuous of Konstantin's play. Had she ever been in love with him? If she had, if their boy-and-girl romance had been closer than mere friendship, they would not have used the formal second person plural when addressing each other throughout the play. Unfortunately, in English it is impossible to convey this subtle shift towards intimacy in the relationship between a man and a woman which is brought about by the change over from second person plural to second person singular. But even so, their dialogue at their first meeting makes their true relationship quite clear: on the one hand, Konstantin, who is 'deliriously happy' at the sound of Nina's footsteps, and who greets her rapturously; on the other, Nina, who pours cold water on his excitement by declaring that she would have to leave in half an hour, that is, almost immediately after her performance. After Sorin's diplomatic departure to summon the audience for the play, Nina shows a rather unenthusiastic response to Konstantin's advances.

KONSTANTIN. We're quite alone.
NINA. I thought there was someone there.
KONSTANTIN. There is no one. (*A kiss.*)

It is Konstantin who kisses Nina. This is not the uninhibited 'lingering kiss' Nina exchanges with Trigorin a few days later at the end of the third act. Far from responding, Nina does her utmost to divert Konstantin's attention from herself.

NINA. What tree is this?

It is hardly credible that a country-girl like Nina should not be able to distinguish one common tree from another. Besides, why this sudden interest in trees?

KONSTANTIN. An elm.

By this time Konstantin is quite obviously put out by Nina's reluctance to respond, and his replies get more and more laconic and resentful.

NINA. Why is it so dark?
KONSTANTIN. Well, it's evening. Everything's getting dark.

He implores her not to rush away after the play, but she is adamant. She does not want him to follow her to her house, and she certainly does not relish the idea of his standing beneath her window all night (in Symbolist plays it is usual for the lover to spend the night looking up at the window of his beloved). She was afraid that the nightwatchman might see him and, besides, their dog was not used to him and would start barking. The sound of approaching footsteps saves her from continuing a dialogue that was becoming more and more strained.

After this welcome interruption, during which Konstantin gives a few instructions to Yakov about the methylated spirit and the sulphur – 'There must be a smell of sulphur,' he insists, little dreaming that the smell of sulphur would ruin his play – Nina changes the conversation to a subject much nearer to her heart. She begins questioning Konstantin about Trigorin, and her questions quite clearly suggest a more than merely literary interest in the celebrated author. She starts by admitting that she feels nervous, but that is not because she is afraid of his mother: it was Trigorin she was terrified of.

NINA. . . . a famous writer. . . . Is he young?
KONSTANTIN. Yes.
NINA. His stories are wonderful!
KONSTANTIN (*coldly*). Don't know. Haven't read them.

Quite a change from his friendly reference to Trigorin a little earlier in his conversation with Sorin, in which he described the novelist as a decent fellow, though he repeated what was obviously the general opinion of Trigorin as a writer, namely that, though charming and able, nobody would want to read him after Tolstoy and Zola.

Nina is stung to the quick by Konstantin's cavalier dismissal of her literary idol. She retorts with quite a blistering criticism of Konstantin's play.

NINA. It is difficult to act in your play. There are no living people in it.

Konstantin dismisses Nina's objections with contempt: in his play, as in other Symbolist plays, there are no living people: in his play all living creatures are extinct! But unimpressed by Konstantin's interpretation of drama as an art form in which life must be shown not 'as it is' but 'as we see it in our dreams', Nina delivers her *coup de grâce*:

NINA. There is little action in your play. It is just good enough to be read aloud.[1] I think there ought to be love in a play.

Fortunately, the arrival of the first spectators makes it impossible for Konstantin to enlighten Nina on the conventionality of such a view. They hurry off to the stage and we do not see them again together till the middle of the second act in which Nina is already head over heels in love with Trigorin. They do not meet at all in the third act, at the beginning of which Nina invites Trigorin 'to come and take' her, an invitation which he accepts with alacrity at the end of it.

The Play

Pauline, whose only aim in life is to be the mistress of the man she loves, is quite naturally plagued with recurrent fits of jealousy which Dr Dorn takes philosophically, except when they are in danger of becoming a bit too loud and violent, when he resorts to humming a snatch from some operatic aria or popular song, a way of escape from a difficult situation which can be compared to Gayev's use of billiard terms on similar occasions.

Shamrayev, a retired regular army officer of low rank, who finished up as the inefficient manager of Sorin's estate, has had a smattering of a classical education which has grown very rusty with the passage of time which leads him to confuse the Latin proverbs *de gustibus non disputantur* with *de mortuis aut bene aut nihil*. He has been something of a stage Johnnie which makes him fond of claiming to have been a close friend of once famous actors and actresses, whom Arkadina dismisses with a laugh as 'antediluvian'. He still has something left

---

[1] Chekhov wrote: *Tol'ko chitka. Tol'ko*—only *chitka*—a theatrical term meaning the preliminary reading of a play by the cast before the start of rehearsals. What Nina meant was that Konstantin's play was just good enough to be read but not to be acted. There can hardly be any doubt that, as was his usual practice, Chekhov was expressing his own opinion through the mouths of his characters, though strictly within the context of the play, that is to say, without departing from the requirements of the dramatic situation and without making anyone speak out of character. Chekhov's own opinion of the *avant-garde* drama of the Symbolists was that it was quite unsuitable for the stage, and, at best, good enough for a public recital. It is a curious fact that it has been accepted as axiomatic by critics in Russia and abroad that a play by Chekhov lacks action, a misconception that arose from a complete ignorance of Chekhov's intention and a fundamental misunderstanding of Chekhov's dramatic art.

of his old enthusiasm for the theatre and is visibly delighted to be in the company of so famous an actress as Arkadina. This is an important point to keep in mind, for when in the second act Shamrayev refuses to provide horses for Arkadina's carriage, he takes the actress's explosive displeasure as a personal insult, with rather dire consequences.

Of the eight spectators of Konstantin's play those most involved are Arkadina and Trigorin who are immediately made the victims of a scathing attack by Konstantin. It was entirely Arkadina's fault in pouring out upon her and her lover the vials of her son's wrath. As soon as Konstantin came out from behind the stage and only within a few minutes of her own appearance on the scene, she put the rather inappropriate question to him: 'When are you going to begin, my son?' This sounded like the expression of a desire to have the performance of his play over and done with, which was not surprising in view of her fear that Trigorin might fancy Nina. But such a question, and its implication, could not help exasperating Konstantin who, in spite of his avowed belief that his mother would 'hate' his play (which was quite justified in view of her known contempt for the *avant-garde* drama of the Symbolist school), hoped against hope that she would be impressed by it. There was, therefore, a distinct note of exasperation in his reply: 'In a minute, Mother. Please, have patience.' It was this unmistakable note of exasperation that provoked Arkadina to choose Queen Gertrude's lines to Hamlet both as a challenge to his disapproval of her relationship to Trigorin and to his pretensions to have written a dramatic masterpiece. It was a disastrous choice. A short while earlier Konstantin had told Sorin that what he resented most about his mother was her 'running about with that novelist fellow'. For a woman of forty-three to attach herself to a man in his mid-thirties seemed quite grotesque to a young man like himself, and that quite apart from his belief that his own presence belied her pretence that she was much younger than her age. Besides, there was always that feeling of inferiority that arose from the fact that his mother despised him for being a 'Kiev artisan', that is to say, that officially he belonged to the despised lower middle class because his father, a famous actor, had been of 'humble birth', while she was a noblewoman; for being 'a nobody' in his mother's circle of well-known actors and writers; for his involvement in the student disturbances and demonstrations, which was such a feature of university life in Russia at that time and which had resulted in his expulsion from the university. There was an even stronger reason for his intense exasperation with his mother and her lover: Nina's coldness towards him, her undisguised contempt for his play, and her unconcealed admiration for Trigorin: was not his mother's jealousy of Nina justified and might not Nina too, for all he knew, soon be 'running about with that novelist fellow'? That Konstantin's recital of Hamlet's lines to Gertrude had some deep personal meaning could not have escaped Arkadina or Trigorin. How would Arkadina and Trigorin have reacted to this furious attack? Chekhov left it to the actors to decide, but one could easily picture Arkadina's ironic contempt for her 'conceited and headstrong boy' and Trigorin's sheepish smile at such a disgraceful *public* demonstration of Konstantin's 'tactlessness'. As for the reaction of the others on the stage, all of whom quite naturally knew of Arkadina's relationship to Trigorin and Konstantin's violent objection to it, each of them would show their embarrassment in conformity with his or her character and personal attitude towards the protagonists.[1]

The sound of the horn off stage brought this painful scene to an end. Konstantin, as he had done earlier in speaking to Masha and Medvedenko, assumed the dictatorial mantle of the stage director: 'Ladies and gentlemen, I'm beginning. Quiet, please, quiet!' But his invocation to 'the venerable shades that hover over the lake' to send the audience to sleep (Chekhov's sly dig at the Symbolist drama) so that they could dream of what things would be like 'in two hundred thousand years' provoked Sorin to the matter-of-fact comment that in two hundred thousand years there would be nothing. Piqued by so philistine a remark (his uncle had quite obviously never read Solovyov), Konstantin replied with some severity, 'Well, let them [that is the venerable shades] show us that nothing.' It was a foolish thing to say and it brought his mother's first sarcastic interjection: 'Let them. We're asleep.' Konstantin ignored it, but these interruptions were beginning

[1] The audience must by now have a clear enough idea of the characters in the play to be able to read what was passing in their minds from the expressions of their faces and their general conduct and in this way to participate actively in the action on the stage by guessing the reaction of each character to any situation. Their failure to do so is not Chekhov's fault: it is the fault of the director and each actor and actress in failing to follow Chekhov's advice to read his play because *it is all there.*

to undermine his morale already shaken by his outburst against his mother and Trigorin. One more and his self-control would snap.

The curtain rose just then and not a moment too soon, revealing the view of the lake, the reflection of the moonlight in the water and Nina 'all in white' sitting on a big stone. The moon also illuminated the small audience, sitting on chairs sideways to the stage, each character plainly visible to the audience in the theatre: Arkadina sitting beside Sorin, Trigorin a little farther off, and the rest grouped in a semi-circle round the roughly knocked up stage. The only recorded comment of Chekhov's about the acting of this scene concerned the actress playing Nina who, he insisted, ought to keep in mind that Nina was a young, inexperienced girl, who found herself for the first time on a stage, who suffered from stage fright and was very nervous. Chekhov did not think it necessary to go into greater detail about Nina or the other characters since he assumed, falsely as it turned out, that a director who took the trouble to read the play would be able to explain the situation to the cast. What was the situation, then, so far as the chief characters were concerned? There was Arkadina, anxious about the impression Nina might make on Trigorin; there was Trigorin who had all his life longed for 'the delightful, poetic love of a young girl' whose mission seemed to be to carry him off 'into a world of dreams', an experience he had never had, for, as he explained to Arkadina in the third act, as a young man he was too busy running from one editorial office to another trying to earn a living; there was that young girl herself who could not take her eyes off him as she nervously recited all that Symbolist rigmarole about the World Soul and Satan. She looked terrified. Not of him, surely! He certainly felt powerfully drawn to her as she (he was quite sure of that) felt drawn to him. Was it possible that this great love had come to him at last? Not if Arkadina could help it. She was watching him intently. Knowing Trigorin as she did, she made up her mind at once to get him away from that girl who possessed all the attractions – youth, beauty, innocence – she herself lacked. She would have to find some excuse for taking him back to town, but in the meantime she must stop them gawking so shamelessly at one another. She would have to stop the play. She interrupted it 'quietly' by whispering audibly as though talking to herself: 'This is something decadent', which immediately brought forth Konstantin's 'imploring and

c

reproachful' appeal: 'Mother!' But her chance came with the smell of sulphur at the approach of Satan.

ARKADINA. There's a smell of sulphur. Is that really necessary?
KONSTANTIN [furiously]. Yes.
ARKADINA (*laughs*). Well, this certainly is a marvellous stage effect!
KONSTANTIN [this time a threatening note in his voice]. Mother!
NINA. He feels lost without man—
PAULINE (*to* DORN). You've taken your hat off. Please put it on or you'll catch your death of cold.
ARKADINA. Why, the doctor has only taken off his hat to the devil, the father of eternal matter!

[The brutal sarcasm of this interjection, which shows how desperate Arkadina was to get Nina off the stage, had its desired effect:]

KONSTANTIN (*flaring up, aloud*). The play's finished! Enough! Curtain!
ARKADINA. What are you so cross about?
KONSTANTIN. Enough! Curtain! Lower the curtain! (*Stamps.*) Curtain! (*The curtain drops.*) Sorry, I forgot that it is only a few chosen ones who can act and write plays. I've infringed the monopoly. I–I— (*tries to say something more, but waves his arm instead and goes out left*).

But what about Nina? Konstantin was too incensed to realise how badly he had let her down. It was Nina's first appearance on the stage, she had put so much work into learning her part, and she had counted so much on her acting to provide her with a chance to go on the stage. Now he seemed to have shattered her dream of becoming an actress, let alone a famous actress, by his inconsiderate outburst prompted perhaps not so much by his mother's sarcasm as by his own jealousy—for he could hardly have failed to notice how terrified she had been of Trigorin and how she had kept looking at him. The thought of his unfair treatment of Nina had not yet sufficiently sunk in when he rushed off into the park, but by the time he returned to find that Nina had gone he must have realised how selfishly he had treated her, which explains not only his despair but also his insistence that he must go and see her at once.

After her son's dramatic exit Arkadina pretended that she did not know what was the matter with him. When Sorin mildly objected that that was not the way to treat a young man's pride, her explanation was that Konstantin had warned her that his play was 'a joke' and that she therefore treated it as a joke. Now it seemed he had written a master-piece, which meant that he had put on his play and nearly suffocated them all with sulphur 'not as a joke but as a demonstration!' That, she felt, was a bit too much. In addition, those constant attacks on her, those 'pinpricks', were enough to try anyone's patience, Why did he not write some ordinary play? Why that 'decadent drivel'? Not that she minded listening even to drivel, but then why all those 'pretensions to new forms, to a new era in art'? Here, again, Chekhov was express-ing his own view of the *avant-garde* movement, skilfully disguising it as an expression of opinion by a professional actress outraged by the ridiculous claims made by someone who had had no experience of the theatre and who put a personal twist to everything she stood for and seemed to enjoy making her look a fool. Why did he not leave her in peace?

At this point Medvedenko's fatuous profundities about the separation of spirit from matter, and his appeal to Trigorin to write a play about the sorry lot of school teachers helped to clear the air. There was also that distant singing of village girls from across the lake which made everything look so much less hopeless. Arkadina's dire forebodings seemed less real, and it was in a more conciliatory mood that she asked Trigorin to sit down beside her and began to tell him about the fun and games that had gone on on the shore of the lake fifteen years before—the laughter, the noise, the shooting and the love affairs, Dr Dorn being the general favourite of the ladies. Stricken with sudden remorse, she remembered her 'poor boy' and gladly accepted Masha's offer to go and look for him. But Masha's departure was followed by Nina's appearance from behind the stage, which revived all Arkadina's anxieties. Not that, good actress that she was, she betrayed them by even the flicker of an eyelid, except perhaps by the exaggerated enthusiasm with which she greeted the young girl. 'Bravo! Bravo! We were charmed, my dear . . . With your figure and your lovely voice it's a shame to bury yourself in the country. I'm sure you have talent. . . . You *must* go on the stage.' Nina, conscious as she was of the mess she had made of her part, was too ingenuous and guileless to see through Arkadina's sham compli-ments. The very mention of the possibility of her going on the stage, makes her exclaim: 'Oh, it's one of my dreams!' And with a sigh: 'I'm afraid it will never come true.' Arkadina's comment is not very hopeful: 'You never can tell', but the introduction to Trigorin which follows makes both of them forget the theatre and anything else. The embarrassment shown by Nina as well as by Trigorin gives them both away and sends a chill through Arkadina's heart. She tries to cover it up by telling Nina not to look so embarrassed, for, though a celebrity, Trigorin is just an ordinary human being: 'Look, he is himself embarrassed.' He was indeed. In fact, the atmosphere becomes so charged with embarrassment that Dorn has to come to their rescue by appealing to Shamrayev to have the curtain raised. 'It gives me the creeps,' he declares, as well it might if only he knew what the future held for the three of them.

Asked by Nina what he thought of Konstantin's 'strange' play, Trigorin admitted that he could not make head or tail of it (he was much more generous to Konstantin earlier when he declared that everyone wrote as he liked and as he could), but that he admired the sincerity of her acting and, besides, the scenery was lovely. After a pause during which the insincerity of his compliment and the irony of his reference to the 'scenery' must have become a little too obvious, he added to Nina's astonishment the down-to-earth observation that he expected there must be lots of fish in the lake. To Nina's rather hesitant 'Yes. . . .' he went on to astonish her even more by declaring that he loved fishing and that nothing gave him greater pleasure than sitting on the bank of a stream and watching the float.[1] 'Surely,' Nina, who had absorbed the Nietzschean ideas so popular at the time, expostulated, 'anyone who has experienced the joys of creation cannot possibly enjoy anything else!' Trigorin made no answer, but looked even more embarrassed than ever: a girl who had so high an opinion of him should prove a much easier catch than he had anticipated. To Arkadina the true reason for Trigorin's embarrassment was too obvious, but her uncalled-for laugh and, particularly, the possessive way in which she spoke about him merely increased his embarrassment. Arkadina's laugh sounded rather

[1] Chekhov was a passionate angler and Trigorin's obsessive passion for fishing is one of the autobiographical traits he attached to Trigorin whose real prototype was Ignatius Potapenko, a prolific writer, who was involved in an affair with a young girl, a friend of Chekhov's family, which bore a close resemblance to Trigorin's affair with Nina.

patronising to Nina, but what she resented most was the way Arkadina spoke to her as if she were a little girl: she knew she was jealous of her, but why was Trigorin so embarrassed? Was he afraid of Arkadina? Did he not realise that she, Nina, had sufficient strength of character to get what she wanted in spite of Arkadina and in spite of her father? No one in the company could think of anything to say to relieve the charged atmosphere. Shamrayev's anecdote about the cathedral chorister who took a note an octave lower than the famous Silva had had no effect. The silence was finally broken by Dorn's comment that an angel of silence must have flown over them. This was the signal for Nina to leave. Arkadina's motherly solicitude for her and her all too evident desire to be rid of her company – shown by her exaggerated protestations that she wanted her to stay – was a little too much to put up with any longer. But again she could not help giving herself away:

NINA. If you knew how I hate to have to go.
ARKADINA. Don't you think someone ought to see you home, my pet?
NINA (*frightened*). No, no!

Arkadina could only have meant that Konstantin should see her home and Konstantin was the last man on earth she wanted to see. It was only Sorin's entreaty that made her hesitate for a moment.

NINA (*after thinking it over, tearfully*). I can't. (*Shakes hands and hurries off.*)

Arkadina's disingenuous commiseration with Nina: 'Poor child, I am sorry for her' is, no doubt, meant as an indirect warning to Trigorin against getting himself too deeply involved with a girl who might prove a financial burden to him later on. They walk off, Sorin complaining about his aching leg, and Shamrayev ignoring his order to let the howling dog off the chain; Arkadina takes Sorin's arm. Shamrayev, as behoves an old army officer, gallantly offers his arm to Pauline – apparently completely unaware of her long association with Dorn – and walks off with her and Medvedenko, still chuckling at the church chorister's scoring over a famous opera singer. Medvedenko, obsessed with the slender pay he is getting, inquires anxiously what were the wages of a church chorister. Trigorin follows in silence: an affair with Nina might have its problems, but by now he had made up his mind to have her whatever the consequences, for she would not be the first mistress he had discarded when he no longer had any use for her.

Dorn is left behind meditating on Konstantin's play, which he liked for its freshness and naïvety. His view of 'the ecstasy artists experience while creating' is as romantic as Nina's. If he had been an artist, he tells Konstantin – who comes in looking heartbroken and still hoping to catch Nina before she leaves for home – 'I should have soared away from the earth higher and even higher.' There was something in his play, he assures the distracted Konstantin rather vaguely. He was quite certain Konstantin had talent and he ought to persevere. But – and it is at this point that Chekhov formulates the central theme of the play:

> There must be a clear and definite idea in every work of art. You must know *why* you are writing. If you don't, if you walk along this picturesque road without any definite aim, you're bound to lose your way and your talent will be your ruin.

It was, too. But Konstantin hardly listened to what the doctor was saying. Not that he would have heeded the warning even if he had listened to it. He was too upset by the thought that he had lost Nina.

KONSTANTIN. Where is Nina?
DORN. She's gone home.
KONSTANTIN (*in despair*). But what am I to do. I want to see her. I must see her. I'm going after her. I must go.

The sudden appearance of Masha, whom he detested, with the news that his mother was worried about him, drives Konstantin into a paroxysm of blind fury.

KONSTANTIN. Tell her I've gone off. And I beg you, all of you, to leave me alone. Leave me alone! Don't follow me about!

And after bidding the doctor goodbye and thanking him for his advice to go on writing, he runs off.

The doctor sighs: 'Youth! Youth!' which gives Masha the opportunity of showing her claws. 'When people have nothing more to say,' she jeers, 'they say: youth! Youth!' And as if to emphasise her contempt for the doctor's opinion, she takes a pinch of snuff, which she must have known that Dorn disliked. The doctor, as was to be expected, snatches the snuffbox away from her and flings it into the bushes with the appropriate comment: 'Disgusting habit!' The ensuing silence is broken by the playing of the piano in the house. Masha refuses the doctor's invitation to go indoors. The doctor's violent action provides her with a not-to-be-missed chance for an exhibition of her 'ruined' life. She appeals to Dorn for help as she might 'do something silly', she might 'make a mess of her life', she might 'ruin' it. She knew perfectly well that the doctor, even if she felt 'close' to him (a hint that he might be her putative father), could do nothing that would be of any use to her in her present predicament, except to be duly impressed by her confession that she was in love with Konstantin. The romantic doctor, who has had many adventures with the ladies of the six country houses on the shore of the lake, quite naturally blames the 'magic' of the lake for all those broken hearts. 'How overwrought they all are! Oh, that spellbinding lake! (*Gently*.) But what can I do, my child? What? What?'

Masha knew perfectly well that he could do nothing: that was not the object of the exercise. Besides, the doctor's last line was just right (from Chekhov's point of view) for bringing down the curtain on the first act of a play in which all the chief characters are involved in the sort of triangular situations that are all too familiar in classical comedy, except that the two main themes in *The Seagull* deal with problems that transcend the aim of the classical comedy, which is merely to provide an evening's entertainment.

Act Two

There is an interval of several days between the first and the second acts. This becomes clear from the remark Arkadina makes to Nina about Konstantin who has been spending 'whole days' at the lake so that she hardly sees him. During that short time a marked change has come over many of the characters. To begin with, Dorn seems to be no longer under the spell of the magic of the lake and in consequence has seen through Masha's sham tragic poses. When Masha goes off to the house on the excuse that it is nearly lunch-time, the following illuminating exchange takes place between Dorn and Sorin:

DORN. Gone to have a couple of drinks before lunch.
SORIN. The poor girl is so unhappy.
DORN. Nonsense!

As for Nina, the change that has come over her after her first meeting with Trigorin can no longer be disguised, even if Nina, whose infatuation with the popular novelist is now apparent to everybody, cared to disguise it or, indeed, was able to disguise it. 'The sun', Konstantin tells Nina half-way through the second act on the approach of Trigorin, 'is still miles away and already you're smiling. Your gaze has melted in its rays.' To Arkadina the situation has become unbearable: accustomed, as her son says in the first act, to acclaim and adulation, she could not allow herself to become the laughing-stock of everybody in the house, including the domestics. She felt she could no longer rely on her dominating role in her relationship with a man who, though weak-willed as Trigorin was, somehow managed to get what he wanted in the end. She therefore decided that the time had come to take him away. She must be careful, however, not to disclose the real reason for their departure: her excuse for it must have nothing to do with her being jealous of a silly 'provincial' girl like Nina; for to reveal it would be an even bigger blow to her self-esteem than allowing Trigorin to carry on with his affair with Nina, an affair that could not possibly last very long.

Arkadina had drawn up her plan of action before the second act. She

had arranged to go to town with Pauline on some pretext or other, for –
as she very well knew, it being harvest time – Shamrayev would not be
able to let her have the horses for her carriage, and she hoped that the
inevitable row with him would give her the needed excuse for leaving
for Moscow with Trigorin.

It was the gap between the ages of herself and Nina that worried
Arkadina most. While waiting for the storm to break with the appearance of Shamrayev, she was trying to persuade herself and everybody
else that in spite of being 'almost' forty-four she was younger than the
22-year-old Masha and, indeed, could still play a girl of fifteen. Dorn
agreed ironically. Masha played up to her by implying that her unhappy
love for Konstantin made her drag her life like an endless train behind
her, which provoked Dorn to give his caustic comment on *that* situation by starting to hum the flower song in which Faust complained of
the suffering caused by love. There followed the reading of a passage
from Maupassant's story 'Sur l'eau' describing the way French society
women try to captivate a famous author by doing their best to please
him. 'That,' Arkadina comments, laying down the book as she catches
sight of the approach of the elegantly dressed Nina accompanied by
Sorin and Medvedenko, 'that may be the French way ... With us
when a woman tries to captivate a writer she usually falls head over
heels in love with him first.' Then, afraid of having given herself away,
she adds quickly: 'Take me and Trigorin, for instance.'

Nina – who must have exchanged a few words with Trigorin who
was fishing by the bathing hut (he might even have boasted to her
about catching the two chub she later mentions in her soliloquy) –
could not conceal the 'happy' look on her face, and Sorin does his best
to explain it away to his sister: Nina, he tells her, was looking so happy
because her father and stepmother had gone away to town for three
days. Nina confirms it. 'I'm awfully happy,' she declares as she sits
down beside Arkadina and embraces her. 'Now I belong to you.'
Sorin makes things worse by asking his sister to admire Nina who
looked 'so sweet today'. Provoked beyond endurance, Arkadina is
pitiless to the young girl. 'Elegant and charming', she comments,
adding caustically: 'I never dreamt you could dress like that. But', she
adds after kissing Nina a little ominously, 'we mustn't praise you too
much, must we? It may bring you bad luck.' Then, anxious to find out
whether Nina had seen Trigorin, she suddenly fires a question at her:

'Where is Mr Trigorin?' She knew perfectly well where Trigorin was and she put the 'Mr' before Trigorin's name as a warning that she would resent any familiarity from her when talking about him. Nina gives herself away at once. 'He's by the bathing hut, fishing,' she replies guilelessly. This immediately provokes Arkadina's enraged reply: 'I can't understand why he doesn't get sick of it!' To remind Nina of her relationship to her son Arkadina asks her where *he* is and why he is 'so moody and bad-tempered'. Nina does not reply. It is Masha who comes up with the answer that Konstantin had not been feeling 'very happy', and to show that she blamed Nina for that she asks her to read 'something from his play'. Nina's reply reveals her complete indifference to Konstantin.

NINA (*shrugging*). Do you really want me to? It is so dull!

It is now Masha's turn to confound Nina. She conjures up a highly idealised picture of Konstantin with eyes blazing and a face turning pale as he reads something himself. 'He has such a beautiful, sad voice and the look of a poet!' she adds, hardly able to control her excitement.

Considering that Masha was the last woman in the world Konstantin would have read anything to, it can be safely assumed that she had made it all up. Indeed, the fact that Chekhov makes Sorin interrupt Masha's panegyric by his loud snoring is a clear indication of how absurd it is to take her seriously.

There follow some bantering exchanges about Sorin's health, Dorn offering his usual specific of valerian drops[1] during which Arkadina is

[1] In a letter to Alexey Suvorin of 27 October 1892, Chekhov mentions valerian drops as his usual treatment for people suffering from attacks of giddiness. ('Don't be alarmed Mother', Konstantin calms Arkadina when Sorin has a fainting fit in the third act. 'It's not serious. Uncle often has these attacks now.') Chekhov wrote to his 58-year-old publisher: 'Swaying, walking unsteadily, accompanied by blackouts and even loss of consciousness for a few seconds . . . is almost a usual occurence with people of your age as well as with women and young people of irregular diet. One has to make the best of it and, remembering your age, try not to walk too fast when your mind is working or when you are wearing a heavy fur coat. I used to suffer from fits of giddiness in my second year at the university and I was greatly worried about it. My father is today suffering from attacks of giddiness with loss of consciousness of ten to twenty seconds and it does not worry me in the least. This is a usual complaint among old peasants and I tell them not to be alarmed, not to change their way of life and, if not feeling too lazy, to take ten valerian drops four times a day, especially if their pulse is weak or just

getting more and more impatient about the delay in Shamrayev's appearance. It is at that point that Arkadina (to relieve the tension under which she was labouring) bursts out with the famous and all too often misunderstood line about there being nothing more boring than the 'delightful' country boredom, followed up by her no longer disguised wish to be back in Moscow or, as she puts it, 'in a hotel room, studying a part'. Arkadina completely ignores Nina's ecstatic agreement, Sorin goes on to rhapsodise on the delights of town life, while Dorn resumes his humming of the flower song, this time as a comment on Arkadina's predicament. It is at this point that at last Shamrayev makes his appearance with his wife. He is in a raging temper which he suppresses only with difficulty.

The moment Arkadina had been waiting for has arrived, but she has badly misjudged Shamrayev's feelings with the result that she overacts her part. Shamrayev had always expressed his admiration for her, he was proud to be daily in the company of so famous an actress, he enjoyed the opportunity it gave him to recount his countless amusing anecdotes about actors with whom he claimed to have been on intimate terms, and now she was treating him as one of her menials who was obliged to carry out her 'phenomenal' order to let her have the horses for her carriage at the height of the harvest! 'I'd gladly sacrifice ten years of my life for you,' he repeated a phrase he had often heard in the theatre, 'but I can't let you have any horses.'

---

medium. However, each patient must be considered individually, but one should not tell lies to one's patients as one usually does in cases of cancer or tuberculosis. It will take a month or two before you get used to it and are able to control your feeling that you are about to collapse in the street. Don't give way to your impulse to walk near a fence so that you could catch hold of something. On the contrary, when you feel that you are about to fall, say to yourself: 'Go on, fall down!' and, I promise you, you won't fall down. There are crowds of people in the street and no one ever falls down. Above all, don't stop going to the theatre or anywhere else for that matter. When going to an exhibition take a light folding chair in the shape of the letter X which will cost you 90 kopeks. After every two or three pictures, sit down and remain sitting. A prolonged conversation leads to a violent rush of blood to the lungs and, consequently, a drop in the flow of blood to the head, resulting in the fatigue of the brain. For that reason you should avoid talking too much. . . . Tolstoy calls us medics scoundrels, but I'm convinced that [during the present cholera epidemic] the country would have been in a devil of a mess without us doctors.'

Arkadina who had heard similar melodramatic declarations made to her on the stage seemed little impressed.

ARKADINA. But what if I have to go? Well, really!

SHAMRAYEV. My dear lady, you have no idea what it means to run an estate.

ARKADINA (*flaring up*). That's an old story! In that case I'm leaving for Moscow today. Tell them to hire horses for me in the village or I shall walk to the station!

SHAMRAYEV. If that's the case I throw up my job! Find yourself another agent! (*Goes out.*)

In the heat of the moment Arkadina, who was too eager to have Trigorin back in Moscow with her, failed to grasp the dire consequences of Shamrayev's threat: declaring dramatically that she had been insulted and would never come back again to her brother's estate, she flounced off in the direction of the bathing hut and could be seen a moment later entering the house, followed meekly by Trigorin with his rod and pail.

By this time the audience should be able to participate fully in the action on the stage by savouring the incongruity of the ensuing scene of general dismay, which is so typical of a comedy: Sorin's anger with Shamrayev at the way he had treated his sister and his absurd demand for the horses to be fetched immediately, followed by an appeal to Nina to join him in 'imploring' Arkadina to stay, and, finally, assuring her that by 'talking it over' with the 'brute' he would be able to persuade him to withdraw his resignation; Nina's failure to realise that Arkadina had engineered the whole scene with Shamrayev in order to get Trigorin away from her, and her comic indignation with Shamrayev for refusing the request of a famous actress 'whose every whim is more important than the whole of the estate'; finally, Dorn's comment that 'the old woman' Sorin as well as his sister were sure to apologise to Shamrayev, followed by another 'tiresome' scene between him and Pauline whose senseless bouts of jealousy contrast so strongly with the fierce and fully justified jealousy of Arkadina who is determined to hang on to her 'last chance' in spite of the hopeless odds against her.

What made the odds so hopeless was, strangely enough, not Nina's youth but rather her guilelessness which Trigorin was quick enough to exploit in the brilliant and meticulously executed seduction scene (a sequel that Arkadina did not foresee) which followed the brief scene between Nina and Konstantin and in which the 'seagull' theme appears for the first time.

Nina's first reaction at the sight of the dead seagull, which Konstantin had laid at her feet, was natural enough.

NINA. What does this mean?
KONSTANTIN. I did a vile thing today: I killed this seagull. Let me lay it at your feet.
NINA. What's the matter with you?

Nina knew perfectly well what was the matter with Konstantin, but her infatuation with Trigorin had made her totally indifferent to the agony he was suffering on account of her changed attitude towards him. She picked up the seagull and gazed at it in silence for some time, but without showing any particular interest in Konstantin's 'vile' act. Nor did she take Konstantin seriously when he declared that he would shoot himself 'in the same way'. His threat merely elicited her cold remark: 'I do not recognise you'. Konstantin's retort that she failed to recognise him only after he had stopped recognising her did not seem to have made any impression on her either: she accused him of having become 'irritable of late' and of expressing himself in some kind of 'incomprehensible symbols', and as she put the dead bird down on the bench, she surmised that the seagull, too, must be some kind of 'symbol'. Two years later, after Trigorin had left her and she herself had to go through the same sort of experience Konstantin had been through, she remembered his words about not recognising her and was overwhelmed by a feeling of guilt at having caused him so much suffering. 'Every night' she tells Konstantin in the last act 'I dream that you look and look at me and do not recognise me.'

For the moment, however, she dismissed Konstantin's complaint about her 'coldness' by saying that she was 'too unsophisticated' to understand him. Konstantin's reply was obvious: there was nothing to understand, for women never forgave a failure, and the failure of his play, for which, curiously enough, he did not blame himself, had made her 'despise his inspiration' and regard him as 'a nonentity like hundreds of others'. Then, stamping his foot in cold fury as he had done earlier when shouting for the curtain to be rung down, he added that his pride was sucking 'his lifeblood like a serpent'. It was his hurt pride that also blinded him to the simple fact that Nina had never been in love with him. He realised it as soon as he saw the change that had come over her and her ineffably sweet, tender smile at the approach of 'the genius' Trigorin: it was this realisation that made him carry out his threat to commit suicide.

Arkadina's hysterical fit and Sorin's attack of asthma should have made it abundantly clear to Trigorin that there could be no question of leaving for Moscow before the problem of propitiating Shamrayev and saving the harvest was satisfactorily solved. On Dr Dorn's arrival to administer the valerian drops to his two patients, Trigorin left the house in the hope of finding Nina who had left only a short while before. The pose he assumed of a writer engrossed in his task of collecting material quite rightly provoked Konstantin's derisive remark: 'Here comes real genius! Walks like Hamlet and with a book, too. (*Mimicking*.) Words, words, words!' Actually it was just an unimportant note about Masha's drinking, wearing black and taking snuff and Medvedenko's being in love with her – nothing, in fact, that he would not have remembered without writing it down. Besides, it was quite an unnecessary effort since he should by now have known how much his very presence affected Nina. But while intent upon the realisation of his 'sweet dream' of possessing Nina, he thought it wise to let her do all the chasing. During the whole of the ensuing scene, therefore, he indulged in a bout of self-depreciation, leaving it to the young ecstatic girl to build him up as 'a great and wonderful' writer. He began by expressing his regret that he might be compelled to leave before finding out what kind of entrancing creature she was and what her thoughts were about. He met so few interesting girls of her age that he had no idea what an 18- or 19-year-old girl was like, which, he added, baiting his hook, was why the young girls in his stories and novels were so unconvincing. No hint of being powerfully 'drawn to her', no mention of 'the delightful, poetic love of a young girl' which, as he told Arkadina a week later, was 'to carry him off into a world of dreams'. No, he preferred to play it very cool, still unsure how far Nina would be ready to satisfy his overpowering desire to possess her. To her wish to be in his place so as to find out what it was like to be a famous writer, he replied that either she was exaggerating his fame or that it was something he was hardly aware of. To her ecstatic assertion that he was 'one in a million', that his life was 'wonderful and full of

significance', he embarked on a long tirade on the torments and tribula-
tions of a writer's life, though admitting reluctantly – in reply to her
question whether 'inspiration and the whole process of creative work'
did not give him 'moments of ecstasy and happiness' – that it was quite
true that when he was writing he felt happy and that he also liked to
read the proofs, but that the moment the wretched thing was published
he felt miserable because he realised that 'the whole thing was a mistake', and that he shouldn't have written it at all. Indeed, he was so sure
of himself by now that he went so far as to tell her of the general
opinion of him as a second-rate writer: 'Charming, talented but a long
way from Tolstoy! Excellent but Turgenev's *Fathers and Sons* is
better!' Why, he even suggested to her the inscription on his tombstone: 'Here lies Trigorin, a good writer but not as good as Turgenev.'
Nina, as Trigorin confidently expected, refused to listen to him: she
was quite certain that the reason why he was so dissatisfied with himself
was that he was working too hard. Nina had fully absorbed the ideas of
Nietzsche,[1] who was very popular at the time, and she was convinced
that a 'great writer' must look down on the 'mob' of his admirers. 'If I
had been a writer like you,' she declared, 'I'd have dedicated all my life
to the mob, but at the same time I'd realise that they could achieve
happiness only by trying to rise to my level, and I'm sure they would
pull me along in a chariot!'

That was too much even for Trigorin. 'A chariot!' he objected, 'I am
not Agamemnon, am I?'

But though both of them smiled at the idea of Trigorin as a second
Agamemnon, Nina refused to allow his quite sensible interjection to
dampen her enthusiasm for 'real fame'.

NINA. For the happiness of being a writer or an actress, I'd put up with
the hostility of my relations, endure poverty and disappointment,
live in an attic, eat nothing but rye bread, suffer agonies from the
realisation of my own shortcomings, but in return I'd demand fame—
real, resounding fame! (*Buries her face in her hands.*) Oh, my head's
spinning!

[1] In a letter to the publisher Suvorin, written in February 1895, at the time he
was working on *The Seagull*, Chekhov expressed the view that Nietzsche's
popularity was a passing phase. 'Nietzsche's philosophy', he wrote, 'is spectacular
rather than convincing.'

Nina's ecstatic hopes for fame were to be cruelly disappointed later, but at the moment she was brought down to earth by Arkadina's call for Trigorin. Casting a last glance at the lake, Trigorin, fearing that he might have to pack after all, could not help lingering for a few more minutes while Nina pointed out to him the house on the other shore of the lake where she was born. It was then that Trigorin caught sight of the dead seagull.

TRIGORIN. ... And what's this?

NINA. A seagull. Konstantin shot it.

TRIGORIN. A beautiful bird. I don't want to leave, not really. I wonder if you would persuade Irina to stay.

An extraordinary request! Did he really expect Arkadina to listen to such a plea from Nina of all people? It was quite in character, though. It was typical of Trigorin's fear of a direct clash with Arkadina in which he knew he was bound to be worsted. Not that he expected Nina to agree to his request. Indeed, he seemed to have forgotten all about it as a sudden thought struck him and he hastened to jot it down in his book.

NINA. What are you writing?

TRIGORIN. Oh, nothing much. Just making a note. Got an idea. (*Putting his notebook away.*) An idea for a short story. A young girl has lived in a house on the shore of a lake since childhood, a young girl like you. She loves the lake like a seagull, and she's as free and happy as a seagull. But a man comes along, sees her, and just for the fun of it destroys her like that seagull there.

It was just at this point that Nina seems to have been seized with a dreadful foreboding that Trigorin's idea for a short story might well be the sequel of her affair with him. As it turned out the seagull 'symbol' – its theme appears here for the first time – was to become one of Nina's most terrible obsessions, a nightmare that nearly drove her out of her mind. Her reaction to Trigorin's 'idea' appears from the line Chekhov (probably out of a desire not to give his plot away too soon) deleted from the final printed edition of the play. The line was:

NINA (*shudders*). Don't, please, don't. Not like that!

At that moment she could not bear her happiness to be clouded by what must have seemed to her an entirely unfounded slur on the character of a man she admired and was in love with. Besides, at that moment Arkadina appeared at the window of the house and called Trigorin a second time.

ARKADINA. Boris, where are you?

TRIGORIN. Coming! (*As he walks towards the house, he turns round a few times to look at* NINA. *Stops by the window. To* ARKADINA.) Well?

ARKADINA. We're staying.

TRIGORIN *goes into the house.*

NINA (*goes up to the footlights; after a moment's reflection*) A dream!

If she had any premonition of disaster, she had now completely driven it out of her mind. More than that: she had taken her fateful decision: 'to take the plunge', run away from home, go on the stage and start 'a new life' with Trigorin.

Act Three

There is an interval of one week between the second act and the third. 'I shall remember you,' Trigorin said to Nina at the beginning of the third act, 'as you were on that bright, sunny day – remember? – a week ago, when you were wearing that summer dress. We had a long talk and—there was that white seagull lying on the seat.' 'Yes', Nina murmured, *pensively*, 'the seagull'. She did not forget the cloud that suddenly darkened her mind when Trigorin had told her of his 'idea for a short story'. But in Trigorin's mind the *white* seagull blended enchantingly with the white dress Nina wore on the stage, the light-coloured dress she wore during their talk, and the general impression of purity that he associated with Nina and that he found so fascinating. It was in memory of that meeting that Trigorin asked Shamrayev, as appears from the fourth act, to have the seagull stuffed for him. During that week, too, Konstantin carried out his threat to shoot himself 'in a moment of insane despair', for, as he told his mother in the third act, he had felt that he had lost everything, that Nina did not love him any more, and that all his hopes were shattered. He had only wounded himself lightly in the head, though. During that week, it would seem, Trigorin and Nina had met frequently. 'Even now', Konstantin taunted his mother, 'he is somewhere in the sitting-room or the garden laughing at us, broadening Nina's mind, doing his best to convince her that he is a genius.' He had challenged Trigorin to a duel (the Symbolists were all for the knightly code of duelling, though only in their plays), a challenge that to Konstantin's great disgust Trigorin had ignored. 'He's running away,' he told his mother when she insisted that Trigorin was 'an honourable man'. 'What an ignominious flight!' But as she watched Trigorin getting himself more and more involved with Nina during that week, she must have been through a more tormenting hell than Konstantin, just because she had had to pretend not to see what was going on. 'Forgive me,' she pleaded with her son after their stormy slanging match, 'I'm so unhappy.'

The person who came off best in this tragi-comic explosion of passions was the exhibitionist Masha. As the curtain goes up on the third act we find her having a high time telling the story of her life to Trigorin while knocking back one glass of vodka after another. 'I'm telling you all this', one can hear her almost bubbling over with delight, 'because you are a writer. You can use it if you like.' If Konstantin had 'hurt himself badly', she assures him 'frankly', she would not have gone on living for 'another minute'. As he had not, she still had sufficient courage, for 'as a matter of fact' she had made up her mind (for the umpteenth time) 'to tear this love' out of her heart 'by the roots'. To Trigorin's puzzled question of how she was going to perform so perilous an operation, she replied that she would do it simply by marrying Medvedenko. Once married she would not have time to think of love, for new worries would make her forget her past. But would she be able to give up so wonderful an opportunity for self-display? She did not seem to be sure. 'Anyway,' she declares light-heartedly, 'it will be a change.' But what about poor old Medvedenko? He was not very clever, he was a good fellow though, and she was, of course, sorry for him and for his widowed mother, too. Well, not sorry enough to miss the chance of another drink. 'Shall we have another?' she asked Trigorin who seemed a little worried by the number of glasses she had already had. But she reassured him: women drank more often than he thought, though not as openly as she. Changing the conversation to Trigorin's forced departure, she could not help wondering why he did not ask 'her' to stay. But Trigorin was quite certain that she would not stay 'now'. He put the blame on Konstantin's 'tactless' behaviour:

'First he tries to shoot himself and now he wants to challenge me to a duel. And what for? He sulks, he snorts, he preaches new forms. Isn't there room enough in the world for everybody? For the new as well as the old? Why get in one another's way?'

But Masha was not going to let him get away with so 'tactful' an explanation. Where others were concerned she was always clearsighted, even brutally so. 'I suppose,' she observed mildly, 'it's jealousy too. However,' she was quick to apologise for her indiscretion, 'it's none of my business.'

At that moment Nina came in and Masha made herself scarce, though not before explaining how sorry she was for Medvedenko whom she was about to nobble, and squeezing a few more drops of sympathy from the reluctant and sceptical Trigorin by asking him to send her some of his autographed books with an inscription emphasising her ill fortune.

Nina had come in with the express intention of making Trigorin come to the point: was he going to help her make up her mind to leave home and go on the stage? Of course this implied that she was ready to go away to Moscow with him. She had carefully prepared a plan to force Trigorin's hand. (Contrary to the belief that Chekhov was the creator of 'forlorn and ineffectual' women, all the women in Chekhov's plays, including Sofia in *Platonov*, Sasha in *Ivanov*, Nina in *The Seagull*, Sonia in *Uncle Vanya*, the sisters in *The Three Sisters*, and Anya in *The Cherry Orchard*, are stronger, more active, more conscious of life and the will to live than the men.) At first Nina tried to make the indecisive Trigorin 'advise' her to go on the stage without seeming to force a decision from him by a direct request.

NINA (*holding out her clenched fist to* TRIGORIN). Odd or even?
TRIGORIN [quite willing to play her game]. Even.
NINA (*sighing*). Wrong I've only one pea in my hand. I was trying to find out whether to go on the stage or not. I wish someone would tell me what to do.
TRIGORIN. I'm afraid it's something you'll have to decide for yourself. (*Pause.*)

Foiled, Nina was trying to think how to produce her trump card in the shape of the medallion which quite unmistakably conveyed the message that she was willing to become his mistress. She began by making it clear that he would lose her if he was afraid to take the decisive step she herself did not shrink from taking.

NINA. You're going away and—I don't suppose we shall see each other again. I'd like you to have this little medallion as a keepsake. I had your initials engraved on it and—on the other side, the title of your book: *Days and Nights*.

No mention of the fact that she had also had the number of the page and the two lines engraved in the inscription on the medallion. She merely asked him to let her have two minutes before he left, so that she could see whether, after he had read her message, he was ready to come up to scratch. As she expected, the number of the page and the two lines aroused Trigorin's curiosity at once. He replied to Arkadina's question whether it was Nina who had left the room with a monosyllabic 'Yes' and did not react at all to her sarcastic apology for having 'disturbed' them.

The following three highly emotional scenes are largely duologues between Arkadina and Sorin, Konstantin and Trigorin. In the first Sorin nearly had a fainting fit after the failure of his repeated attempts to get Arkadina to do something for her son. Konstantin had made a most thorough and far from sympathetic study of his mother's character. He had told Sorin in the first act that Arkadina had seventy thousand roubles in an Odessa bank, but that she was so stingy that she burst out crying if anyone tried to borrow money from her. In the scene with Sorin, she burst into tears several times. Her references to Konstantin clearly showed that she was not interested in Konstantin's literary ambitions, that she never tried to understand him, let alone sympathise with him, and that her plans for his future did not go further than the somewhat vague wish that he should get himself a job in the civil service 'or something'. He was a great trial to her, she moaned, and, a rather reluctant admission on her part, she feared that the chief reason for his attempted suicide was jealousy, so that the sooner she took Trigorin away the better.

It was the mention of Trigorin that was responsible for the malevolent row between mother and son in the second scene, though the rumblings of the impending storm could be heard at its beginning when Konstantin suggested, not without a touch of sarcasm, that she might for once bring herself to be generous and lend Sorin two thousand roubles to make it possible for him to spend a year in town since he fretted too much in the country.

ARKADINA [with cold fury]. I have no money. I'm an actress not a banker.

There was an uneasy pause: Konstantin, reflecting that it would be useless to pursue the matter, seemed to have sensed Arkadina's unhappiness and for a moment he felt sorry for her. He asked her to

change his bandage, adding propitiatingly: 'You do it so well, Mother.'
There followed a short, almost idyllic, interlude during which both
indulged in a reminiscence of Konstantin's childhood.

KONSTANTIN. These last few days, Mother, I loved you as I used to
love you when I was a little boy, so dearly and tenderly. I've no one
left now in the whole world except you, Mother.

But the confession of his love for his mother brought another
and, perhaps, no less strong motive for his jealousy of Trigorin. It
was his exclamation: 'Why, oh why, Mother, are you under the
influence of that man?' which started the storm that ended in his abject
collapse.

Konstantin taunted his mother not only with not being able to keep
her lover. He suggested almost in the same breath that Trigorin was not
the genius she took him to be. He was quite right, of course; and he was
quite right to tell Arkadina – who, in her turn, taunted him for being
one of those mediocrities who turned up their noses at men of real
genius – that he had got 'more genius' than Trigorin. For that is what
the whole play is about: for unlike some of the men of real genius in the
Russian Symbolist movement who realised its fundamental weaknesses
and rose above them, Konstantin when at last he realised that he had
been wrong in 'walking along that picturesque road without any
definite aim', did not have enough strength of character to make the
break. On the other hand, his attack on 'the dealers in stale ideas' who
'usurped the supremacy in art' and thought that 'everything they did
was real and legitimate', was perfectly justified.[1] Unfortunately, it
degenerated into a personal squabble. His mother called him a decadent, a low-born parasite and – what hurt him most – a nonentity. He
called her a miser and accused her of acting 'in miserable third-rate
plays.' Both collapsed in tears and the highly charged emotional scene
ended in a reconciliation, which was as inevitable as their malevolent
rows. She asked him to forgive her and, embracing her, he bewailed his
loss of 'everything'.

[1] The two main themes of the play, the theme of the seagull and the theme of the
aim of art, appear briefly in the third act, first in Nina's reflective reiteration of
Trigorin's reminder of the 'white seagull' and in Konstantin's outburst about
possessing greater genius than any of them.

ARKADINA. Don't despair. Everything will come right. He'll be gone soon and she'll love you again. (*She wipes his tears.*)

He seemed willing to believe that Nina would return to him although all the omens were against it. He even agreed not to insist on his preposterous challenge. All he wanted was that Arkadina should not insist on his meeting Trigorin, for he could not stand that: it would be too painful. At that moment Trigorin came in, 'carrying a book' and feverishly trying to find the page and the two lines engraved on Nina's medallion. It was Konstantin's cue for a hurried exit.[1]

Barely recovered from the scene with her son, Arkadina, who was used to highly emotional scenes on the stage, prepared herself for another tense emotional scene with Trigorin, though even she could hardly have expected to have to deal with a situation she had secretly dreaded but never really thought she would ever be confronted with. One glance at Trigorin, however, told her that something had happened that seriously endangered their relationship. There was a harsh note in her question: 'You've finished packing, I hope?' Trigorin's impatient reply: 'Yes, yes,' prepared her for the worst. The scene between them, therefore, lacked any trace of the tenderness that was never far from the surface in her scene with Konstantin. The masks were off. No question of tact either on his part or on hers. The second person singular in which they addressed each other emphasised the intimacy of a relationship that had passed the borderline of 'civilised' behaviour. It was no longer possible either for her or for him to be, as he pleaded, 'reasonable, sensible, wise.'

It was Chekhov who gave the clue to the basic flaw in Trigorin's character, namely that he had 'no iron in his blood'. Both Nina and Arkadina, convinced that Trigorin's popularity put him in the first rank of Russian writers (he was 'the only hope of Russia', Arkadina never for a moment hesitated to tell him, and she believed it), were also so strongly attracted to him because he was so obviously a weakling. He himself realised, as he told Nina in the second act, that as a writer he also had certain obligations towards 'his country, towards science, towards the rights of man, and so on,' yet he did nothing to carry out these obligations. He was the sort of writer who, as Chekhov wrote to the publisher Suvorin in November 1892 – that is only three years

---

[1] See also *Chekhov the Dramatist*, pp. 194–8.

before *The Seagull* was written – was 'talented and charming', but whose writings were not permeated by 'a consciousness of a definite aim' which made the reader feel 'not only life as it is but as it should be'. In his long tirade meant to impress Nina, Trigorin was not afraid to touch upon the painful subject of his standing in the literary world because nothing that he would say could affect her round-eyed adoration of him. Both Arkadina and Trigorin were good professionals, but he alone lacked confidence in the lasting value of his fame. Not so Arkadina. Unlike the reputation of a writer, an actor's fame is by its very nature transient and, quite naturally, Arkadina did not care about what posterity would think of her. To Trigorin, however, the inscription that would be on his tombstone was important. Unlike Arkadina, he did not care about his appearance and completely disregarded the social conventions (which Nina found so attractive about him), but the nagging thought that he was only a 'minor writer' never left him and that was why he felt the constant need of being bolstered up in his opinion of himself. The extravagant praise of his genius by Arkadina could not fail to have an effect just because it was absolutely sincere ('I alone know how to appreciate you'), and because Arkadina's flair for social life and her position in artistic and literary circles added weight to it. That is why he had in the end to give in to her: he could not do without her. He, too, was quite sincere in asking Arkadina to take him away with her, to carry him off and not to let him out of her sight 'for a single moment'. But was he as 'listless, flabby and submissive' as he wanted her to believe? Realising at last the hold she had over him – 'Now he is mine!' – she generously proposed that he should stay behind for another week and have the silly girl if she really meant so much to him. For she knew perfectly well how much his claim that there could be 'no greater happiness on earth than the love of a young girl' was worth. But Trigorin refused what in his present state of mind he could only regard as a dishonourable proposal. Besides, he was quite used to having his cake and eating it. He was, in fact, determined to have Nina on his own terms if she was really serious about her message 'to come and take' her life which he regarded as 'an appeal from a pure heart', an appeal that filled his soul 'with sadness' and made his heart 'contract with pain'. After everybody had left the dining-room, he ran breathlessly back and, to make sure that no one would suspect his real motive, shouted: 'I've forgotten my walking stick. Must have left it on the

veranda'. At the door to the veranda he met Nina, who was not going
to let him run off immediately after he had told her where to meet him
in Moscow and had given her his address. She, too, had to make certain
that he was hers.[1]

[1] See also *Chekhov the Dramatist*, pp. 199–201.

Act Four

After the magnificently worked-up climax of the third act with the brief interval between the first and second acts, the fourth act opens two years later. The great changes in the lives of most of the characters during this time can be perceived immediately on the rise of the curtain: a large drawing-room has been converted into Konstantin's study: a writing desk, books on windowsills and chairs, a bookcase—all bear signs of a writer who is busy at work. Even a large glass door leading on to a terrace makes it 'more convenient' for Konstantin, as Masha informs Dorn, 'to go out into the garden to do his thinking'. Indeed, Konstantin's Symbolist stories have appeared in journals to which such a popular writer as Trigorin is also a contributor. To everybody's surprise, for no one, as Pauline naïvely tells Konstantin, had ever dreamt that he'd be a 'real' writer one day, he has even been receiving money for his stories. But so far success has eluded him. The papers, Shamrayev observes, have been 'going for him' and Trigorin attributes his failure to gain critical recognition to his inability to create 'living characters'. His 'queer stuff' at times reminded Trigorin 'of the ravings of a lunatic'. Surprisingly enough, Konstantin himself seems for once to agree with Trigorin: he is acutely dissatisfied with his work, as becomes apparent from his long soliloquy shortly before Nina's visit, and he no longer conceals his disappointment with the whole Symbolist philosophy. What is worse, he realises to his dismay his own inadequacy as a writer, camouflaged, as it were, by 'the new forms' he was so keen about. 'I've talked so much about new forms, but I can't help feeling that little by little I am lapsing into clichés myself.' He has even a good word to say for Trigorin: 'Trigorin has his methods worked out. He finds it easy. The neck of a broken bottle gleaming on the milldam, the black shadow of the water wheel—and there's your moonlight night. But I have to bring in the tremulous light, the gently twinkling stars, and the distant strains of a piano dying away in the still, scented air. Oh, it's dreadful!' And what conclusion does he draw from it all? 'New forms! No! I'm coming more and more to believe that it isn't old or new forms that matter. What matters is that one shouldn't think about forms at all. Whatever one has to say should come straight from one's heart.'

There is another, more personal, reason for his despondency: the loneliness of being immured in an ivory tower. 'I'm alone in the world,' he tells Nina. 'I have no one whose affection can warm me. I'm cold, cold, as though I lived in some dungeon, and everything I write is dry, harsh, gloomy.' There was one faint glimmer of light in the darkening gloom: the unexpected arrival of Nina. She had now been staying for five days at a hotel in a near-by town. He had gone to the hotel several times a day, he had stood under the window of her room 'like a beggar', but she refused to see him. Masha, too, had tried to see her and she was told that Nina would not see anyone. Medvedenko had seen her walking across the fields in the direction of the town. He spoke to her and she told him that she would come and see them. Konstantin had a feeling that she would come and that was, as he told Nina on her sudden appearance in his study towards the end of the last act, why he had felt so restless all day. Driven out of his study by Masha's predatory, prying eyes and Pauline's dark hints, Konstantin ran to the drawing-room where the piano was to play a 'melancholy waltz'. 'That means', Pauline commented, 'that he is unhappy.' The Russian verb *toskovat'*, translated in this context to be sad or unhappy, means much more than that. It also means 'to pine for someone', 'to miss someone'. Konstantin was longing for Nina to come in the vain hope that she might come back to him, for that alone would help him snap out of his depression. No longer able to stand his mother's ecstatic account of her stage triumphs, he left the room again to play the same 'melancholy waltz'. As he was leaving, he stopped for a moment to kiss his mother on the head. Was it a farewell kiss? Did he even then contemplate suicide? 'Whirled about in a maze of dreams and images,' he was to tell Nina a short while later, 'and not knowing what it was all about or who wanted it,' the thought of suicide might well have occurred to him, for, fearing that there was no future for him as a writer and despairing of Nina's return to him, he must have regarded it, in the words of Hamlet whom he liked to quote, as 'a consummation devoutly to be wish'd'. Hence his intense excitement when Nina did come at last, and his terrible despair when she refused to have anything to do with him.

What about Nina? Why did she come back? Her affair with Trigorin had ended in disaster and Trigorin's 'idea for a short story', which had filled her with dread foreboding, was to be enacted in life. Like the dead seagull, which Konstantin had shot and laid at her feet, she was about to be destroyed just as Trigorin had planned for the heroine of his story. Just for the fun of it! It was the dreadful spectre of the seagull, with which she began to identify herself, that she hoped to exorcise by returning to the place where she had first met Trigorin and where Trigorin had outlined the plot of his story to her.

When after his return from Italy, Dorn asked Konstantin where Nina was and how she was, he replied evasively that as far as he knew she was well. Pressed for more information, he gave a brief account of Nina's life after she had run off to Moscow to become Trigorin's mistress and go on the stage. She had a child, the child died, and Trigorin left her to return 'to his old attachments'. 'Nina's personal life', he told Dorn, 'has been a complete failure.' Konstantin, who had followed Nina 'for months' in spite of her refusal to see him, did not seem to think much of her stage career, either, although he did admit that occasionally and for a few moments only 'she would utter a cry that showed some talent or do a death scene really well'. What mystified him was that she signed herself 'The Seagull' in the 'warm, sensible, interesting letters' he had received from her. He could only assume that the disastrous ending of her love affair with Trigorin and her lack of success on the stage had affected her mind.

Though still obsessed with the spectre of the seagull in the scene with Konstantin at the end of the play, in which Chekhov is very careful to show how Nina frees herself gradually from the obsessive image of the seagull,[1] Nina gives a much fuller account of her life with Trigorin whom she blames for her initial lack of success on the stage. 'He did not believe in the theatre', she says.

He was always laughing at my dreams, and little by little I stopped

[1] The chief difficulty of getting the relevance of the seagull theme through to the audience is due, curiously enough, to the fact that Russian has no articles, either definite or indefinite. What Nina actually repeats three times in the last scene which actresses find so difficult to act is: 'I am the seagull', referring to the shot seagull in Act II. This is conventionally translated into English as 'I am a seagull' which completely obscures the meaning of that vitally important part of her dialogue. Chekhov made her meaning clear in the Russian text by putting a dash after 'I am' and before 'seagull': *Ya-chaika*. If he had wished Nina to say 'I am a seagull' he would not have put the dash but would have simply written: *Ya chaika*.

believing in them myself and lost heart. Besides, I had the worries of love to cope with: jealousy, constant anxiety for my little one, I grew trivial, cheap. I acted badly, I didn't know what to do with my hands, how to stand on the stage, how to control my voice. You've no idea what it feels like to know that you're acting badly.

What was Nina doing during the five days since her return to the scenes of her childhood? She had been walking by the lake and she had been near the house many times, but could not bring herself to go in. She also told Konstantin that the night before she had gone to see 'if our stage was still in the park. Well,' she went on, 'it was still there. It was then that I cried for the first time in two years and . . . I felt more at ease in my mind.' When out in the grounds that night, Medvedenko walked past the stage, 'standing there, bare and hideous like a skeleton, the curtain flapping in the wind', and it was Nina he had heard crying, but he failed to see her in the dark.

Oddly enough, Trigorin, too, as he told Konstantin, had a good reason for coming to spend one day at Sorin's country house: he wanted to have a look 'at your stage' at the place 'where your play was performed'. He did not mention Nina or the dead seagull. Indeed, when Shamrayev reminded him of his request to have the seagull stuffed, he pretended to have forgotten all about it. What he came for was 'to refresh in memory' the scene where it had all happened. Now that he knew 'what a young girl of eighteen or nineteen feels or thinks', he hoped, no doubt, that his story of a young girl wantonly destroyed by a man who happened to pass by would not be so 'unconvincing'. After all, he was a professional writer first and foremost and every experience was grist to his mill. The important thing was that his affair with Nina was now sufficiently of the past for the subject of his story to have 'matured'.

The only change that has taken place in the lives of the other characters before the beginning of the fourth act has been Masha's expected marriage to Medvedenko and the birth of their child for whom Masha did not display any perceptible maternal affection. The failure of Konstantin's pursuit of Nina and her refusal to see him after her reappearance, childless and jilted, at the hotel of the near-by town seemed to Pauline an excellent opportunity for Masha to step in and get her man instead of being content to go on threatening to tear her love from her heart 'by the roots'. It was unfortunate that Medvedenko had not gone yet when she and Konstantin came into the room to make up Sorin's bed. But she ignored him. Walking up to Konstantin's desk where he had sat down a moment earlier she pretended to examine one of his manuscripts. The following scene is remarkable not so much for her, and for that matter Masha's, total incomprehension of Konstantin's literary aims and ambitions, let alone the crisis he was going through, as for the utter humiliation the two women subjected him to without regard to his personal feelings in attempting to persuade 'dear Konstantin' to be 'more affectionate' to 'darling Masha'.

PAULINE (*looking at the manuscript*). No one ever thought you'd be a real writer one day, Konstantin. Now, thank God, you're even getting money from the magazines. (*Smooths his hair.*) And you've grown so handsome, too. Dear, dear Konstantin, please try to be kinder to Masha.

The pained look of horror on Konstantin's face at the silly woman's patronising air, and the all too obvious meaning of her quite shameless suggestion that he should become the lover of a young woman whom he regarded as an 'insufferable creature' and with whose husband he had only a minute earlier shaken hands in silent sympathy for the way his wife and mother-in-law were treating him, must have moved even Masha to intervene to stop her. But the insulting familiarity of her interjection: 'Leave him alone, Mother', made things worse: they were treating him just as if he were another Medvedenko! Still he did not react, but sat there mutely with anger seething in his breast. Pauline quite naturally paid no attention to her daughter's danger signal.

PAULINE (*to* KONSTANTIN). She's such a nice girl. [A pause to see what effect her words had made on Konstantin, and, realising that he was anything but receptive, she proceeded to sum up her philosophy of life in one sentence:] All a woman wants, Konstantin, is that a man should look kindly at her. [And like Arkadina on a similar occasion, she concluded:] Don't I know that?

The scene was getting quite ludicrous: a true comedy situation in which the man was fuming with rage at the stupidity of the woman, while the woman was convinced that what she was proposing was quite right and proper. His patience with the two of them was at an end.

Unable to bring himself to speak for fear that he might say something he would regret, he got up from his desk and left the room without a word.

What followed is typical of the whole comic situation of the scene: the two characters are utterly unable to understand one another because the true motives of their behaviour are buried too deep in their subconscious for them to understand why they have to act in the way they do.

MASHA. You've made him angry. Why do you pester him, Mother?
PAULINE. I'm sorry for you, my child.
MASHA. A lot of good that does.
PAULINE. My heart's been bleeding for you, dear. Do you think I don't know what's going on? I see everything and understand everything.

That is exactly what she did not do: for how could it have occurred to her that what Masha found so exciting in that situation was that it gave her the opportunity to flaunt her unhappiness.

MASHA. It's just nonsense, Mother. It's only in novels you read about unhappy love. It's nothing. The only sensible thing is not to brood over it, not to sit about to wait for something to happen. If you're silly enough to fall in love with a man who doesn't care for you, then you must get over it. They've promised to transfer Simon to another district. As soon as we have moved I shall forget it all. I shall tear it out of my heart by the roots.

When they hear Konstantin playing a 'melancholy waltz' in the next room, Pauline immediately concludes that he is unhappy, the implication being that she was right in trying to exploit the situation in her daughter's favour. But Masha merely 'dances a few waltz steps noiselessly', clearly unaffected by Konstantin's unhappiness or the conclusion her mother draws from it. The chief thing, she insists, is not to see Konstantin because 'all this is so damned silly'.

And she never spoke a truer word.

Masha's hopes that the transfer of 'my Simon' to another district would make her 'forget it all' were somewhat shattered at the appearance of the luckless schoolmaster accompanied by the much-travelled but broke Dorn, and Sorin, now permanently confined to his bathchair.

For, hearing her husband as usual complaining of having now to feed six mouths on his meagre salary, her resentment against him for constantly reminding her of her duty towards their child broke out with barely controlled fury.

MASHA (*to her husband*). Haven't you gone yet?

MEDVEDENKO (*guiltily*). Well, how can I when your father won't let me have a horse?

MASHA (*with bitter annoyance, in an undertone*). I wish I'd never set eyes on you!

Medvedenko walked off 'with a hangdog expression' to the other end of the room, leaving Dorn to comment on the changes in the house after his return, followed by the usual half-bantering and half-serious exchange of words between the doctor and Sorin about Dorn's lack of sympathy with Sorin's worsening health. Their dialogue is interrupted by the entry of Konstantin, who, in that strange melancholy mood of expectancy and despair, seemed particularly anxious to show his affection for his uncle and his mother, and sat down at Sorin's feet. The mention of Genoa and the 'collective personality' he seemed to acquire in the dense, milling crowds of that city, led Dorn to associate it with 'the world soul' Nina had acted in Konstantin's play and, quite naturally, inquire where Nina was and how she was getting on. Konstantin's reluctant and rather unfavourable account of Nina's private life (there was not the slightest touch of pity for her either in his voice or in his words) and her stage career concluded with the characteristically egotistical observation: 'How awfully easy it is, Doctor, to be a philosopher on paper and how damned difficult to be one in life.'

The arrival of Shamrayev, vociferous and gallant as ever, Arkadina and Trigorin – 'our great man', as Arkadina unctuously described him – put an abrupt end to the conversation about Nina, who in the following scenes was never mentioned in the presence of Arkadina and Trigorin. Trigorin tried his best to cover up his embarrassment at the now inevitable meeting with Konstantin. His jovial way of greeting Sorin and Masha was anything but genuine, especially his question to Masha: 'Happy?' which he did not venture to pursue in view of her obviously dissembling smile. He approached Konstantin 'diffidently'. The reconciliation scene between the two had obviously been prepared by him and Arkadina. 'Your mother has told me', he said to Konstantin propitiatingly, 'that you have forgotten the past and are no longer angry with me.' Konstantin just held out his hand to him in silent agreement. Arkadina stepped in with an even more propitiatory announcement: 'Boris has brought you the magazine with your new story.' He accepted the magazine with a cold 'very kind of you'. But Trigorin's diffidence did not last. As soon as the awkward moment of the meeting of the two rivals had passed over without any 'tactless' remark by Konstantin, he no longer thought it necessary to conceal his real feelings. 'Your admirers', he declared with ill-concealed irony,

want to be remembered to you. You'd be surprised how interested they are in you in Moscow and Petersburg. They're always asking all sorts of questions about you. What you are like, how old you are, whether you are dark or fair. For some reason they all assume that you can't be young. And no one knows your real name because you write under a pseudonym.

Finally, the knock-out blow: 'You're as mysterious as the Man in the Iron Mask.' Konstantin's reply was disdainfully cool: 'Will you be staying long?' he inquired with the clear enough implication that the sooner 'the genius' went the happier he would be. Trigorin was not slow to get his meaning. He was thinking of leaving for Moscow 'tomorrow', he replied, for he had a novel to finish and a short story to write which he had promised for an anthology of short stories. 'As you see,' he added, 'it's the old, old story.' A highly successful novelist who, now that he had no longer to impress a guileless young girl whom he had made up his mind to seduce, had no need to complain of his 'crazy sort of life' or boast of being continually harassed by friends who kept asking him what masterpiece he was going to write for them next, or to pretend to be constantly haunted by the thought of being 'dragged off to a lunatic asylum'.

Konstantin's contemptuous comment on opening the journal with his own and Trigorin's stories: 'He has read his own story but hasn't even cut the pages of mine', shows how little he was impressed by Trigorin's account of the interest shown in him by the literary world in Moscow and Petersburg: he had reached the moment of truth and nothing that Trigorin or the literary world could say was of any interest to him.

The game of lotto was about to start and most of the company

E

seemed to be glad of the diversion it provided. Even Pauline held out her hand, though reluctantly, for her son-in-law to kiss before walking off to his home and baby in the cold and howling wind. 'He'll get there all right', was Shamrayev's parting comment. 'He's not a general, is he?' Konstantin refused to join in the game, but he did not go out for a stroll as he had told his mother. Instead, he went back to resume playing his 'melancholy waltz'. The scene of the 'lotto' game emphasises more than anything else in the play Konstantin's utter loneliness in his family circle. Masha, in particular, gets so absorbed in calling out the numbers that she forgets even to glance at Konstantin when he comes back into the room.

ARKADINA. The stake is ten kopecks. Put it down for me, Doctor, will you?
DORN. Certainly, madam.
MASHA. Have you all put down your stakes? I begin. Twenty-two.

What she began was the count-down on the shot before the fall of the curtain.

ARKADINA. Got it.
MASHA. Three.
DORN. Right.
MASHA. Have you put three down? Eight. Eighty-one. Ten.
SHAMRAYEV. Don't be in such a hurry.
ARKADINA. What a wonderful reception I had in Kharkov. My goodness, my head's still swimming!
MASHA. Thirty-four.

A melancholy waltz is played offstage.

ARKADINA [she pays no attention to her son's playing. Too excited by her own triumph]. The students gave me an ovation. Three baskets of flowers, two bouquets and – this! (*Takes a brooch off her dress and throws it on the table.*)
SHAMRAYEV. Ah, that is something!
MASHA. Fifty.
DORN. Did you say fifty?
ARKADINA. I wore a lovely dress. Say what you like but I do know how to dress.

PAULINE [tries unsuccessfully to draw Arkadina's attention to Konstantin's playing]. Konstantin's playing again. Poor boy, he's unhappy.

Arkadina is not interested in her son's unhappiness: she ignores Pauline's remark. Shamrayev, however, explains Konstantin's unhappiness as the result of the bad press he is getting.

SHAMRAYEV. They've been going for him in the papers.

MASHA [utterly unconcerned either with Konstantin's unhappiness or the attacks on him in the press]. Seventy-seven.

ARKADINA. Why worry about it?

TRIGORIN. He's unlucky. Quite unable to find his own individual style. Writes such queer stuff, so vague. At times it almost reminds me of the ravings of a lunatic. Not one living character!

MASHA. Eleven.

ARKADINA (*looking round at* SORIN). Are you bored, Peter dear? (*Pause.*) He's asleep.

DORN. Regular State Councillor Sorin is asleep.

MASHA. Seven. Ninety.

TRIGORIN. Do you think I'd ever have written anything if I lived in a house like this by a lake? I'd have conquered this mania and spent all day fishing.

MASHA. Twenty-eight.

TRIGORIN. To catch a roach or a perch – that's my idea of heaven.

It was obviously not Dorn's idea of heaven: he is the only one to realise that Konstantin is a much better writer than Trigorin and it is through his mouth that Chekhov once more criticises the *avant-garde* Symbolist movement for lacking any definite aim.

DORN. Well, I believe in Konstantin. There's something in him. He thinks in images. His stories are vivid, brilliant. They affect me strongly. A great pity, though, that he hasn't any definite aim. He produces an impression and that is all. But you can't go far by just producing an impression. Aren't you glad your son is a writer, Irina?

Arkadina's answer reveals more than anything else how little she thinks of Konstantin's ability as a writer and her ingrained conviction that he is a nonentity compared with a 'genius' like Trigorin.

ARKADINA. I'm ashamed to confess it, Doctor, but I haven't read any of his things. I can never find the time.

MASHA. Twenty-six.

KONSTANTIN *comes in quietly and goes to his desk.*

He came in just in time to hear Trigorin express his complete, brutal indifference to the mental crisis through which Nina was passing because of him though, since he is quite unaware how much the seagull symbol was preying on Nina's mind, it is the audience rather than Konstantin who should be able to appreciate the hidden meaning of the following brief scene.

SHAMRAYEV (*to* TRIGORIN). I forgot to tell you Mr Trigorin. We've still got something of yours here.

TRIGORIN. Oh? What's that?

SHAMRAYEV. You remember the seagull Konstantin shot down. You asked me to have it stuffed for you.

TRIGORIN. Did I? I don't remember. (*Thinking it over.*) I don't remember.

MASHA. Sixty-six. One.

KONSTANTIN (*flings open the window and listens*). How dark it is! I can't understand why I should be feeling so restless.

Konstantin is still hoping that Nina will come to see him, but Arkadina who has no idea what it is Konstantin is listening to, only feels the draught.

ARKADINA. Shut the window, Konstantin. There's an awful draught.

KONSTANTIN *closes the window.*

MASHA. Eighty-eight.

TRIGORIN. My game, ladies and gentlemen.

ARKADINA (*gaily*). Bravo! Bravo!

SHAMRAYEV. Bravo!

ARKADINA [the bitter irony of her statement can only be appreciated by the audience]. What marvellous luck that man has! He always wins! (*Gets up.*) Now let's go and have something to eat. Our great man hasn't had any lunch today. We'll carry on with the game after dinner. (*To her son.*) Leave your manuscripts. Let's go in to dinner.

KONSTANTIN. I don't want to, Mother. I'm not hungry.

ARKADINA [with complete indifference: her indifference to her son is almost on a par with Trigorin's indifference to Nina]. As you wish. (*Wakes* SORIN.) Dinner, Peter dear. (*Takes* SHAMRAYEV's *arm.*) Let me tell you about that marvellous reception I had in Kharkov.

PAULINE *puts out the candles on the table; then she and* DORN *wheel out the chair. All go out by door on left;* KONSTANTIN *alone remains on the stage, sitting at his desk.*

Konstantin's soliloquy establishes the fact that he has done with his Symbolist past, but it makes it no less clear that it would require a deal of effort on his part to become a writer 'who writes because what he has to say comes straight from the heart'. The knock on the window throws him suddenly into feverish activity, he rushes out on to the terrace and comes back with Nina: his premonition that she would come had turned out to be right after all.

The following scene between Nina and Konstantin is a good example of the incongruities that typify a classical comedy situation, except that in a Chekhov comedy such a situation is never resolved into a so-called 'happy ending', endings which, according to Chekhov, merely 'lull people in their golden dreams . . . that there is nothing to worry about in this world'. The scene is remarkable for the complete lack of under-standing or, as Medvedenko would put it, of 'a point of contact', between the two characters: Nina has no idea of the mental crisis through which Konstantin is passing nor that Konstantin has cast her in the role of his deliverer; Konstantin has no idea of Nina's seagull obsession nor of her determination to exorcise the spectre of the seagull – that threatened to destroy her and her stage career – by going back to the place where it first originated. It was only natural, therefore, that Nina should be appalled by Konstantin's delirious avowals of love, and that Konstantin should be no less shocked by Nina's reaction to them.

This scene contains the clue to the whole play. It is a scene that is invariably misunderstood. It is a scene that actors find almost im-possible to play. It is a scene in which the two great themes of the play meet and coalesce: the theme of the seagull and the theme of the aim of art. At the end of it Nina gets rid of her obsession with the spectre of the seagull, while Konstantin, balked of his last hope that Nina might save him by reciprocating his love, commits suicide.

The scene opens quietly. Overcome by memories of a past that seems so far away as to be almost unbelievable, Nina lays her head on Konstantin's chest and sobs 'quietly'.

KONSTANTIN (*deeply moved*). Nina! Nina! It's you – you! I had a feeling you'd come. All day I've been so restless. (*Takes off her hat and cloak.*) Oh, my darling, my precious darling, so you've come! Don't let's cry, don't!

But Nina knows that Arkadina is in the house and she feels apprehensive that any meeting with her might revive the agony of her final rift with Trigorin.

NINA. There's someone here.
KONSTANTIN. There's no one, no one.
NINA. Lock the doors. Someone may come in.
KONSTANTIN. No one will come in.
NINA. I know your mother's here. Please lock the doors.
KONSTANTIN (*locks the doors on right; going to the door on left*). There's no lock on this door. I'll put a chair against it. (*Puts an armchair against the door.*) Don't be afraid. No one will come in.
NINA (*scanning his face intently*). Come, let me look at you. (*Looking round the room.*) Warm, nice. . . . This used to be a drawing-room. Have I changed much?
KONSTANTIN. Yes, you are thinner and your eyes are larger. Nina, it's so strange to be seeing you. Why wouldn't you let me see you? Why haven't you wanted to come all this time? I know you've been here almost a week. I've been to your hotel several times a day. I stood under your window like a beggar.

Forced to give some explanation why she had been walking by the lake but could not bring herself to visit the house she had been drawn to so powerfully before, Nina was overcome for the first time in this scene by her obsessive dread of the spectre of the seagull to the great alarm of Konstantin.

NINA. I was afraid you might hate me. Every night I dream that you look and look at me and don't recognise me. If only you knew! Ever since I got back I've been coming here to walk by the lake, but I couldn't bring myself to come in. Let's sit down. (*They sit down.*) Let's sit down and talk and talk. Oh, it's so nice here, cosy, warm.

Listen to the wind! There's a passage in Turgenev: 'Happy is he
who on a night like this has a roof over his head, a warm corner' I'm
the seagull—no, that's not what I was going to say. (*Rubs her forehead.*) I'm sorry. What was I saying? Oh, yes. Turgenev: 'And may
the lord help all homeless wanderers.' Never mind. (*Sobs.*)
KONSTANTIN. Nina, again? Nina, Nina!

Konstantin's obvious concern for her (the mention of the seagull
must have awakened his fears for her sanity) makes Nina lift the veil a
little on the reason for her visit, and, inevitably, she cannot help com-
paring her dreams of fame before she left home with her far from
glamorous engagement in a small provincial town where she would
have to put up with the sordid advances of cultured businessmen.
Unfortunately, she also mentioned her child-like 'joyous' life when she
used to be 'so happy' and when she 'loved him'. Misinterpreting the last
phrase (Nina only meant to say that she had been very fond of him: she
still used the formal second person plural), Konstantin burst into such
a torrent of words that Nina was at first stunned and when he actually
appealed to her to stay with him or let him follow her, she 'quickly put
on her hat and cloak' and was about to rush out of the house to her
waiting cab:

NINA. It's nothing. I feel much better now. I haven't cried for two
years. Late last night I went out to see if our stage was still in the
park. Well, it was still there. It was then that I cried for the first time
in two years, and I felt much better, I felt more at ease in my mind.
See? I'm not crying any more. (*Takes his hand.*) And so you're a
writer now. You—a writer and I—an actress. We're right in it now,
the two of us. I used to be so happy, like a child. I'd wake up early as
merry as a lark. I loved you. I dreamed of fame. And now? Early
tomorrow morning I shall have to leave for Yelets. Travel third
class, with peasants. And in Yelets cultured businessmen will
pester me with their attentions. Life is sordid.
KONSTANTIN. Why are you going to Yelets?
NINA. I've an engagement there for the whole winter.

The Yelets engagement was an unexpected blow: Konstantin, like
Trigorin, had little faith in Nina's stage career, hence his impassioned
account of his own suffering because she had left him the first time.

KONSTANTIN. Oh, Nina, I cursed you, hated you, tore up your letters and photographs, but every minute I knew that I belonged to you, that my heart was yours for ever. Nina, I can't stop loving you. Ever since I lost you and my stories began to appear in print, life has been unbearable. I suffered agonies. It was as though my youth was suddenly snatched away. I felt as though I were an old man of ninety. I prayed for you to come back, I kissed the ground you had walked on. Wherever I looked, I saw your face, your sweet smile which had brought sunshine into the best years of my life.

NINA (*bewildered*). Why does he talk like this? Why does he talk like this?

KONSTANTIN. I am alone in the world, Nina. I have no one whose affection can warm me. I'm cold, cold, as though I lived in some dungeon, and everything I write is dry, harsh and gloomy. Please, stay, Nina. I implore you. Or let me go with you. (NINA *quickly puts on her hat and cloak.*) Nina, why? For God's sake, Nina! (*Looks at her while she puts on her things; pause.*)

NINA. My cab's waiting for me at the gate. Don't see me out, please. I'll find my way alone. (*Bursts into tears.*) Could you give me some water, please?

Konstantin's impassioned plea makes Nina realise for the first time that she is not without blame for Konstantin's 'loneliness'. But what about his mother? Wasn't she at home after all? Couldn't she be of some help, seeing how fond they were of each other? Konstantin's explanation that his mother was there because of Sorin's illness deepens Nina's feeling of responsibility for ignoring the pain she had caused him. His declaration that he kissed the ground she trod on wrings the cry from her that she ought to be killed. Overwhelmed by this additional emotional stress, she is once more overcome by the dread spectre of the seagull, by the feeling that she deserved to be destroyed. The laughter of Arkadina and Trigorin in the dining-room brings her back to reality. It is after she has run to the door and peeped through the keyhole to make quite sure that she was not mistaken that she tries to explain to Konstantin that one of her reasons for her break with Trigorin was, that his lack of faith in her stage career made her acting so bad; and that that, together with her other troubles, brought about her nervous breakdown and her identification with the seagull which

Konstantin had killed and which Trigorin had thought he could use for a
short story about the destruction of a young girl 'just for the fun of it'.
Even before her return she was beginning to feel that she was 'a real
actress', and since her return she felt that the powers of her mind and
soul were 'getting stronger every day', or, in other words, that she was
at last succeeding in exorcising the spectre of the seagull.

Nina's profession of faith and Konstantin's confession of failure to
find a way out of 'the maze of dreams and images' provide the key to an
understanding of Chekhov's intention in writing *The Seagull*:

KONSTANTIN (*gives* NINA *a glass of water*). Where are you going
   now?
NINA. Back to town. Isn't your mother here?
KONSTANTIN. Yes. Uncle was taken ill on Thursday, so we wired her
   to come.
NINA. Why did you say that you kissed the ground on which I had
   walked? I ought to be killed. (*Leans over the table.*) Oh, I'm so tired.
   I want to rest, rest. (*Raises her head.*) I'm the seagull. No, that's not
   so. I am an actress. Yes! (*Hearing* ARKADINA *and* TRIGORIN
   *laughing, she listens for a minute, then runs to the door on left and looks
   through the keyhole.*) He's here too. (*Returning to* KONSTANTIN.)
   Oh well, it doesn't matter. . . . No, he didn't believe in the theatre.
   He was always laughing at my dreams, and little by little I stopped
   believing in them myself and lost heart. Besides, I had the worries of
   love to cope with; jealousy, constant anxiety for my little one. I grew
   trivial, cheap. I acted badly. Didn't know what to do with my hands,
   how to stand on the stage, how to control my voice. You've no
   idea what it feels like to know that you're acting badly. I'm the
   seagull. No, that's not so. Remember you shot a seagull? Quite by
   accident a man came along and just for the fun of it destroyed it. An
   idea for a short story. No, that isn't so. (*Rubs her forehead.*) What
   was I saying? I was talking about the stage. I'm different now. I'm a
   real actress. I enjoy acting. I revel in it. The stage intoxicates me. I
   feel that I'm peerless. But now, while I've been here I've been walking a lot and thinking, thinking, and feeling that the powers of my
   mind and soul are growing stronger every day. Now I know, now I
   understand, Konstantin, that in our calling, whether we act on the
   stage or write, what matters is not fame, nor glory, nor the things I

used to dream of. What matters is knowing how to endure, to know how to bear your cross and to have faith. I have faith, and it doesn't hurt so much. And when I think of my calling, I'm no longer afraid of life.

KONSTANTIN (*sadly*). You have found your path, you know which way you are going. But I am still whirled about in a maze of dreams and images, not knowing what it is all about and who wants it. I have no faith and I do not know what my calling is.

All the hopes Konstantin cherished about Nina's visit, which had filled him with such wild excitement when at last she did come, were shattered by her refusal to stay or let him go with her, by the light-hearted way in which she invited him to come and see her when she became 'a famous actress', and even more by her confession that she was still in love with Trigorin. After her somewhat theatrical exit (she had to convince him that she was a *real* actress by reciting the beginning of his play she had made such a mess of in the first act), he decided to destroy himself, for he realised that there was no future for him as a writer since, like a fanatical Symbolist, he had spent too long a time immured in his ivory tower (the usual place of refuge for the Symbolists) and let life pass him by. Nina no longer existed for him. His last thought was for his mother. A very strange thought: for had he not himself asked Nina a little earlier to stay and have supper, or would not his suicide have upset his mother more than Nina's visit, or, which was more likely, did he fear that his mother would hold Nina responsible for his suicide, as, indeed, practically every director and critic of *The Seagull* has done? But he was no longer capable of rational thought, all he was concerned about was to tear up his manuscripts before he shot himself. As if to emphasise the deliberateness of this action, Chekhov insists in his stage direction that it takes Konstantin *two minutes* (a very long time for an actor to remain on the stage alone) to tear up his manuscripts. For by destroying his manuscripts, Konstantin was destroying everything he had lived and worked for: he was destroying his life. His final act of self-destruction was merely the physical expression of a *fait accompli*.

While confessing that she was still in love with Trigorin (in her last speech) Nina could not help recalling Trigorin's 'idea for a short story', which caused her to dwell rather sadly on the 'joyful' memories of the boy-and-girl romance she had had with Konstantin. Chekhov, who made Nina speak contemptuously of Konstantin's obsession with symbols, was not averse to using a symbol himself by making Shamrayev not only mention the stuffed seagull to Trigorin earlier on, but actually produce it at the very end of the last act: a clear indication that the spectre of the seagull, which had nearly driven Nina out of her mind, was nothing but a stuffed bird which was not likely very much longer to haunt a girl who was determined to achieve her aim in life in spite of the hard and slogging path ahead of her.

The shot behind the scenes made everybody start, but Dorn's explanation reassured them. Attempts have been made in some recent productions of *The Seagull* to show that neither Arkadina nor Masha were deceived by Dorn's explanation. There is nothing in Chekhov's stage directions to justify such a gross interference with the audience's participation in the play, one of the most important features of Chekhov's new form of drama of indirect action. From the very beginning of the play the audience is always ahead of the characters on the stage. This is no less true of its end. Chekhov leaves no doubt in the mind of the spectator what the reaction of every character in his play will be when he or she learns of Konstantin's suicide or what the lives of his characters will be like after the fall of the curtain.

UNCLE VANYA

Introduction

Chekhov described *Uncle Vanya* (completed in 1897 shortly after *The Seagull*) as 'old-fashioned' and subtitled it 'Scenes of Country Life in Four Acts'. This description as well as the subtitle (one of the echoes from Alexander Ostrovsky's plays) can be explained by the fact that *Uncle Vanya* is an adaptation of Chekhov's earlier 'Tolstoyan' comedy *The Wood Demon* which he refused to include in the complete edition of his works. Chekhov took one of the principal themes of *The Wood Demon*, namely the conflict between Ivan Voynitsky and Professor Serebryakov, which had nothing whatever to do with the Tolstoyan ideas propagated in that play, and constructed around it an entirely new play. He did so by incorporating almost the entire second and third acts of his earlier play into *Uncle Vanya* (he did, however, introduce an important change: instead of shooting himself, Ivan Voynitsky tries unsuccessfully to shoot the professor). Chekhov also introduced a radical change into the other important theme of his earlier play: the theme of the conservation of forests, which in *The Wood Demon* is treated as some kind of aberration of the eccentric landowner Khrushchov (*khrushch*, a cockchafer which is so destructive of trees, emphasises by contrast the 'wood demon's' mania for the preservation of trees). In *Uncle Vanya* this theme assumes the much greater significance of the destruction of the environment, anticipating almost by a hundred years the modern preoccupation with this problem. Khrushchov becomes in *Uncle Vanya* Dr Astrov, a conscientious and overworked country doctor, whose name is symbolic of the man whose work for humanity at large has no trace of eccentricity about it. The two chief themes of *Uncle Vanya* – one dealing with a selfish idealist like Ivan Voynitsky, who suddenly realises that he has been deluded in wasting his life on a 'demigod' with feet of clay, and the other dealing with an unselfish idealist like Dr Astrov, who is entirely free from any delusions and whose only hope is that in 'a thousand years' his work for the preservation of forests might, in however small a way, have contributed to 'the happiness of mankind' – form the real dramatic kernel of the play. These two themes, however, do not coalesce nor do they lead inevitably to the denouement in the last act, as do the two chief themes of *The Seagull*, and that, no doubt, is another reason why Chekhov declared the play to be 'old-fashioned'. In *Uncle Vanya*, the characters are static: they do not show any growth or development as the characters of *The Seagull* do: they remain the same at the end of the play as at the beginning. As a result, the audience of *Uncle Vanya*, while feeling for, and sympathising with, the characters of the play, remain mere spectators who do not participate in its dramatic action, for at no point do they know more than the characters on the stage. By 'lifting' the main theme of *Uncle Vanya* from his earlier play Chekhov has had to sacrifice the 'new form' of indirect action play he had invented and perfected for *The Seagull*.

The action of the play takes place on the estate belonging to Sophia (Sonia), the young daughter of Professor Alexander Serebryakov. It was bought by Sonia's grandfather, Peter Voynitsky, a high court judge, as a dowry for his daughter on her marriage to Alexander Serebryakov, an eminent professor of the fine arts. Her brother, Ivan Voynitsky (Uncle Vanya), who would normally have inherited the estate on the death of his sister, had renounced his rights to its ownership in favour of his niece Sonia. The play opens about a year after the retirement of Professor Serebryakov. Professor Serebryakov and his young wife Helen (Yelena), finding life in town too expensive, have moved into the large country house on the estate, where they intended to stay permanently, as appears from Uncle Vanya's reply to a question by Dr Astrov at the beginning of the first act:

ASTROV. Are they going to stay here long?
VOYNITSKY (*grimly*). A hundred years. The professor has decided to stay here for good.

Chekhov gives only Helen's age in the list of characters in the play: she is twenty-seven years old. Sonia's age can be gathered from the first version of the play where her age is given as twenty-one. From internal evidence the age of Dr Astrov can be assumed to be in the late thirties, while Uncle Vanya himself gives his age as forty-seven, an age old enough to make his hopes of 'a new life' rather pathetic, and certainly justify the 'uncle' of the title.

The duration of the action of the play is left rather vague by Chekhov. The first act opens between two and three o'clock in the afternoon on a hot June day, the second act on a night at the beginning of July (the mention of the haymaking by Sonia would justify such a date[1]), and the third and fourth acts on an evening and the following morning in September. The whole play, therefore, covers at most three months. In the first act Helen remarks that Astrov had been three times while she had been staying at the estate; since Astrov usually visited the Voynitskys once a month, she and the professor arrived only about three months before the opening of the play.

[1] In a letter to Stanislavsky on 23 November 1903, Chekhov states that haymaking usually takes place between 20 June and 25 June.

F

Act One

Chekhov's descriptive stage direction is, like all similar stage directions in his plays, extremely scanty. The only interesting features which provide the spectators with a glimpse into the past and present life of the characters are: part of the large country house, the old poplar tree, the guitar and the swing, and the table set for tea. The only word that seems to forebode the gathering storm concerns, apparently, the state of the weather: 'overcast', a word which has a distinctly emotive overtone of despondency in Russian when applied to people.

This feeling of deep-seated dissatisfaction with life verging on despondency becomes evident in the very first scene between Dr Astrov and the old nurse Marina who has known the doctor for over eleven years. During that time he has aged considerably and, Marina observes deprecatingly, grown a little too fond of vodka. The doctor admits it, but tries to excuse it on the grounds of overwork and the 'dull, sordid and stupid life' he is forced to live. 'So far as my personal life is concerned,' he tells Sonia in the second act, 'I wish I could say there was something good in it . . . I work harder than anyone in our district, fate is forever hitting out at me and sometimes I suffer unbearably . . . I don't expect anything any more for myself.' He has come to dislike people: the peasants were all 'uncivilised' and lived in squalor, and he found it difficult to get on with the 'intelligentsia', the majority of whom he found stupid, while those who were more intelligent were hysterical and given to morbid introspection. They thought him odd because of his obsession with the conservation of forests and because he was a vegetarian. 'They no longer', he declared, 'have a spontaneous, pure and objective attitude to nature and to men.'

Helen, perhaps because she was 'a little in love with Astrov', was more clear-sighted about him than anyone else in the play. 'It is not only a question of forests and medicine', she tells Sonia at the end of the second act, 'it is his genius that matters', by which she meant his 'courage, independence of mind and bold initiative. He plants a tree', she observes, 'and already he is thinking what the result of it will be in a thousand years, already he is dreaming of the happiness of mankind in

a thousand years. . . . He drinks and is occasionally a little coarse, but
. . . just think what his life is like: muddy, impassable roads, frosts,
blizzards, enormous distances, coarse savage peasants, widespread
poverty, disease—how can you expect a man . . . to keep himself sober
and spotless working and struggling like that, day in, day out, and in
such surroundings?' Astrov himself is well aware of the reason for
having grown 'a different man' in eleven years. 'Overwork, Nannie,
overwork,' he tells Marina. 'On my feet from morning till night. Don't
know the meaning of rest. At night I lie awake under the bedclothes in
constant fear of being dragged off to a patient. Haven't had a single free
day ever since I've known you.' He then proceeds to give her a terrifying account of a typhus epidemic during which he had to spend a whole
day among the sick peasants who were lying on the floor with calves
and pigs beside them. On his return home he had to perform an
emergency operation on a railway signalman who died under the
chloroform. 'It was then,' he says,

> when I didn't want them that my feelings awakened and my con-
> science pricked me, as though I had killed him on purpose. I sat down,
> closed my eyes and thought to myself: will those who will be living
> a hundred or two hundred years after us spare a thought for us who
> are now blazing a trail for them? Will they have a good word for us?
> No, Nanny, they won't, they won't!

MARINA. Men won't, but God will.
ASTROV. Thank you, Nanny. You spoke well.

It was at this point that Uncle Vanya made his first appearance after
his afternoon nap: he did not seem to have quite recovered from his
sleep and, as he sat down on the garden seat, he kept straightening his
'fashionable' tie, which, as it were, personified his attempt to keep up
appearances as behoved a landed gentleman, and in this way emphasise
the difference between him and the low-born professor with whom he
was now at daggers drawn. When Helen asks him at the end of the first
act why he always quarrels with the professor at breakfast, the only
reply he gives her is: 'But what if I hate him!' Why did he hate him?
Principally because he considered that the professor had been responsible for wasting his life. 'Day and night,' he tells Helen in the second
act, 'the thought that my life has been irretrievably wasted weighs

heavy upon me like a nightmare. I have no past. It has been stupidly squandered on trifles. And the present terrifies me by its senselessness.' A little later in the same act he tells his niece that 'where there is no real life one has to live on illusions'. What illusions? The greatest illusion of his life was his idealisation of Professor Serebryakov, an illusion that was only shattered after the professor's retirement from his university post. The Herr Professor, as Uncle Vanya keeps on referring to Serebryakov contemptuously, is usually represented on the stage as seen through the eyes of Uncle Vanya. But he could hardly be blamed for the extravagant view Uncle Vanya had had of him before his retirement from the chair of fine arts, nor for the fact that Uncle Vanya had not the commonsense to realise that he was just a distinguished academic and not the 'demigod' he had imagined him to be. It was not the professor's fault that Uncle Vanya, as he himself admits in his soliloquy in the second act, 'adored' Serebryakov and was 'proud of him and his scholarship', or that he regarded everything that the professor uttered and everything he wrote as 'the highest achievement of genius'. The Herr Professor, to be sure, had a rather exaggerated opinion of his own importance, but that is not such a rare thing among 'eminent' academics. Indeed, it was only to be expected of a man who had risen from utter obscurity to the highest position in his profession and was generally acknowledged to be a great authority on his subject. If, again as Uncle Vanya maintains in the first act, Serebryakov had been writing and lecturing for twenty-five years 'without knowing anything about art', it was not for Uncle Vanya to assume the mantle of an art critic, particularly as such an accusation can be, and indeed has been, levelled against many another 'distinguished' academic in that exceptionally vulnerable field of learning. Chekhov had never had a particularly high opinion of academics and there certainly is a great deal in Uncle Vanya's vitriolic attacks on the Herr Professor that expresses Chekhov's own opinion of them. It is no accident, for instance, that the professors of Moscow University should have been so incensed by this play that they decided to boycott its performances. What Chekhov objected to was the propensity of academics to stick labels on everything and, particularly, to accuse him and his plays of 'realism, naturalism and all sorts of other nonsense', which, incidentally, they still persist in doing.

So great was Uncle Vanya's shock on discovering that the 'great man was an impostor that he gave up doing any work on the estate. 'Before,' he tells Astrov in the first act, 'Sonia and I were working, now Sonia is the only one who does any work while I sleep, eat and drink.' At the age of forty-seven he had fallen in love with the professor's 27-year-old wife whom he imagined he could have married when she was seventeen. The picture of the idyllic life he could have had with Helen which he conjures up in the second act is almost as childishly absurd as his ludicrous overestimation of the professor's intellectual stature. It is as absurd as his belief that if he had had 'a normal life' he might have been 'a Schopenhauer or a Dostoevsky'. It is true it was the professor's taunt in the third act that he was 'a nonentity' that provoked that preposterous assessment of his own creative powers which he himself dismissed a moment later as sheer nonsense. But such an idea must have lain buried in his subconscious mind ever since he began to be worried over the way the professor had achieved fame and general recognition. A soap bubble! A learned minnow! 'And what success he's had with women!' he exclaims in reply to Astrov's teasing remark that he was simply jealous of the professor.

No Don Juan has ever known such amazing success! His first wife, my sister, loved him as only pure angels can love beings as pure and beautiful as themselves. My mother still dotes on him to this day and he still inspires a feeling of reverential awe in her. His second wife . . . married him when he was already an old man. She sacrificed her youth, her beauty, her freedom, her glamour for him. Whatever for?

Uncle Vanya could find no satisfactory answer to the enigma of the professor's fame or his phenomenal success with women. Nor, for that matter, why he of all people should have allowed the professor 'to turn their life upside down'. He went to sleep at the wrong time, he had early lunch, dinner at seven, ate 'all sorts of fancy concoctions', drank wine. Marina, too, found 'the goings on' at the house since the arrival of the professor and his wife objectionable. They had completely disorganised their traditional way of life: no more 'tea at eight o'clock in the morning, dinner at one, and supper in the evening' and, what was even worse, 'no more noodles for dinner!' 'Moreover, the professor', Marina wailed, 'spends the night reading and writing and all of a sudden at two in the morning he rings his bell. What is it now? Why, tea, if you please! Wake the servants for him! Put on the samovar!' The samovar has, indeed, been on the boil for hours in expectation of the return of the professor, his wife and his daughter from a country walk. They all appear presently, 'the eminent scholar', as Uncle Vanya remarks sarcastically, 'wearing an overcoat, galoshes and gloves and carrying an umbrella'. The short scene that follows their entry is characteristic of the professor's condescending way with his intellectual 'inferiors', 'the stupid people' he was obliged to see every day with 'their absurd talk'.

SEREBRYAKOV. Excellent, excellent. Wonderful scenery.

TELEGIN [a nephew of the former owner of the estate and Sonia's godfather, now reduced to the state of an impoverished retainer and nicknamed Waffles because of his pockmarked face]. Remarkable, sir.

SONIA. Let's go to the plantation tomorrow, Father. Would you like to?

VOYNITSKY. Let's have tea, ladies and gentlemen.

SEREBRYAKOV. My friends, be so kind as to send my tea up to my study. I've still some work to do today.

SONIA. I'm sure you'll like the plantation, Father.

But Serebryakov did not seem to pay any attention to his daughter's repeated invitation to visit Astrov's plantation: he had the utmost contempt for the country doctor and his 'crazy' ideas.

After Serebryakov, Helen and Sonia have gone into the house (the professor 'strutting like a demigod', as Uncle Vanya was not slow to observe), the conversation quite naturally turned to the professor's beautiful wife. There is a tense relationship between Helen and Sonia, which should be brought out at their first entrance in spite of the fact that they do not exchange a single word. 'How long are you going to be cross with me?' Helen asks Sonia in the second act.

Why should we be enemies? . . . You and I have not been speaking to one another for weeks. You're angry with me because you think I married your father for selfish reasons. But . . . I swear I married him for love. I fell in love with him because he was such a famous man. It was not real love. It was so insincere, so artificial, but it seemed real to me at the time. It's not my fault. And since our marriage you have never stopped accusing me with those clever, suspicious eyes of yours.'

It was perfectly true: Helen had not married the eminent professor for any 'selfish' reasons. Like Helen of Troy, Helen is a *passive* destroyer, a predator who is too indolent to be unfaithful to her old husband, a fact she seems to disguise by her talk of loyalty, purity and a capacity for self-sacrifice. But Uncle Vanya was much nearer the truth when he described Helen's loyalty to her husband as 'false from beginning to end'. In fact, he claimed, it was 'immoral' because it was immoral to stifle one's natural feelings. Telegin, whose goodness verges on silliness and who always finds an excuse for the darker sides of human nature (he forgave his wife who had left him for her lover on the day after their wedding because of his 'unprepossessing appearance' and spent all the money he had on educating his wife's illegitimate children), objects violently to Uncle Vanya's statement on the grounds that people who betray their husbands or wives could not be trusted even to be loyal to their country, an objection Uncle Vanya brushes aside with a contemptuous: 'Dry up, Waffles!' Chekhov uses Telegin, as he does the simpleminded Medvedenko in *The Seagull*, to make the audience aware of the tense atmosphere in the Voynitsky household by a statement that is completely the reverse of the truth. It is just after Uncle Vanya's sarcastic remark about the professor and his expression of admiration for Helen's beauty that Telegin gives utterance to his extraordinary expression of universal love and harmony.

TELEGIN. Whether I drive through the fields or take a walk in the garden in the shade of the trees or look on this table, I experience a feeling of indescribable bliss! The weather is enchanting, the birds are singing, we all live in peace and harmony – what more do we want?

What more indeed? The answer comes immediately in Uncle Vanya's harangue against his mother, 'the old crow', who has one foot in the grave, but still goes on 'looking in her clever books for the dawn of a new life', followed by a much longer invective against the professor who spends all his time writing in his study, 'wracking our wits, with furrowed brows, odes, odes, odes we write without a word of praise either for them or us.'[1] He follows it up by a vitriolic biographical sketch of the professor's advance from obscurity to fame, his

---

[1] A quotation from an eighteenth-century Russian poet, famous for his satires, in one of which he attacked the contemporary literary fashion of ode-writing.

self-conceit, his absurd pretensions to greatness, his success with women. But Uncle Vanya was not by any means the only contributor to the tense atmosphere. One need only quote two outsiders, Helen and Astrov, on it:

HELEN [speaking to Uncle Vanya in the second act]. There's something the matter with this house. Your mother hates everything except her pamphlets and the professor. The professor is in a state of exasperation: he doesn't trust me and he's afraid of you. Sonia is angry with her father, angry with me and hasn't spoken to me for a fortnight. You hate my husband and don't conceal your contempt for your mother. I was exasperated and was about to burst into tears a dozen times today. There's something the matter with this house.

ASTROV [speaking to Sonia in the second act]. I don't think I'd survive a month in your house. The atmosphere would stifle me. Your father can think of nothing but his gout and his books. Uncle Vanya with his depressions, your grandmother and, last but not least, your stepmother . . .

It was an attack of gout (or rheumatism) that brought Astrov to the estate in the first act. But when Astrov, on the return of Helen and Sonia to the garden, complained that he had galloped 'like mad' for twenty miles to attend on the professor, who was supposed to be very ill, only to find that he seemed to be in the best of health, he received a rather lame excuse from Helen, who apparently had grown used to her husband's hypochondriac tantrums. Astrov seemed to take her excuse in good part: at least he hoped he could stay and have a good night's sleep. But it was not to be: an urgent summons to see an injured man at a near-by factory put an end to that hope. Two incidents follow upon each other to shatter still further the 'peace and harmony' so poetically described by Telegin. In the first, curiously enough, it was Telegin himself who was involved. Telegin had taken offence at being addressed by his wrong name and patronymic by Helen, particularly as he had been dining with her every day, which, he opined, must not have escaped her notice. This gave Sonia an opportunity to snub Helen, first, by informing her that Telegin was their right-hand man and by asking him, 'tenderly', to have another cup of tea. The second incident blew up into a violent quarrel between Uncle Vanya and his mother, who

was outraged that some academic should have contradicted everything
he had defended seven years earlier, which, she declared, was 'terrible'!

VOYNITSKY. There's nothing terrible about it. Drink your tea,
Mother.

MARIA. But I want to talk!

VOYNITSKY. You've been talking for fifty years, talking and reading
pamphlets. Time you put a stop to it.

MARIA. I don't know why you always seem to find my conversation
disagreeable. I'm sorry, Jean, but you've changed so much during
the last year that I simply cannot recognise you. You used to be a
man of definite convictions, a man of enlightened views.

VOYNITSKY. Oh, yes, to be sure! I was a man of enlightened views
which did not enlighten anyone. (*Pause.*) A man of enlightened
views! What a cruel joke! I'm forty-seven now. Till a year ago I did
my best to hoodwink myself with that pedantic stuff of yours so as
not to see what real life was like. And I thought I was doing the right
thing! And now, if you only knew! I can't sleep at night, so vexed,
so furious, am I with myself for having so stupidly frittered away my
time when I could have had everything that my age now denies
me.

SONIA. Uncle Vanya, this is boring!

MARIA (*to her son*). You seem to be putting all the blame for something
on your former convictions. But it is not they that are at fault but
yourself. You seem to forget that convictions are nothing by themselves, a dead letter. You should have been doing some real work.

VOYNITSKY. Some real work? Not everyone has the ability to be some
sort of scribbling *perpetuum mobile* like that Herr Professor of yours.

MARIA. What are you suggesting by that, pray?

SONIA (*imploringly*). Granny, Uncle Vanya, please!

VOYNITSKY. All right, all right. I shut up and apologise. (*Pause.*)

The somewhat uneasy pause was interrupted by Helen who tried
to smooth the ruffled feelings of the two contestants.

HELEN. It's such a lovely day. Not too hot.

But Uncle Vanya refused to bury the hatchet.

VOYNITSKY (*grimly*). A lovely day to hang oneself.

The ensuing interlude with Marina clucking for a stray hen and her chicks and Telegin playing a polka on his guitar with everybody listening in silence helped to soothe the frayed tempers. The playing, however, was soon interrupted by a labourer who came to summon Astrov to attend someone who seemed to have had an accident at a factory. It provided a natural changeover to the second theme of the play: the destruction of the environment through the indiscriminate felling of trees. It was Helen who brought up the subject by wondering whether Astrov's preoccupation with the preservation of forests did not interfere with his 'real' work and whether such a preoccupation was really as 'interesting' as he claimed it to be. 'Nothing but trees and trees', she said disingenuously, 'must be awfully monotonous.' It was at this point that Sonia intervened by expounding Astrov's work of conservation with an enthusiasm which betrayed her personal feelings for the doctor. The word she used most frequently when describing her idea of a perfect world is 'refinement': in this ideal world men's speech would be more 'refined', their movements more 'graceful' and their attitude towards women 'full of exquisite refinement'. In asking Astrov to give up drink in the second act, Sonia again gives it as her reason that drunkenness did not become a man of such 'refinement' as Astrov. Deeply religious as she is, Sonia even pictures life beyond the grave as 'bright, beautiful and refined'. No wonder Uncle Vanya finds her enthusiasm 'charming but hardly convincing'. But his unrepentant insistence 'to go on stoking my stoves with logs and building my barns with wood', left Astrov with no option but to try to tone down the impression of himself as the architect of the golden age by an eloquent plea to stop the destruction of the natural riches of the world, or, as he put it, 'what we cannot create'. All he would be content with was the thought that 'if in a thousand years men are happy, I shall have done my bit towards it.' But he did not deny that he also found a great aesthetic satisfaction in his work. 'When I plant a birch tree and then see its green branches swaying in the wind, I cannot help being proud and thrilled that —' He did not finish the sentence for at that moment the labourer appeared with his glass of vodka. He emptied it and, scanning the sceptical faces around him, dismissed the subject. 'All this, I suppose,' he said, 'is just the talk of a crank, when all is said and done.' He went out with Sonia who inquired anxiously when he would be coming back, and got a rather curt 'don't know' in reply. Uncle Vanya and Helen, too, walked off towards the house, Helen inquiring angrily why he had to irritate his mother and why he had to talk about the *perpetuum mobile*. At breakfast he was again quarrelling with the professor. How petty it all was!

VOYNITSKY. But what if I hate him!

HELEN. There is no reason why you should hate Alexander. He is just like everyone else. No worse than you.

But Uncle Vanya was too obsessed with the imaginary wrongs the Herr Professor had done him to appreciate the truth of her remark. To change the subject he became personal again, this time about her indolence, her being 'too lazy' to live. Her reaction was quite explosive, quite unlike that of a woman who 'was too lazy to live'. Indeed, her fierce resentment against people who were looking at her with compassion because she had married an old husband showed that she was beginning to feel (as she was later to confess to Sonia) the serious disadvantages of what Uncle Vanya described as 'stifling her natural feelings'. But in her vehement approval of what she claimed to be Astrov's views of 'a devil of destruction in all of you', we hear also Chekhov's voice: it is one of those rare instances where the dramatist's own sentiments are so deeply felt that he simply has to express them although they may not be strictly in the character of the particular person in the play:

> You're all recklessly destroying the forests, and soon there will be nothing left on the earth. In the same way, you're recklessly destroying human beings, and thanks to you there will be no more loyalty, no more purity, nor any capacity for self-sacrifice. Why can't you ever look with indifference at a woman if she doesn't happen to belong to you? Because, again the doctor is right, there's a devil of destruction in all of you. You don't care what happens to the forests, to the birds, to the women, or to one another.

No wonder that a man like Uncle Vanya, pursuing selfish ends in spite of realising the hopelessness of achieving them, finds such a 'philosophy' distasteful. What Helen finds distasteful is to have Uncle Vanya talking to her about his love when he himself admits that the chances that she should return his feelings are 'nil'. Especially when she herself was beginning to feel that she was greatly attracted to Astrov.

She finds his 'tired, sensitive' face 'interesting', and feels sorry that her 'shyness' with him prevented her from 'being nice' to him or speaking to him as she would have liked. A sudden feeling of apprehension that her 'natural feelings' might get out of control makes her turn on the luckless Uncle Vanya with his maudlin talk of love. 'This has gone far enough', [literally: This is sheer torment . . .] she murmurs as she goes into the house.

As the curtain falls on the first act, Telegin, who does not seem to have noticed anything unusual, 'strikes a chord on the guitar and plays a polka', while the old bluestocking Maria Voynitsky 'writes something in the margin of the pamphlet', another disgraceful lapse of the Kharkov academic, no doubt, to which she must draw the attention of 'Alexander'.

Act Two

The action of the second act takes place on a stormy night of August in 'the dining-room of Serebryakov's house' and is divided into seven scenes (in *The Wood Demon* Chekhov preserved this 'old-fashioned' division by marking each scene separately). Of these only the two longer ones are of importance in so far as they advance the dramatic action of the play: the first leading up to the climax in the third act by concentrating on Professor Serebryakov's dissatisfaction with country life ('We are not made for country life', is how he puts it grandly in the third act) and his towering rage against the 'insipid' people adverse circumstances had forced him to live with; and the sixth scene illustrating the dichotomy in Sonia's character: the active, level-headed manager of an estate and the naïve, helpless young girl utterly incapable of coping with a situation in which her deepest emotions are involved, in spite of the many transparent hints Astrov gives her of his inability to reciprocate her feelings, because – he makes no secret of it, either – of his infatuation with Helen.

The first scene gives a finely-etched portrait of a selfish hypochondriac who makes life a hell for his wife and everyone else in the house by his nagging complaints. He summons the country doctor but refuses to accept his diagnosis of his ailment. 'Please, don't send for me to see your father again', Astrov tells Sonia. 'I tell him it's gout and he tells me it's rheumatism. I ask him to stay in bed and he will sit in a chair. And today he refused to talk to me at all.' When Sonia asks her father why he won't see the doctor whom he himself told her to send for, his reply is typical of the academic who looks down on people whose qualifications are too low to earn his respect.

SEREBRYAKOV. What good is your Astrov to me? He knows as much about medicine as I do about astronomy.
SONIA [who stands no nonsense from her father]. You don't want us to send for the whole medical faculty for your gout, do you?
SEREBRYAKOV. I refuse even to talk to that crazy fellow.

The dining-room table is littered with bottles of medicine. 'Look at these prescriptions!' Astrov says to Uncle Vanya. 'From Kharkov, from Moscow, from Tula . . . Every town [in Russia] must be sick and tired of his gout.' But when Serebryakov, who was sitting in an arm-chair at the open window, asks Sonia to fetch him one of the bottles from the table and she passes him the wrong one, he shouts 'irritably': 'You can't ask anyone for anything!' It is at this point that Sonia, unlike Helen who is too passive to assert herself, reveals her strength of character:

SONIA. Kindly keep your temper. Some people [a transparent dig at Helen] may put up with it, but I won't. . . . I haven't the time, either. I have to get up early in the morning. We are haymaking.

Helen does, indeed, put up with her husband's hypochondriac tan-trums. Not because like Serebryakov's first wife (as Marina reveals at the end of the scene) she is in love with her husband any longer, but out of sheer 'indolence'. She hardly listens to his complaints. She never bothers to reply when he asks her what time it is or wants her to get him some book from his library in the morning.[1] It is only when he starts talking of his old age, for which, as Helen says, he seems to be blaming them all, that she gets up from her chair by the window, where she has been dozing and 'sits down farther away'. But the professor is not to be shut up so easily.

SEREBRYAKOV [who had just remarked that ever since he had grown old, he had become disgusted with himself]. You most of all must find me repugnant. And you're quite right, of course. I'm not a fool and I understand. You're young, healthy and beautiful. You want to live, while I am an old man, almost a corpse. Isn't that so? Don't you think I realise it? And, of course, it's stupid of me to go on living. But wait, I shall soon set you all free. I shan't last much longer.
HELEN. I can't stand it any longer. For God's sake, be quiet.
SEREBRYAKOV. What it comes to is that, thanks to me, all of you are worn out, bored, wasting your youth, and only I am satisfied and enjoying life. Why, of course.

[1] The book Serebryakov wanted to look up was by Professor Fyodor Batyush-kov, a literary historian and critic, the editor of the Russian section of the international journal *Cosmopolis*, to which Chekhov, at Batyushkov's request, contributed two short stories: 'The Man in a Case' and 'A Visit to Friends'.

HELEN. Do be quiet! You've exhausted me.

SEREBRYAKOV. I've exhausted all of you. Of course.

HELEN (*through tears*). It's unbearable! Tell me, what do you want of me?

SEREBRYAKOV. Nothing.

HELEN. Well, in that case be quiet. I beg you.

SEREBRYAKOV. A funny thing. Every time Ivan or that old idiot Maria starts talking, no one objects, everyone listens. But I've only to open my mouth and everyone begins to feel miserable. Even my voice disgusts them. Well, suppose I am disgusting, suppose I am an egoist, or despot, but haven't I got some right to be an egoist even in my old age? Haven't I earned it? Haven't I the right, I ask, to enjoy a quiet old age, to be treated with consideration by people?

The professor seems to have forgotten that, as Marina reminds him at the end of this scene, he had been a damned nuisance to his first wife when he could hardly have blamed his old age for it. She too, like Helen, had to sit up night after night with him. He reduced her, too, to tears by his constant complaints. All Helen could say was that no one disputed his rights, without specifying what rights she had specially in mind. Fortunately, the windows began banging in the wind and the nightwatchman began knocking and singing in the garden, putting a brief end to the professor's recriminations. When he resumed talking, he was no longer insisting on his right to be a nuisance. Instead, he made it quite clear that he was no longer going 'to be buried alive in this tomb', listening to the insipid talk of stupid people. 'I want to live!' he cried, for once disclosing the hidden thought at the back of his mind. 'I like success, I like fame, I like to hear people talk about me, and here—why, it's like living in exile! Every minute to be grieving for the past, watching others make a name for themselves, being afraid of death! I can't put up with it! I haven't the strength!'

The entrance of Sonia and her straight talk to her father brought some fresh air into the stifling atmosphere of the sick room. Not for long, though. At that moment Uncle Vanya entered 'in his dressing-gown and with a lighted candle' and, to the accompaniment of thunder and lightning, announced his willingness to replace Sonia and Helen in looking after his sick brother-in-law. Serebryakov protested violently that he would not be left alone with him because he would 'talk me to death'.[1]

VOYNITSKY. But you must let them have some rest. It's the second night they've had no sleep.

SEREBRYAKOV. Let them go to bed, but you go, too. Thank you. I beg you. In the name of our past friendship, don't raise any objections. We'll talk another time.

VOYNITSKY (*with a wry smile*). Our past friendship – our past —

SONIA. Do be quiet, Uncle Vanya.

SEREBRYAKOV (*to his wife*). My dear, don't leave me alone with him. He'll talk me to death.

VOYNITSKY. This is becoming really ridiculous.

Here the Russian word used by Serebryakov quite obviously carries the meaning of 'casting an evil spell', for otherwise Uncle Vanya's retort that the situation was becoming 'ridiculous' is pointless. There is, of course, no reason at all why on the two occasions Serebryakov expressed his fear of being left alone with Uncle Vanya, he should say: 'He'll cast an evil spell on me.' It is in character, considering his background, that he should use it.

Marina's appearance solved the problem of how to get rid of the professor. Again, he feels at home with a woman of the people and lets her lead him away to give him 'some lime tea' and 'warm his feet'. Sonia accompanies them, leaving Uncle Vanya alone with Helen. He, too, has not been asleep for two nights: he has been drinking with Astrov, a fact which becomes apparent to Helen when he starts talking to her about his love and, barring her way as she was about to go out, tells her that what makes him so miserable is the thought that 'by my side in this very house another life is being wasted— yours!'

HELEN (*looking at him intently*). You're drunk!

VOYNITSKY. Possibly, possibly . . .

HELEN. Where's the doctor?

---

[1] The Russian word *zagovorit'*, usually translated in this context as 'talk one to death', has also the meaning of 'casting an evil spell', which, coming from the son of a sacristan, suggests that the professor was so terrified at the prospect of being left alone with Uncle Vanya because he was deeply superstitious.

VOYNITSKY. He's in there. He's staying the night with me. Possibly, possibly — Everything is possible.

HELEN. Have you been drinking again today? Why do you do it?

VOYNITSKY. At least it's something like life. Don't stop me, Helen.

HELEN. You never used to drink before and you never used to talk so much. Go to bed. You bore me.

VOYNITSKY (*pressing his lips to her hand*). My darling—my wonderful one!

HELEN (*with vexation*). Leave me alone. This is really the end! (*Goes out.*)

Uncle Vanya's soliloquy has already been discussed and the appearance of the tipsy Astrov that follows it emphasises Helen's statement that a talented person in Russia 'cannot keep himself entirely spotless'. His coarseness shows itself in his treatment of the submissive Telegin and, more particularly, in his statement that a woman can be a man's friend by being first 'a good companion', then 'a mistress' and only then a friend. A piece of cynicism that is characteristically described as 'a vulgar idea' by Uncle Vanya, who a moment ago had conjured up the highly romantic picture of being awakened in bed at night and holding Helen, frightened by the storm, in his arms and whispering: 'Don't be afraid, darling, I'm here.' Astrov was quite ready to admit that he was growing vulgar and that, as a rule, he got drunk once a month. 'When in this condition,' he says, 'I become brazen and insolent . . . and don't care a damn for anything. I don't hesitate to do the most difficult operations, and', he declared a little too rashly perhaps, 'I do them beautifully. I make the most ambitious plans for the future . . . and am convinced that I'm being of enormous service to humanity—enormous! At such a time I have my own philosophic system and all of you, my friends, seem to me such tiny insects, such microbes.' But his gruff exhortation to Telegin to play, and his invitation to Uncle Vanya to finish what was left of the bottle of brandy, are interrupted by Sonia's entry and his quick exit, followed by Telegin. The brief scene between Sonia and Uncle Vanya terminates in Uncle Vanya's bursting into tears because Sonia looked at him like her mother used to, no doubt, in somewhat similar circumstances of mental collapse. Left alone, Sonia immediately knocks on the door of Astrov's room; she is still in full control of herself, she upbraids Astrov for letting

G

her weakling uncle get drunk, she invites him to have something to drink, she even joins him in a drink herself. It is only then, sensing the reason why she is so eager to be with him, that he declares bluntly that it is years since he cared for anyone.

SONIA [alarmed by his bluntness]. Not for anyone?
ASTROV [firmly]. Not for anyone. I feel a certain affection for your old nurse—for old times' sake.

It is when he is about to drink, that her control of herself begins to weaken.

SONIA (preventing him). Don't, please. I beg you. Don't drink any more.
ASTROV. Why not?
SONIA [giving herself away completely]. Because you're not that kind of man. You are so refined, you have such a nice, gentle voice and— more than that. You are—you are beautiful! Why do you want to be like ordinary people, who drink and play cards? Oh, please don't do it, I implore you! You keep saying that people do not create, but only destroy what Heaven has given them. Then why do you destroy yourself? You mustn't, you mustn't, I beg you, I entreat you!

It was time, Astrov realised, to make her understand that he did not love her, that, in fact, he was in love with Helen. A little earlier, he told her that what was wrong with Helen was that, while she was very beautiful, all she did was 'eat, sleep, go for walks, fascinate us all by her beauty', and—nothing more. She had no duties. Other people worked for her. And an idle life could not 'be pure'. Now he had to make it clear to Sonia that he could not form any lasting attachment to anyone. The only thing that still exercised 'the strongest possible appeal' on him was beauty. He could not remain indifferent to it. Having said so much, he could see that she still did not take the hint, and it was necessary to make her understand that it was not her but Helen he wanted. He tried to convey it to her gently. 'I can't help feeling', he went on, 'that if, for example, Helen wanted to, she could turn my head in one day'. There was a sudden gleam of alarm in her eyes, and he hastened to add: 'But then that is not love, that is not affection.'

Her sudden alarm brought back the memory of the railway signalman, who had died while he was operating on him, and he covered his eyes and shuddered.

SONIA. What's the matter?

ASTROV. Oh, nothing. In Lent one of my patients died under chloroform.

SONIA. It's time you forgot about it.

Somehow, in the ensuing pause Sonia recovered from her alarm and tried to broach the subject of her love in a more direct way.

SONIA. Tell me, if I had a friend or a younger sister, and if you were to discover that—well, that she had fallen in love with you, what would your reaction be to that?

To Astrov that was the signal to go: her ingenuousness was so shattering that only a brutal statement of the truth would have made her realise that her love for him was quite hopeless. That he could not bring himself to make. Instead he preferred to prevaricate.

ASTROV (*shrugging*). Don't know. I'd give her to understand that I couldn't care for her and – er– that I had other things on my mind. Well, if I am to go, [he brought the conversation to an abrupt end] I must go now. Goodbye, my dear child, or we shall not finish till morning. (*Presses her hand.*) I'll go through the drawing-room or else your uncle might detain me. (*Goes out.*)

Sonia was left in suspense. 'His heart and mind', she murmured in her soliloquy, 'are still hidden from me.' And yet she was happy, for in spite of appearances she felt that the last word had not been spoken yet.

I told him: you're so refined, you have such a nice, gentle voice. . . . Shouldn't I have said that? His voice trembles, it is so caressing. . . . I can almost still feel it in the air. But when I spoke to him about a younger sister, he didn't understand. (*Wrings her hands.*) [She recalled his words that beauty was the only thing that still moved him deeply.] Oh, how awful I'm not beautiful! How awful! And I know I am not beautiful. I know. I know. Last Sunday when people were coming out of church, I heard them talking about me, and one woman said: 'She's such a good and generous girl, what a pity she is so plain.' So plain.

Astrov's characterisation of Helen as a woman whose 'idle life cannot be pure' and whom he could not really love or feel affection for, made it easier for Sonia to make it up with Helen.

HELEN. How long are you going to be cross with me? We've done one another no harm. Why should we be enemies? Don't you think it's time we made it up?
SONIA. Oh, I've been wanting to myself. (*Embraces her.*) Don't let's be cross ever again.

They drink *Bruderschaft*, that is to say, drink out of one glass and go on addressing one another in the second person singular. Both are moved to tears by the occasion; Helen goes on to explain that she did not marry Sonia's father for any ulterior motive and, asked by Sonia whether she would not have preferred to have a young husband, confessed with a laugh that she would indeed! This confession made it easier for Sonia to broach the subject of her being in love with Astrov. Helen cannot help being carried away in her appreciation of the sort of man Astrov is, but she is very careful not to arouse any suspicion in Sonia's mind. She kisses her and wishes her all the happiness in the world. 'You deserve it', she adds generously. She goes on to draw a not entirely untruthful portrait of herself as a tiresome, 'episodic' character, and ends up by confessing that she is 'very, very unhappy'. Pacing up and down the stage in agitation, she cries: 'There's no happiness for me in this world', and is a little put out by Sonia's laughter.

HELEN. What are you laughing at?
SONIA (*laughs, hiding her face*). I'm so happy, so happy!

She was brimming over with happiness because Helen's apparent confidence in her future and her apparently sincere regret at having made an unhappy marriage filled Sonia with hope of a happy ending to her relationship with Astrov. She responded enthusiastically to Helen's proposal 'to play something'. The only trouble was that music irritated Serebryakov when he was not well. Sonia goes out to ask him if he would object to Helen's playing.

The final short scene seems to teeter on the brink of expectation and is brought to an end by a rather too obvious curtain line: the knocking of the nightwatchman, Helen's eagerness to play—'I'll play and play and cry and cry like a fool', the short dialogue between Helen and the nightwatchman, who whistles for his dog and walks away, a short pause, then Sonia's return, Helen's questioning glance, and the fateful monosyllable:

SONIA. No!

Act Three

The third act takes place 'in a drawing-room of Serebryakov's house'. The exact time is a quarter to one. It is a month after the second act. During that time Astrov, contrary to his custom, had been visiting the family every day. 'The doctor', Sonia says at the beginning of the act, 'used to come and see us very rarely before – once a month. It was difficult to coax him into coming. But now he is here every day. Neglects his forests and his patients.' Neither had she any doubt about the reason for Astrov's visits: 'You are', she says to Helen, 'a witch.' But while admitting Astrov's infatuation with Helen, Sonia does not seem to be perturbed about it: she seems to be quite certain that Helen would never be unfaithful to her husband. Besides, did not Helen wish her 'all the happiness in the world'? Sonia was too naïve to realise that Helen herself was no longer able to control her 'natural feelings', although all she would admit was that she was 'a little in love' with Astrov. Hence her agitation at the opening of the third act ('*Helen*', Chekhov's stage direction runs, '*is pacing up and down the stage, deep in thought about something*'), hence her outbursts of anger when Uncle Vanya is teasing her about 'walking about, swaying lazily', hence also her admission that she 'does not know what to do' although, like Arkadina in the second act of *The Seagull*, she disguises her real meaning by claiming that she was 'bored to death'. Sonia, naïvely, takes her literally and expresses surprise that she should be bored when there was so much work to be done, while Uncle Vanya unwittingly adds fuel to the flames by telling Helen to be 'sensible' and, suggesting that she has 'mermaid blood' in her veins, advises her 'to fall head over ears in love with some water goblin, plunge headlong into the whirlpool with him, and leave the Herr Professor and all of us breathless with surprise.' Uncle Vanya, even less than Sonia, little suspects that Helen has fallen 'head over ears in love', though not with a 'water goblin' but with a 'wood demon'. That is why Helen shouts 'angrily' at him: 'Leave me alone! How can you be so cruel?' and is about to rush out of the room, but is mollified by Uncle Vanya's apology and his promise to present her 'as a token of peace and harmony' with some 'autumn roses: so sad and so lovely', little dreaming that it would be his bunch of roses that would open his eyes to the real situation between Astrov and Helen.

The second theme of the play – Uncle Vanya's conflict with his brother-in-law which reaches its dramatic climax at the end of the act – is only hinted at in the opening scene of the third act:

VOYNITSKY. The Herr Professor has been so good as to express the wish that we should meet him in this room at one o'clock today. (*Looks at his watch.*) It is a quarter to one. He wishes to make some communication to the world.

Uncle Vanya's rather forced sarcasm shows that he had not the slightest idea what the professor's communication was about. Helen apparently has no idea, either, of what her husband is up to.

HELEN. I suppose it's some business matter.
VOYNITSKY. He has no business matters. All he does is write rubbish, grumble and be jealous. Nothing else.

There was nothing to warn him that coming on top of the shock of discovering the woman he loved in the arms of his best friend, he would have to suffer the even greater shock of the professor's proposal to sell the estate he had laboured for twenty-five years to save from debt and the humiliation of firing at the professor twice and missing him each time.

But there was nothing to indicate the approaching storm as he went out to fetch the bunch of roses he had picked for Helen that very morning, leaving the two young women looking out of the window. Helen was wondering how she was going to live through the winter in a house in which everyone seemed to be at loggerheads with everyone else. In the ensuing pause she could not help but wonder whether 'to run away from this hell' with 'a handsome, interesting, fascinating man' like Astrov was not the solution she was looking for. She had fallen under the spell of that man, she felt bored when he was not in the house with her, she found herself smiling when she thought of him, she could no longer deny that she was in love with him. Uncle Vanya said that she had mermaid blood in her veins and advised her to let herself go for once in her life. Well, why not? In her soliloquy after persuading Sonia to let her talk to Astrov in order to find out whether he loved her or not, she admits that running away with Astrov was 'what I really ought to do'. Except that she was 'cowardly and timid' and that 'my conscience would not let me'. But was there not another reason also? At the beginning of her soliloquy she described Astrov as merely 'a country doctor' for whom an unattractive girl like Sonia would make an excellent wife. Astrov might be handsome and fascinating, but he was only an obscure country doctor who was regarded as odd by the people of the district. To marry a celebrity like Serebryakov was one thing, but to run away with a mere country doctor like Astrov was quite another. But all the same she could not resist seeing him at her feet, even at the risk that she would not be able to control her own feelings. 'You're a cunning one!' Astrov says, 'a beast of prey . . . who must have her victims . . . I'm mad with desire for you and you're awfully pleased about it. Well, I'm conquered. I surrender. Come and eat me up.'

HELEN. You're crazy.
ASTROV (*laughing through his teeth*). And you—are afraid.

She was, too, but she found her resistance wilting under the overwhelming force of his passion. Her futile attempts to resist it, her declaration that she was 'better and higher' than he thought, were of no avail. She wanted to leave the room, but he barred her way: he sensed that she was as much in love with him as he with her, and that, provided they were not interrupted, he would prevail.

ASTROV (*taking her arm and looking round*). Where can we meet? Tell me quickly: where? Someone may come in. Tell me quickly. (*Passionately.*) You're so beautiful, so lovely . . . . One kiss. . . . Let me just kiss your fragrant hair. . . .
HELEN. I swear to you —
ASTROV (*not letting her speak*). Why swear to me? There's no need to. No need for unnecessary words. Oh, how beautiful you are! What lovely hands! (*Kisses her hands.*)
HELEN. That's enough—go away, please. (*Taking her hands away.*) You're forgetting yourself.
ASTROV. But tell me, tell me, where we shall meet tomorrow. (*Puts his hand round her waist.*)[1] You see it is inevitable. We must meet. (*He*

---

[1] As he feels her resistance collapsing, he changes to the second person singular.

kisses her; at that moment UNCLE VANYA *enters with a bouquet of roses and stops at the door.*)
HELEN (*not seeing* UNCLE VANYA).[1] Have pity on me. Let me go. . . . (*Lays her head on Astrov's chest.*) No! (*Tries to go out.*)
ASTROV[2] (*holding her back by the waist*). Come to the plantation to-morrow – at two o'clock. You will come – yes? You will?
HELEN (*seeing* UNCLE VANYA). Let me go! (*In great confusion goes to the window.*) This is awful!

But what about Sonia? She had agreed that Helen should talk to Astrov, but she was not sure that her present state of uncertainty was as dreadful as Helen suggested. 'No,' she murmurs as she is going out of the room to tell Astrov that Helen was waiting for him to show her his maps, 'uncertainty is much better. At least there is hope.' And she was right. What Helen had done by her self-interested interference was to make quite sure that Astrov would never contemplate marrying Sonia. For the thought of marrying the girl whom he greatly respected had occurred to him before his involvement with Helen. He was disappointed with Helen's lack of interest in his ecological maps.

ASTROV (*coldly*). . . . I can see from your face that this does not interest you.
HELEN [a little taken aback]. But I understand so little about it.
ASTROV [grimly: he resented having wasted the time with her and even more the fact that it didn't seem to matter]. There's nothing to understand. You're simply not interested.
HELEN. To tell you the truth, I was thinking of something else. I'm sorry. I have to put you through a little interrogation and I'm not quite sure how to begin.
ASTROV [surprised]. An interrogation?
HELEN. Yes, an interrogation but—a rather innocent one. Let's sit down. (*They sit down.*) It concerns a certain young lady. We will talk like honest people, like good friends, without beating about the bush. Agreed? [Helen's stiff approach seemed a little baffling, but Astrov

---

[1] Her appeal for pity shows how close she is to giving in to him. She lays her head on his chest, and her final cry is merely a last attempt to stave off her surrender.
[2] Still addressing her in the second person singular.

surely must have guessed what she was driving at, though he was still uncertain what her real purpose was.]

ASTROV. Agreed.

HELEN. It concerns my stepdaughter Sonia. Do you like her?

ASTROV. Yes, I respect her.

HELEN. But do you like her as a woman?

ASTROV (*after a slight hesitation*). No.

HELEN. A few words more and I've done. You have not noticed anything?

ASTROV. Nothing.

HELEN (*taking him by the hand*). You are not in love with her. I can see it from your eyes. She's terribly unhappy. Please, understand that and—stop coming here. [Helen has not mentioned marriage, but by now it has become obvious what she was driving at.]

ASTROV (*gets up*). I'm afraid I'm too old for that sort of thing. Besides, I have no time for it. (*Shrugging.*) When could I? (*He looks embarrassed.*)

And well he might, for he had not expected Helen to appear in the role of a matchmaker.

HELEN. Oh dear, what an unpleasant conversation. . . . Well, thank goodness, that's over. Let's forget it all, just as though we'd never discussed it and . . . go away. You're an intelligent man, you'll understand. (*Pause.*) [During the pause, it became clear to Helen that Astrov did not understand.] Goodness, I'm hot all over.

ASTROV. If you had told me that a month or two earlier, I should have considered it, but now . . . (*Shrugging.*)

So he had seriously considered marriage to Sonia, but now that Helen had forced him to confess that he did not care for her and as good as told him not to come and see her any more, the subject could never be taken up again. That was one result of Helen's 'interrogation'. Why, then, should Helen have interfered if she really had Sonia's interests at heart? It did not take Astrov long to put his own construction on Helen's motives, and he nearly succeeded in proving that he was not far off the truth. Uncle Vanya's appearance with his bunch of roses put both Astrov and Helen in a rather awkward situation. Astrov simply walked out of the room after trying, rather unsuccessfully, to brazen it out, but it was not so easy for Helen, who was caught, as it were, in *flagrante delicto*. All she could do in the circumstances, was to walk up quickly to the shattered Uncle Vanya and tell him, rather ironically, to use 'all your influence to arrange that my husband and I leave here today. Do you hear? Today!'

VOYNITSKY (*mopping his face*). What? Why, yes . . . All right. . . . I saw it all, Hélène. . . .

HELEN (*tensely*). Do you hear? I *must* get away from here today! Today!

Why 'must'? Could she no longer face Uncle Vanya or could it be that now that her secret was out she might be driven to take the desperate step she so dreaded. However, neither she nor Uncle Vanya could possibly have foreseen at that moment the way Uncle Vanya would 'use his influence' to bring about just that result.

The great scene of the third act has, as already mentioned, no real connection with what has gone before. It starts with the entrance of Professor Serebryakov, Sonia, Telegin and Marina. The last two had nothing whatever to do with the professor's proposal to sell the estate: he had roped them in anticipating Uncle Vanya's objections to his plan and hoping that their presence, and especially the presence of Telegin, would help to relieve the atmosphere should it become a little too charged. Indeed, Telegin's first very respectful words on entering with the professor, who would hardly have exchanged any civilities with him on any other occasion, show that the professor's hope was not entirely without foundation. That he was not quite sure that his plan, which would not only deliver him from the uncongenial company of his relations, but would also enable him to realise his cherished dream of possessing 'a small country house in Finland', would not meet with violent objections, is shown by the impatience with which he rings the bell to summon the absent members of his family. In his impatience he does not even notice the distraught Helen, who was in the room all the time. His formal invitation to the 'ladies and gentlemen' to be seated emphasised the importance he attached to the occasion. Sonia was too preoccupied with her own thoughts to pay much attention to her father: she was anxious to know what was Astrov's answer to Helen.

SONIA (*going up to* HELEN, *impatiently*). What did he say?

HELEN. Later.

SONIA. You're trembling? You're agitated? (*Looks searchingly at her.*) [Not knowing what has passed between Astrov and Helen, she naturally assumed that Helen was so agitated because she was reluctant to tell her the worst.] I understand. . . . He said he won't come here again. . . . Yes? (*Pause.*) Tell me – yes?

Helen nods. Sonia interprets it as the end of all her hopes and up to the end of the scene she seems to be in a state of shock.

Resuming, the professor first addresses himself to Telegin, who had been complaining that he, too, had not been very well for the past two days. What worries him, Serebryakov says, is not so much ill-health, but to have to live in the country, which gives him the feeling of having been dropped on another planet. Having in this roundabout way hinted at his reason for summoning the family council, he repeats his invitation for everybody to sit down and, noticing that Sonia is not listening to him, but 'standing with her head drooping sorrowfully', he calls her again, but she doesn't hear. Receiving no reply, Serebryakov invites Marina, too, to be seated. He then turns to the business of the meeting, laughing at his own jocular invitation to 'the ladies and gentlemen' to suspend their ears on the nail of attention. His laughter, though, was a bit premature, for he is immediately pulled up by Uncle Vanya, who certainly does not seem to be amused.

VOYNITSKY (*agitated*). You don't want me, do you? Do you mind if I go?

SEREBRYAKOV. I do. It's you I want here most of all.

VOYNITSKY. What do you want with me? [Uncle Vanya addressed the professor in the second person plural which, coming from a brother-in-law, sounds much too formal to be friendly.]

SEREBRYAKOV. You. . . . [Repeating the second person plural in a hurt voice.] Why are you [second person singular] so cross? (*Pause.*) [During the pause they look at each other in silence for a moment, trying to find out what each has at the back of his mind. The professor decides to assume a more conciliatory tone.] If I am to blame for anything I have done to you, then, please, forgive me.

But this friendly approach arouses Uncle Vanya's suspicions in good earnest.

VOYNITSKY. Drop that tone. Let's get down to business. What do you want?

The entrance of Maria Voynitsky relieves the tension which threatened to jeopardise the professor's plan before he had time to expound it. He feels that he has to be more circumspect: perhaps another joke with just a hint at the serious consequences that his plan would involve for the family of his first wife.

SEREBRYAKOV. Ah, here's *maman*. Ladies and gentlemen, I begin. [He pauses to make sure that he has everybody's attention and then proceeds to quote the first line of Gogol's *The Government Inspector* with which the mayor creates dismay among the town officials.] I have invited you here, ladies and gentlemen, to announce that a Government Inspector is about to pay us a visit. [His second joke, too, misfires: they all look uncomprehendingly at him, and he is quick to dismiss it.] However, joking apart. This is a serious matter.

It is, indeed. For what he was about to propose would have destroyed the lives of Uncle Vanya, his mother-in-law and his daughter, who had all laboured selflessly to assist him with his work and research and, in addition, make sure that he had no financial worries. He, therefore, began by asking them all for their 'help and advice'. He was only a scholar who spent his life among books and had always been a stranger to practical affairs. Among the people of 'practical business experience' he included not only Uncle Vanya, but also, astonishingly enough, 'Mr Telegin' and his mother-in-law, on whose support he knew he could count. He then went on to draw tears from everybody's eyes by expatiating, after an appropriate quotation from Horace on the transience of human life, on his old age and illness and on his wish to settle his worldly affairs so that his young daughter, in particular, would not be left penniless after his death. He paused to see what effect his words had produced, but finding that no one was particularly impressed, least of all by his reference to his daughter, who had been keeping him in comfort for many years, he at last got down to business. He admitted that he found it quite impossible to go on living in the country, while life in town on the income 'we' derived from the estate, was quite impossible. One might, he threw out a tentative suggestion, sell the woods, but that was an emergency measure that could not be repeated every year. Some scheme, therefore, must be found that would guarantee 'us' a more or less stable income. He had thought of just such a scheme and he was only too happy to submit it for their consideration.

Serebryakov then proceeded to outline his plan for the sale of the estate: 'Our estate', he pointed out, 'returns an average of no more than two per cent. I propose to sell it. By investing the money in gilt-edged securities, we should get from four to five per cent, and I think there might even be a surplus of a few thousand, which would enable us [that is to say, him and his wife] to buy a small country house in Finland. [Apparently to realise an old dream of his, for he would be able to spend the winter months in Petersburg near his university colleagues and his adoring ladies and the summer months in his 'little country house in Finland'.]

But however 'reasonable' he tried to make his 'scheme' sound, the sheer enormity of his proposal did produce the explosion that he had feared.

VOYNITSKY. One moment . . . I think my ears must be deceiving me. Repeat what you've said.

Serebryakov was so convinced of the fairness of his proposal that he was only too glad to oblige.

SEREBRYAKOV. Invest the money in gilt-edged securities and use the surplus to buy a small country house in Finland.
VOYNITSKY. Never mind Finland. There was something else you said.
SEREBRYAKOV. I propose to sell the estate.
VOYNITSKY. Yes, that's it! You're going to sell the estate. That's rich! An excellent idea. And how do you propose to dispose of me and my old mother and Sonia here?

But the professor dismissed the question as of no particular importance.

SEREBRYAKOV. We shall discuss it all in good time. You don't expect me to settle everything at once, do you?

The professor seemed to have forgotten the fact that the estate did not belong to him. It belonged, Uncle Vanya pointed out to him with a touch of sarcasm, to Sonia. The professor admitted it.

SEREBRYAKOV. Yes, the estate belongs to Sonia. I'm not disputing it. Without Sonia's consent I shouldn't dream of selling it. Besides [he added, revealing for the first time how little he understood or cared for his daughter], I'm proposing to do it for Sonia's benefit.

It evoked the expected reaction from Uncle Vanya:

VOYNITSKY. This is beyond everything! Beyond everything! Either I've gone stark raving mad, or —

It was at this point that 'the old idiot Maria' revealed herself as a staunch supporter of the great scholar.

MARIA. Don't contradict Alexander, Jean. Believe me, he knows much better than you or I what is good and what isn't.

His mother's intervention left Uncle Vanya speechless: he had told Astrov earlier that she worshipped the professor who inspired a feeling of reverential awe in her, but that she should actually let him throw her out of her house and home was something that stumped him completely.

VOYNITSKY. No . . . Give me some water (*Drinks water.*) Say what you like, what you like. . . .

Serebryakov seemed utterly incapable of communicating with Uncle Vanya, and his efforts to appear *reasonable* merely further exasperated his brother-in-law.

SEREBRYAKOV. I don't understand why you are so upset. I don't say that my plan is ideal. If *all* of you [having just received his mother-in-law's *carte blanche* endorsement of his plan, the professor was now quite sure to be able to carry it out] think it's no good, I will not insist on it.

It was now Telegin's turn to intervene, but Uncle Vanya brushed aside his attempt to find some way of lowering the temperature. He embarked on a long disquisition of the way the estate had been bought and how he had worked 'like an ox' for ten years to clear it of debt and now that he was growing old, he was to be kicked out. The professor still tried to keep his temper. He said that he was sorry to have started the discussion and that he was at a loss to know what Uncle Vanya was driving at. But when Uncle Vanya began complaining that he had never received a word of thanks from Serebryakov and that it never occurred to his brother-in-law to add 'a single' rouble to his beggarly salary, the professor was given his chance of delivering his first shrewd blow.

SEREBRYAKOV. My dear fellow, how was I to know? I am not a practical man and I know nothing of such things. Why didn't you increase your salary by as much as you pleased?

It was quite a fair rebuttal of the last charge, but by this time Uncle Vanya's excitement had reached such a pitch that he began accusing Serebryakov of regretting that he was not a thief.

VOYNITSKY. You mean why didn't I steal? Why don't you all despise me because I didn't steal? That would be only fair and I shouldn't have been a pauper now!

MARIA (*sternly*). Jean!

His mother's rebuke – just because it was just – broke down the only remaining barrier that still kept him from the last desperate act: the physical annihilation of his enemy who now seemed to be bent on destroying him. Telegin sensed this and tried to plead with him.

TELEGIN (*alarmed*). Vanya, my dear fellow, don't – don't – I'm trembling all over.... Why spoil a good relationship? (*Kisses him.*) Please, don't.

But there was no stopping Uncle Vanya now.

VOYNITSKY. For twenty-five years I sat like a mole within these four walls with this mother of mine. All our thoughts and feelings belonged to you alone. By day we talked about you and your work. We were proud of you. We uttered your name with reverence. We wasted our nights reading books and periodicals for which I have now the utmost contempt!

TELEGIN. Don't, Vanya, don't.... I can't stand it.

SEREBRYAKOV (*angrily*). What is it you want?

VOYNITSKY. We looked upon you as a being of a higher order, and we knew your articles by heart. . . . But now my eyes are opened. I see it all. You write about art, but you don't understand a thing about art. All those works of yours which I used to love aren't worth a brass farthing! You've humbugged us!

SEREBRYAKOV. Won't any one of you stop him? I—I'm going!

HELEN. Be silent, Vanya! I insist. Do you hear?

VOYNITSKY. I won't be silent! (*Stopping in front of Serebryakov and barring his way.*) Wait, I haven't finished! You've ruined my life! I haven't lived! I haven't lived at all! Thanks to you I've wasted, destroyed, the best years of my life! You're my worst enemy!

TELEGIN. I can't stand it – I can't. . . . I'm going. . . . (*Goes out in great agitation.*)

SEREBRYAKOV. What do you want from me? And what right have you to talk to me like this? Nonentity! If the estate is yours, take it! I don't want it!

HELEN. I shall run away from this hell this very minute! (*Screams.*) I can't stand it any longer!

Uncle Vanya, who had told Sonia in the second act that he preferred to live on illusions because he could not face real life, now, when 'real life' has become too unbearable because, as he rightly felt, his life had been irretrievably ruined, sought refuge in the greatest illusion of his life, namely, that if he had lived a normal life, he might have been a second Schopenhauer or Dostoevsky. But that illusion only lasted for a moment. He realised that he was talking nonsense, that he was going mad and, in his despair, he went even so far as to appeal to his mother to come and save him:

VOYNITSKY. . . . Mother, I'm in despair! Mother! [*Mátushka* – 'dear mummy' – for a moment he seems to have become a little boy running to his 'mummy' for comfort, but there was neither love nor sympathy to be got out of the old woman.]

MARIA (*sternly*). Do as Alexander tells you.

SONIA [who had been standing mute and unhappy during the whole of this scene, now knelt at the feet of her old nurse, clinging to her]. Darling nanny! Darling nanny!

VOYNITSKY [once again appealing to his mother]. Mother, what am I to do? Oh, never mind! I know myself what I must do! (*To* SEREBRYAKOV.) You will not forget me in a hurry! (*Goes out through middle door, followed by his mother.*)

H

The professor appeared baffled, but not particularly impressed by the implied threat in Uncle Vanya's parting words. Neither did it occur to him that he might have to leave before the question of selling the estate was settled. All he demanded was that Uncle Vanya should find some lodgings in the village, for otherwise he would himself move to other quarters, for, he declared, 'I will not stay in the same house as he.'

He got a shock when Helen told him firmly that they were going to leave that very day and asked him to make all the necessary arrangements at once. He must have connected Helen's sudden decision to leave with Uncle Vanya's outburst, for he knew nothing about her involvement with Astrov. The firmness of her demand left him no option but to accept his defeat and he gave vent to his resentment by calling Uncle Vanya 'an utter nonentity', which made even Sonia, stunned as she was by her own sorrow, turn furiously on her father:

SONIA (*still kneeling, turning to her father; nervously, through tears*). One must be charitable, Father! Uncle and I are so unhappy. (*Restraining her despair.*) One must be charitable! Remember how, when you were younger, Uncle Vanya and Granny sat up all night translating books for you, copying your papers – night after night, night after night! Uncle Vanya and I worked without a moment's rest, afraid to spend a penny on ourselves and sent it all to you. . . . We earned our bread and butter. I am sorry, I seem to be saying it all wrong, but you must understand us, Father. One must be charitable!

HELEN (*agitatedly, to her husband*). For God's sake, Alexander, go and talk it over with him. I implore you.

SEREBRYAKOV. Very well, I'll talk to him. I'm not accusing him of anything, but you must admit his behaviour is extraordinary, to say the least. I'll go to him, if you insist. (*Goes out through middle door.*)

HELEN (*following him out of the door*). Be gentle with him. Try to calm him.

They leave Sonia and Marina behind, Sonia still clinging to the nurse, who is trying to comfort her, when a shot behind the door makes her start violently. Presently Serebryakov runs in, staggering and looking terrified and shouting for someone to stop Uncle Vanya. He is followed by Uncle Vanya and Helen. They struggle in the doorway,

Helen trying to snatch the revolver away from Uncle Vanya, who frees himself, fires at the professor again and misses him a second time.

VOYNITSKY. . . . Missed him again! (*Furiously.*) Oh, damn, damn, damn! (*Bangs the floor with the revolver and sinks exhausted in a chair.*)

The fact that in attempting to shoot the professor, Uncle Vanya should miss him twice is for some inexplicable reason taken to be very funny by certain critics. This is because they fail to realise the significance of Chekhov's stage direction: '*Bangs the floor with the revolver and sinks exhausted in a chair*'. Uncle Vanya banged the revolver repeatedly on the floor not so much because he had missed the professor twice as because he always missed everything in life, for he was the type of idealist who could never bring himself to face 'real life'. It is true that Sonia, too, collapsed and, like a little hurt child, clung to her 'darling nanny' for protection when her idea of 'refined' behaviour had been shattered. But it did not take her long to recover and once more face life courageously. 'I am perhaps no less unhappy than you,' she tells her uncle in the last act, 'but I do not give in to despair.' Indeed, she not only carried on herself, but helped Uncle Vanya to face up to his responsibilities.

Act Four

Evening of the same day as Act Three. Uncle Vanya's office-cum-bedroom. Apart from the usual office equipment, it includes a table for Astrov with paints, drawing material and a portfolio. The only incongruous article in the room is the map of Africa on one of the walls, a map 'apparently of no use to anyone here', Chekhov notes, except, of course, that it was of great use to Chekhov, for it gives Astrov one of the most telling lines in the play, a line that Stanislavsky, whose Astrov was one of his most successful parts, knew how to get the most out of. 'When he [Stanislavsky] walked up to the map of Africa in the last act', Chekhov's wife, Olga Knipper, who played Helen, wrote forty years after the first performance of *Uncle Vanya*, 'and, looking at it, said "I expect it must be frightfully hot in that Africa – simply terrific heat" – how much of his [Astrov's] bitter experience of life he [Stanislavsky] used to put into that sentence. And he said those words with a kind of bravado and even with a kind of challenge.' Bravado, certainly, for it provided Astrov with a way of escape from an awkward situation by an implied apology for having hurt Uncle Vanya's feelings so deeply, a much subtler attempt 'to brazen it out' than his rather uncomfortable exit in the third act or his rather coarse gesture of cocking a snook at Uncle Vanya when reminded of embracing Helen at the beginning of the last act.

The last act in which no trace of the earlier play remains, opens very quietly with Telegin and Marina scarcely able to conceal their *schadenfreude* at the discomfiture of the professor and his wife; Telegin retailing the latest developments in the family row: the professor and Helen, both scared, leaving in a hurry, travelling light, going to Kharkov (the professor's dream of a villa in Finland completely shattered) to look around for a place to live and then send for their things. 'So much the better', Marina repeats twice, smiling contentedly, foreseeing a return to the good old days when, 'like good Christians', they used to have tea at eight o'clock in the morning, dinner at one, and supper in the evening. 'Haven't tasted noodles for a long time', she adds with a sigh.

Telegin concurs: 'Aye, it's a very long time since we had noodles at dinner.'

Meanwhile Sonia and Astrov have been looking anxiously for Uncle Vanya in the garden, 'afraid', Telegin explains, 'he may lay hands on himself.'

MARINA. And where's his pistol?

TELEGIN (*in a whisper*). I've hidden it in the cellar.

MARINA (*with a smile*). Such goings-on!

Both are turned out of the room by Uncle Vanya, still fuming at the 'disgrace' of having missed the professor twice, on his return with Astrov from the garden. Chekhov, who was very sparing with his advice to actors, did make two remarks on the way Astrov should be played in the last act. The first rather puzzled Stanislavsky. 'Look here,' Chekhov said to Stanislavsky in his usual cryptic manner, 'Astrov whistles! Whistles! Understand? Uncle Vanya weeps, but Astrov whistles!' He refused to say anything more and for a long time Stanislavsky, who was quite convinced that a Chekhov play was full of 'melancholy and hopelessness', could not understand why Astrov should suddenly be whistling. As usual, Stanislavsky put Chekhov's cryptic remark to the test and, as usual, arrived at the completely wrong conclusion. Chekhov's remark, Stanislavsky wrote, 'came to life' at one of the subsequent performances of the play.

One evening I made up my mind to try it out and see what happened, and the moment I did it I felt that Chekhov was right. Uncle Vanya is dejected and broken-hearted, but Astrov is whistling. Why? Because he has lost faith in people and life so completely that his mistrust has turned into cynicism. Nothing that people do can surprise him any more. Fortunately, he loves nature and can serve her faithfully: he plants trees and the woods preserve the moisture which is so necessary for the rivers.

The idea that Astrov has lost faith in people and life is, to say the least, quite absurd. Far from losing faith in people and life, he believed (and here he expressed Chekhov's own views) that the people 'who will live a hundred or two hundred years after us and who will despise us for living such stupid, such insipid lives, will, perhaps, find a way to be happy.' The 'perhaps' merely expressed Astrov's doubt about the length of time it would take to reform human nature. Far from 'his mistrust having turned into cynicism', he had no doubt that it was bound to happen some day. In *The Three Sisters*, Vershinin, another Chekhov idealist, expresses the hope that 'life on earth will become incredibly beautiful in two or three hundred years'. Both Astrov and Vershinin had no doubt that one day, however remote, people 'will find a way to be happy'. Astrov alone, however, is actively doing something to help future generations to achieve that happiness. It was his faith in man and not his 'love of nature' that made him 'plant trees' so that the woods 'preserve the moisture which is so necessary for the rivers'. (What a trivial description of Astrov's efforts to halt the destruction of the environment so that in 'a thousand years' his work might contribute to 'the happiness of mankind'!)

Chekhov's other remark on the way Astrov should be played dealt with the last scene between Astrov and Helen after Sonia had succeeded in wheedling the bottle of morphia from Uncle Vanya and had gone off with him 'to make it up' with Serebryakov. According to Chekhov, Stanislavsky completely misinterpreted this scene. He talked to Helen like 'a passionate lover' which, Chekhov pointed out, completely distorted Astrov's real feelings. 'This is wrong, absolutely wrong!' Chekhov wrote to Olga Knipper on 30 September 1899.

> Astrov likes Helen, she appeals to him strongly because of her beauty, but in the last act he knows already that nothing will come of it, that Helen is going away from him for good – and he speaks to her in this scene in the same tone as he speaks of the heat in Africa, and he kisses her simply because this seems to be the only thing to do. If Stanislavsky acts this scene passionately, he will ruin the whole mood of Act IV – quiet and languid.'

But the appeal of Helen's beauty is too strong for Astrov not to try to put off her departure.

ASTROV. Why not stay? What do you say? And tomorrow on the plantation . . .
HELEN. No, it's all settled. And I look at you so bravely because it is is settled. There's only one thing I'd like to ask you: think well of me. Yes, I'd like you to respect me.

Astrov does not comment on her wish to be respected and his

following words hardly suggest any feeling of respect for her. She must realise, he says, still hoping that he might persuade her to stay, that she has nothing to do, that she has no aim in life, that there never was anything to occupy her mind so that it was inevitable that sooner or later her natural feelings would get the better of her – 'so don't you think it had better be here in the open country than somewhere in Kharkov or Kursk? More poetical at all events. . . .'

But she would not have it, though she does go so far as to confess that she was 'a little in love' with him. A little peeved, he agrees that she'd better go, but he goes on to point out that though she was a good, warm-hearted person, there was something terribly wrong with her and that he was right in his first impression of her as a predator:

> The moment you came here with your husband, all of us, instead of going on with our work, instead of doing something, left everything and did nothing all summer except attend to you and to your husband's gout. You and your husband have infected us all with your idleness. I became infatuated with you and have done nothing for a whole month, and all the time people have been ill and the peasants have been grazing their herds in my newly-planted woods. And so, wherever you and your husband go, you bring ruin and destruction in your wake. . . . I'm joking, of course, but all the same it's – it's strange, and I'm quite sure that if you had stayed here much longer, the devastation would have been enormous. I should have been done for, but – you, too, would not have got off scot free. Well, go! *Finita la commedia!*

HELEN (*takes a pencil from his table and hides it quickly*). I shall keep this pencil to remember you by. [A pencil is as good a phallic symbol as anything else.]

ASTROV. It's all so strange. . . . We've met and, suddenly, for some unknown reason, we shall never see each other again. Everything in the world is like that. . . . But while there's no one here, before Uncle Vanya comes in with his bunch of flowers, let me kiss you. . . . A farewell kiss. . . . Yes? (*Kisses her on the cheek.*) Well – that's the end of that.

HELEN. I wish you all the happiness in the world. (*Looking around.*) Oh, I don't care! For once in my life! (*Embraces him impulsively and both at once draw quickly away from each other.*) I must go.

ASTROV. Hurry up and go. If the carriage is at the door, you'd better set off.

HELEN. I think they're coming.

Both listen.

ASTROV. *Finita!*

The entrance of Serebryakov, Uncle Vanya, Maria Voynitsky with her inevitable book, Telegin and Sonia is followed by the farewell scene which concludes the play. Professor Serebryakov generously accepts Uncle Vanya's 'apologies' and declares that he has been through so much 'during these last few hours' that he could write a whole treatise on the art of living for the benefit of posterity. Uncle Vanya assures him that he would receive the same amount as he did before 'regularly in the future', Maria asks Alexander to have his photograph taken and sent to her. Serebryakov even condescends to shake hands with Astrov, then thanks everybody for the pleasure of their company and asks their indulgence for 'just one single observation: We must work, ladies and gentlemen, we must work!' After exchanging bows, the old 'soap bubble' departs majestically, accompanied by Maria and Sonia. Helen and Uncle Vanya exchange a last farewell: 'We shall never meet again' – are Uncle Vanya's words to her. The constant refrain as one after another they return to the room is: 'They've gone!' Astrov collects his things, Sonia and Uncle Vanya settle down to make up the overdue accounts. Astrov, about to leave the house in which he had spent so many enjoyable hours, exchanges a few curt sentences with the reluctant Uncle Vanya. He obviously feels a little guilty at having to part on such bad terms with his best friend, but the map of Africa gives him the chance to conceal his confusion. After emptying the glass of vodka offered to him ceremoniously by Marina, he bids a general goodbye. When Sonia asks him when they might see him again, he replies dryly: 'Not before next summer.' He leaves accompanied by Sonia 'with a candle'.

On Sonia's return Uncle Vanya could no longer contain his feeling of utter deolation. But when he turned to Sonia with the despairing cry: 'My child, I'm so unhappy! Oh, if only you knew how unhappy I am!', she replied that there was nothing to be done about it. They had to go on living. They had to steel themselves to bear patiently whatever trials fate had in store for them. They must work for others so that when their time came, they would die without a word of complaint in the full consciousness that they had done their duty to their fellow-men and that they would find their reward in the 'bright, beautiful and refined' life to come. Deeply religious as she was, it was natural for Sonia to seek consolation in a brighter future beyond the grave. But it would be a mistake to interpret this as an admission of a frustrated life. On the contrary, now that her dream of a happy married life had been shattered she could devote herself wholly to a life of service.

Unfortunately, the last words Sonia uses as a refrain to her speech – the last chord of a beautiful musical composition, delivered to the accompaniment of a guitar, can only be translated as 'we shall rest', the verb 'to rest' in this particular context having the implication in English of 'eternal rest' or 'death'. The Russian verb has no such connotation. Here we are dealing with one of those literary echoes which Chekhov uses with such telling effect to evoke the right mood in the audience. The verb was used by the Russian poet Lermontov in his wonderful translation of Goethe's famous lyric poem '*Ueber allen Gipfeln ist Ruh*'. Lermontov translated the last line of this poem – *Ruhest du auch* – literally: *otdokhnyosh ee ty*, you too will rest, which evokes a much more serene mood in Russian than the English verb does in the same context. There is a sense of finality in the sound of the English mono-syllable as compared with the Russian trisyllabic *otdokhnyom*, we shall rest, ending in a long drawn out consonant, suggesting not the horror of the rest in the grave, but a serene and happy rest after a task well and truly done.[1]

[1] The last paragraph is a condensed version of the last page of Chapter XX (p. 224) from my book *Chekhov the Dramatist*.

THE THREE SISTERS

Introduction

In no other play of Chekhov's has the dramatist's intention been so distorted, disregarded and sentimentalised as in *The Three Sisters*. Yet Chekhov has taken infinite pains to make his intention crystal clear by ensuring audience participation at every step of the development of its main themes, and, most particularly, of the Moscow theme. Indeed, this dual method of treatment of the dramatis personae and the audience provides the spectator with a glimpse into the future which is completely hidden from the characters and in this way tends to intensify the play's suspense. He achieves this mostly by his subtle treatment of the literary echoes, a fact that, unless carefully brought out in the translation, puts an English or American audience at a disadvantage. He further strengthens this aspect of audience participation by a lavish scattering of symbols which help to reveal the hidden nature of each character, such as the great bell in the case of Andrey, the green belt and lighted candle in that of Natasha, the lost key to the grand piano and the dead tree in that of Tusenbach, the silver samovar and the porcelain clock in that of Chebutykin, the hands and bottle of scent in that of Solyony, the grand piano in that of Masha and many more.

Chekhov deliberately placed the action of the play in a remote town of Russia ('The action takes place', he wrote to Gorky on 16 October 1900, 'in a provincial town like Perm'. Perm is a town on the Kama river west of the Ural Mountains and over 800 miles from Moscow). Far away from Moscow, in fact, to emphasise the delusory character of the desire of the sisters to return to Moscow and give weight to Vershinin's statement that 'there is no town so dull and depressing for an intelligent and educated person to be superfluous in'.

The action of the play, which Chekhov described, again deliberately, as 'a drama' (neither a comedy, as some of the actors of the Moscow Art Theatre thought it to be, nor a tragedy, as Stanislavsky was convinced it was), covers about three and a half years: the first act starts in the morning of 5 May, the second act a year later at eight o'clock in the evening in mid-February (Shrove-tide), the third act between two and three in the morning, probably over a year after the second act, and the fourth act at noon on an autumn day, probably a year after the third act. It is certainly curious that Chekhov should have been most precise about the time of the start of the action of each act, but rather vague about the actual period of time between the acts.

Chekhov does not give the ages of the characters, except for Anfissa, the old nurse, whose age is given as eighty in the cast list, but they are either mentioned in the text or they can be easily deduced from the context. At the start of the play Olga is twenty-eight; Masha twenty-three or twenty-four (she was married to Kulygin at eighteen and, according to her husband's statement in the third act, had been married then for seven years); Irene is twenty (the play opens on her twentieth birthday); Andrey's age cannot be established with any certainty, but it is safe to assume that he was the second one in the family and that his age must be about twenty-five; and Natasha is most probably in her early twenties. Vershinin is forty-two, Tusenbach is probably twenty-eight (about the same age as Solyony), Chebutykin is sixty, and Kulygin is probably in his late thirties.

In all his plays Chekhov gives expression to his own social and political views by putting them into the mouths of his characters. He was very conscious that a writer's duty was to show an active interest in the social and political problems of his day. 'As a writer,' he makes Trigorin say in the second act of *The Seagull*, 'I must speak of the common people, of their sufferings, of their future. I must speak of science, the rights of man, and so on.' In *Uncle Vanya* it is the problem of the destruction of the environment that preoccupies Astrov. In *The Three Sisters* Chekhov, aware of the ever increasing impetus of the revolutionary movement in Russia, makes Tusenbach say in the first act: 'The time is coming when something huge is about to overwhelm us. A mighty hurricane is on the way; it is quite near already, and soon, very soon, it will sweep away idleness and complacency from our society, as well as prejudice against work, and effete boredom.' He was never impressed by the facile optimism of the revolutionaries who believed that by sweeping away the old order they would establish peace and harmony on earth. In his plays he expresses the view that it would take at least two to three hundred years, or perhaps even a thousand years, to bring about a cardinal change in human nature, and in *The Three Sisters* he makes the idealist Vershinin his mouthpiece on the future of mankind, taking, as usual, great care that the expression of his views should be strictly in character.

Act One

The first act of *The Three Sisters* opens, as stated, on 5 May, Irene's twentieth birthday, and exactly a year after the death of her father, a General in command of an artillery brigade. He had been transferred from Moscow eleven years earlier, when Irene was only a child of nine, Masha was about thirteen and Olga seventeen. The General's death meant a considerable decline in their social status. 'When Father was alive', Masha says at the beginning of the first act, 'we always used to have thirty or forty army officers at our birthday parties, but today we have only a man and a half.' Later in the play, she again refers to the fact that they no longer had a batman to help them with the running of the house. This certainly gave an additional impetus to the desire of the sisters to return to Moscow. The General seemed to have been a strict disciplinarian at home. 'He inflicted education on us,' Andrey remarks in the first act, and at the beginning of the same act Olga says: 'Father trained us to get up at seven o'clock.' Their mother had died in Moscow before the General's transfer to the remote provincial town, and the death of their father left the two unmarried girls hard up and rather uncertain of their future: Olga teaching at school all day and giving private lessons in the evenings, and Irene, convinced that 'work alone gives a meaning and a purpose to life', unable to find a satisfactory job. Masha is in an even worse plight. 'I was married off', she tells Vershinin in the second act, 'when I was eighteen. I was afraid of my husband because he was a schoolmaster and I had only just left school. He seemed to me terribly learned, clever and distinguished. Now, I'm sorry to say it is quite different.' Irene remarks earlier in the first act: 'Masha got married when she was eighteen. At the time her husband seemed the most intelligent man in the world to her. It's quite different now. He is the most good-natured but not the most intelligent of men.' It was, indeed, quite different: the situation was almost the same as that of Helen and Serebryakov in *Uncle Vanya*, but Masha was not Helen, although both, curiously enough, were talented pianists: she was not afraid of breaking with convention or speaking her mind or 'snatching at happiness piecemeal'. She was the only one of the sisters not to join in their wish to go back to Moscow (their brother Andrey, in love with 'a local girl', says ironically to Vershinin on learning that he has just arrived from Moscow: 'I congratulate you: now my sisters won't give you any peace'). She had come to Irene's birthday partly in the hope – a sort of premonitory feeling she could not suppress – that something might happen to dispel her 'melancholy mood', but as nothing did, she decided to go home. Irene protested, but Olga, who was perfectly well aware that Masha's marriage was a failure, merely remarked 'tearfully': 'I understand you, Masha.' But something or rather someone did turn up and her life was changed for the next three years. It was a change that gave meaning to her life and the strength she lacked before to carry on, to start 'a new life'.

A significant feature of *The Three Sisters* is Chekhov's widening of the scope of his new form of drama. In the opening scene he does it by bringing on a number of characters who seem to be engaged in some private conversation, but allowing his audience to hear snatches of it, which serve not only as a comment on the views and intentions of the other characters on the stage, but also as a forecast of the inevitable outcome of their plans. This gives the audience the opportunity to know more than the dramatis personnae, an indispensable way of assuring audience participation in the dramatic development of the play. To achieve this, Chekhov divides the stage into two parts separated by a colonnade, the front representing a drawing-room, and the back representing part of a dining-room. The six characters in the opening scene are then divided into two groups, the three sisters in front of the columns and Chebutykin, Tusenbach and Solyony, appearing after the first part of Olga's dialogue, are in time to comment on the plan of two of the sisters to go back to Moscow.

Chekhov's stage direction for the opening scene is very precise: 'Noon; it is a bright, sunny day. In the ballroom [converted into a dining-room on the occasion of Irene's birthday party] the table is being laid for lunch.' Olga wears the regulation dress of a grammar-school mistress and, standing or walking about the room, is correcting exercise books; Irene, wearing a white dress, is standing 'lost in thought' while Masha, who, like Masha in *The Seagull*, is wearing a black dress, but has no trace of the selfish exhibitionist about her, is sitting reading a book, her hat on her lap, apparently not listening to her sisters, 'daydreaming and whistling a tune softly'.

OLGA. It is just a year since Father died, on this very day, the fifth of May – your birthday, Irene. It was dreadfully cold: it was snowing then. I felt as though I'd never be able to live through it, and you were lying in a dead faint. But now a whole year has gone by and the thought of it no longer troubles us. You're wearing a white dress again; you look so radiant. (*The clock strikes twelve.*) Then, too, the clock struck twelve. (*Pause.*) I remember the military band playing at Father's funeral, and they fired a salute at the cemetery. Though Father was a General and a brigade commander, there were not many people at his funeral. It is true, it was raining then. Pouring with rain, and snowing.

IRENE [visibly annoyed with Olga for damping her gay spirits by recounting the events of their father's death and his military funeral, attended by very few people, which seems to show that the disciplinarian General was not particularly popular, though Olga tries to blame the poor attendance on the weather]. Why must you talk about it?

It is at this point that Baron Tusenbach [Tusenbach was a Baltic German by birth, which accounts for his title; the Russian nobility had only two titles: prince, which had no royal connotation, and count, introduced by Peter the Great], the old army doctor Chebutykin, and the subaltern Solyony, who are to act as the chorus, appear near the table behind the columns.

OLGA [goes on with her recital of past events, revealing that she was a girl of seventeen when the Prozorov family left Moscow and the only one to have such a vivid recollection of the day of their departure]. It is a warm day today – the windows can be opened wide – but the birch trees are not yet in leaf. It is eleven years since Father was given his brigade and left Moscow with us and, I distinctly remember it, the flowers were out in Moscow just at this time – the beginning of May. Oh, it was so warm then, and everything was drenched in sunlight. Eleven years have passed, but I can remember everything just as if we had left Moscow only yesterday. My goodness! When I woke up this morning and saw the bright sunshine, saw the spring, my heart leapt for joy, and I felt such a passionate longing to be back home!

I

Her remark that the bright sunshine of the spring morning made her feel 'a passionate longing to be back in Moscow' at once brings the withering comment from Chekhov (using Chebutykin and Tusenbach as the chorus, whose words are heard only by the audience):

CHEBUTYKIN. The devil you did!
TUSENBACH. It's all nonsense, of course!

It is at this point that the daydreaming Masha, unimpressed by Olga's reminiscences, whistles to the annoyance of Olga, who is interrupted at the most poignant point of her speech.

OLGA. Don't whistle, Masha. How can you? [A pause, during which she contemplates the far from joyful reality of her daily life.] I suppose it's because I'm at school all day and giving private lessons in the evenings that I'm getting these constant headaches and these thoughts, just as if I were old already. And really, all these four years while I've been working at school, I've felt as though my strength and my youth were draining out of me drop by drop. And one longing only grows stronger and stronger —
IRENE. To go to Moscow! Sell the house, finish with everything here, and leave for Moscow.
OLGA. Yes! To Moscow as soon as possible.

Chebutykin and Tusenbach laugh: a comment that requires no comment.

Irene, once more revealing how little substance there was in her plans for a return to Moscow, expresses the hope that 'probably' her brother Andrey, who had long given up all hope of an academic career, would become a professor of Moscow University and join them in Moscow. Her only regret is that 'poor Masha', married to a dull-witted schoolmaster, would not be able to join them. But Olga finds an easy solution to that problem: 'Masha', she says unhesitatingly, 'could come to Moscow every year and stay with us the whole summer.' Masha goes on whistling her tune softly, paying little attention to the bright future her two sisters are mapping out for themselves. This time she is not rebuked by Olga, for by now both Olga and Irene have convinced themselves that everything, in Irene's words, 'will turn out all right'. There is one fly in the ointment, though, so far as Olga is concerned. 'Everything is all right,' she agrees, 'everything is as God wills,' she adds cautiously, 'but I can't help thinking that if I got married and stayed at home all day, things would be much better.' She pauses, reflecting perhaps that in that case she might even not miss Moscow. Indeed, she adds: 'I'd have loved my husband.' She would not have hesitated to marry anyone who asked her, she tells Irene in the third act, 'provided he was a decent man. I'd even marry an old man.' But even her dream of marriage is dismissed as inexorably as her plans to return to Moscow:

TUSENBACH [talking to Solyony, but still in the role of chorus, addressing the audience]. What nonsense you talk. I'm sick of listening to you.

Tusenbach now joins the ladies and announces the coming visit of Lieutenant-Colonel Vershinin, the newly-appointed battery commander. His name does not seem to mean anything to any of the three sisters. Olga says that she would be very glad to meet him and Irene merely inquires how old he is and whether he is 'an interesting man'. Masha does not comment at all. However, at this point Chebutykin and Solyony join the company in the drawing-room. Both of them seem to be preoccupied with their own thoughts and, strangely enough, pay no attention either to one another or to the company at large. Solyony is preoccupied with his hands – the hands of a killer – on which Chekhov concentrates the attention of the audience.

SOLYONY (enters the drawing-room with CHEBUTYKIN). I can lift only half a hundredweight with one hand, but with two I can lift a hundredweight and more. From which I infer that two men are not only twice but three times or even more as strong as one.

A little later, commenting on Tusenbach's assertion (or is it Chekhov's prophecy?) that in twenty-five or thirty years everyone would be working, Solyony, who, like Tusenbach, was in love with Irene, utters the threat, so far not taken seriously by anybody, that one day he might lose his temper and put a bullet through his head. This is followed by the stage direction: 'Takes a bottle of scent from his pocket and sprinkles the perfume over his chest and hands.' Towards the end of the second act and in the middle of the third Chekhov makes him take out the bottle of scent again and sprinkle his hands. It is only in the fourth act, when he is on the way to his duel with Tusenbach, that he explains his action.

SOLYONY (*taking out his bottle of scent and sprinkling his hands*). . . . I've emptied a whole bottle on my hands today and still they smell – smell like a corpse.

Chekhov added this stage direction to the text of the play published in 1902, over a year after its first performance by the Moscow Art Theatre in January 1901, which shows how much importance he attached to Solyony's efforts to get rid of the smell of decomposition which his hands seemed to exude.

Chebutykin's constant preoccupation is with newspapers. While entering the drawing-room his whole attention is absorbed in an item he is reading out from a popular newspaper: 'For falling hair, one hundred and thirty grains of naphthalene in half a bottle of spirits. Dissolve and apply daily. (*Writes it down in his notebook.*) Let's make a note of it.' His medical knowledge had been reduced to taking down some absurd prescription from a newspaper. He has never done a stroke of work, he declares in the first act. 'As soon as I left the university, I never lifted a finger or opened a book. I only read newspapers. (*Takes another newspaper out of his pocket.*) Here. . . . I know from the papers that we have had a critic by the name of Dobrolyubov, but I have no idea what he wrote about.' When Andrey asks him in the second act to tell him what to do about his asthma, Chebutykin replies: 'Why ask me? I can't remember. I don't know.' Chebutykin's complete dissociation from life in spite of, or, perhaps, because of, his reading of the popular press, is best demonstrated by his present of a silver samovar to Irene in the first act. He had wanted to give an expensive present to the daughter of the only woman he ever loved, and a silver samovar (usually given as a silver-wedding present) was the only thing he could think of. He is quite incapable of understanding the gasp of horror his present produced.

OLGA [who had earlier warned the company that Chebutykin was 'always doing something silly', could only cover her eyes in horror]. A samovar! This is awful! (*Goes out into the dining-room.*)
IRENE. Oh, you poor darling, what are you doing?
TUSENBACH (*laughs*). I told you.

MASHA. Really, doctor, you ought to be ashamed of yourself.

CHEBUTYKIN. My dear, sweet darlings. You are all I have. You're all I hold most dear in the world. I shall soon be sixty. I am an old man, a lonely, insignificant old man. There's nothing good about me except my love for you. But for you I should have been dead long ago. (*To* IRENE.) My darling child, I've known you ever since you were born. I used to carry you about in my arms. I loved your mother. . . .

IRENE. But why such expensive presents?

CHEBUTYKIN (*through tears, crossly*). Expensive presents! Don't talk such nonsense! (*To his orderly.*) Take the samovar to the other room. (*In a mocking voice.*) Expensive presents!

It was while discussing Chebutykin's birthday present, which he had gone out to fetch, that Masha had uttered her first words: the first two lines from Pushkin's fairy-tale poem *Ruslan and Lyudmilla*, lines full of magic and mystery that provide a key to Masha's character. It is Chekhov's first use of a literary echo in the play. It is unfortunately one of those literary echoes that defy translation. She then gets up and puts on her hat. 'Today', she tells Irene, 'I'm not feeling particularly cheerful, so you'd better not pay any attention to me. (*Laughing through tears.*) We'll have a good talk later. Goodbye for now, my darling. I'll just go somewhere . . . anywhere.' Irene is disappointed but Olga understands her and bursts into tears. Masha turns on her and says crossly: 'Don't howl!' She next turns on Solyony who, as usual, makes one of his idiotic remarks, this time derogatory of women's intellect. 'What do you mean by that,' she asks and referring mockingly to Solyony's assumed pose of Lermontov's romantic heroes, adds, 'you frightfully terrible man?' Solyony replies: 'Nothing!' and, commenting on the way Masha had pounced on him, quotes two familiar lines from a Krylov fable: 'He had barely time to catch his breath / Before the bear was hugging him to death.' This is the second literary echo, so familiar to a Russian audience, that its association with the dialogue of the scene that follows it would immediately spring to mind. The scene describes the arrival of a birthday present – a cake – from Andrey's boss, the chairman of the Agricultural Board and, as appears from a remark of Masha's in the first act, a close friend of Andrey's fiancée, Natasha. Though he never appears on the stage Protopopov will be responsible for the eviction of the three sisters from their home and the installation of Natasha and himself in it.

MASHA. I don't like this Protopopov, this Mikhail Potapych [this bear] or Ivanych. You shouldn't have invited him.
IRENE. I didn't invite him.
MASHA. Excellent.

Mikhail Potapych is the name given by Russian peasants to a bear, familiarly described in Russian as Mishka, the diminutive of Mikhail (Michael). Masha pretends not to be certain of Protopopov's patronymic, although Anfissa had mentioned it a moment earlier. But Protopopov's reputation as 'a bear' must have been well known in the town, though none of the characters suspects the role Protopopov is to play in the life of the three sisters. A Russian audience, however, would perceive something ominous about the connection of Protopopov with the bear from Krylov's fable. Chekhov repeats the Krylov lines again twice in the last act, and again with the ominous undertone: the death of Tusenbach in the duel with Solyony.

The entrance of Vershinin at first makes no impression on the three sisters. Even the fact that he had known them as three young girls (he even remembered their names – 'You must be Olga, the eldest one, and you Maria, and you, the youngest, Irene. . . .') does not arouse their interest. When he tells Masha that he remembers her face, her reply is: 'I don't remember you!' It is, of course, the fact that he has arrived from Moscow that immediately creates a sensation:

IRENE. . . . you are from Moscow. . . . What a surprise!
OLGA. You see, we're going to live there.
IRENE. We hope to be there by the autumn. It's our home town. We were born there. . . . In Old Basmany Street. (*Both laugh happily.*)
MASHA [trying to explain the strange behaviour of her sisters]. It's meeting a fellow townsman so unexpectedly.

Then she suddenly remembers: as a young girl of thirteen she must have found Vershinin very attractive. She may even have secretly had a crush on the 'lovesick Major'. Why else should she have burst into tears a moment later on realising how much older he looked?

MASHA (*excitedly*). I remember now. Remember, Olga, there was someone we used to call 'the lovesick Major'. You were only a Lieutenant then and you were in love with some girl and everyone used to tease you by calling you 'Major' for some reason.

VERSHININ (*laughs*). That's it. . . . That's it. The lovesick Major. Yes, that's quite true.

MASHA. In those days you had only a moustache. Oh, how you've aged! (*Through tears.*) How you've aged!

VERSHININ. Yes, when I was known as the lovesick Major, I was still young, I was in love. Now it's different.

OLGA [trying to soften the effect of Masha's outburst]. But you haven't a single grey hair. You've grown older, but you're not an old man.

VERSHININ. I'll soon be forty-three all the same. [Quickly changing the subject.] How long have you been away from Moscow?

IRENE. Eleven years. What are you crying for, Masha, you funny girl? (*Through tears.*) You'll be making me cry too.

MASHA. I'm all right. And where did you live?

VERSHININ. In Old Basmany Street.

OLGA. We lived there, too.

VERSHININ [commenting for the first time on the way Olga and Irene seemed to be possessed by their memories of Moscow, points out that Moscow can also be a dreary place to live in]. At one time I lived in German Street. I used to walk from there to the barracks. I had to cross a gloomy bridge on the way there. The water rushed so noisily under it and I could not help feeling lonely and sad. (*Pause.*) [His words seemed to have produced an unfortunate impression on the two sisters.] But here [Vershinin went on inexorably, pricking the bubble of their excitement about Moscow] you have such a fine river, such a wonderful river!

OLGA [rather lamely]. Yes, but it's very cold here. Cold and lots of mosquitoes.

Chekhov's voice is quite unmistakable in Vershinin's reply:

VERSHININ. You can't mean it. Here you have such a good, healthy climate, a real Russian climate. Forest, river, and . . . also birch trees. Dear, modest birch trees. I love them more than any other trees. It's good living here.

It is curious how much Chekhov is admired as a superb artist and how little he is thought of as a thinker. And yet in Vershinin, more than in any other of his characters, he gives expression to views which show a profound understanding of the destiny of man. It is after Masha's remark about how quickly the memory of people fades after their death, that Vershinin comments on how the newest trends are taken seriously and considered 'important and significant' and how quickly they are forgotten and dismissed as trivial. 'What is so interesting', he continues,

> is that we cannot possibly know now what will be thought of as great and important in the future and what will be considered pitiful and ridiculous. Did not the discoveries of Copernicus or, say, Columbus appear to be useless and ridiculous at the time, while some utter drivel, written by some crank, seemed to be a great truth? It is quite possible that our present life, to which we seem to be so reconciled, will in time appear to be strange, uncomfortable, unintelligent, not particularly clean and even perhaps immoral.

Tusenbach's rather futile objections that there were no longer any 'tortures, public executions, or invasions' – which come curiously from a man who was to be publicly executed, and who did not live long enough to learn that 'tortures and invasions' were not a matter of the past, and that even 'the sufferings we can observe today . . . show a certain degree of moral uplift already achieved by our society' – receive merely a polite and not very enthusiastic endorsement from Vershinin.

VERSHININ. Yes, yes, of course.

The following scene, introducing Andrey, about whose many talents Vershinin is informed by his doting sisters, again gives Vershinin the chance of emphasising that it will take a long time for mankind to make life on earth 'unimaginably beautiful and marvellous'. 'Man', he declares, 'must have a life like that. If it isn't here yet, he must be able to anticipate it, to dream about it, and to prepare himself for it. To make sure of it, he must be able to see and know more than his father and grandfather did. (*Laughs.*) And you [he turned to Masha who claimed that to know three languages in a provincial town like theirs was an "unnecessary luxury", and that "we know a lot that isn't of any use to us"], are complaining that you know a lot that is of no use to you!'

It was at this point that Masha realised that Vershinin was different from anyone she had known before. At first, she was to tell her sisters in the third act, Vershinin seemed 'strange' to her, next she felt 'sorry for him' and then she 'fell in love with him'. After his speech about the 'marvellous' life on earth 'in two or three hundred years', she thought him interesting enough to change her mind about leaving.

MASHA (*taking off her hat*). I'm staying to lunch.

Vershinin's admiration for their 'wonderful place' and his statement that all his life he had lived in lodgings with two chairs, a sofa, and a stove which always filled his rooms with smoke, and that, if he could start his life all over again, he would get himself a place like theirs with lots of flowers and 'full of light', made Masha feel genuinely sorry for him, particularly as he had a nagging wife, who was 'always complaining of her poor health'. The appearance of Kulygin at that moment must have brought home to her how unhappy her own home life was. Kulygin was 'in excellent spirits' apparently because of the outing arranged for the afternoon by the headmaster for the teachers and their families. Masha, who found Kulygin's colleagues 'coarse and ill-bred' (she tells Vershinin in the second act that she suffered agonies in their company), at first refused to go.

KULYGIN (*chagrined*). My dear Masha, why not?
MASHA. We'll talk about it later. (*Crossly.*) Oh, very well, I'll come, only leave me alone, please.

The prospect of spending the evening at the headmaster's ('A most excellent man', Kulygin rhapsodises, 'a man of irreproachable character, who is doing his best to be sociable.') merely increased her feeling of discontent.

MASHA (*crossly, but trying not to be overheard by her husband*). Damn, another boring evening at the headmaster's!
TUSENBACH. If I were you, I wouldn't go. Very simple.
CHEBUTYKIN. Don't go, my dear.
MASHA. Don't go, indeed! What a damnable, unbearable life! (*Goes into the ballroom.*)

Masha certainly had good reason to sympathise with Vershinin's unhappy family life. If nothing else, their common experience was enough to form a bond between them.

Left alone with Irene after the rest of the company had gone into the dining-room, Tusenbach asked her what she was thinking of, which she could not possibly have told him, for, as she confessed to Olga in the third act, what she was always thinking of was that it was only in Moscow that she hoped to meet the man she'd fall in love with. She therefore replied evasively that she was afraid of Solyony, a fear that was justified in the event but that Tusenbach thought to be unreasonable because it was only in company that Solyony tried to cover up his shyness by behaving like a coarse bully. (Chekhov incidentally, warned the actor playing Solyony not to make him 'too coarse', that is to say, not to make him into a melodramatic villain.) Tusenbach went on to tell Irene how much he loved her.

TUSENBACH. . . . You're twenty and I'm not yet thirty. Think of the years we have still ahead of us. A long succession of days, each one full of my love for you.

IRENE. Please, don't talk to me of love.

TUSENBACH (*not listening*). I've such a passionate yearning for life, for work, for striving for a better life. This yearning has, somehow, become mingled with my love for you, Irene. And, as luck would have it, you are beautiful and life also seems beautiful to me. . . .

IRENE. You say life is beautiful, but what if it only seems so? Our life, I mean my life and the life of my two sisters, has not been particularly beautiful so far. Life has choked us like a weed. I'm crying. I'm sorry, I mustn't. (*Quickly dries her eyes and smiles.*) We must work, work, work! We are unhappy, we have such a gloomy view of life because we don't know the meaning of work. We are the children of people who despised work.

It was a very painful tête-à-tête and Irene must have been grateful to Natasha for entering at that moment in her pink dress and shiny green belt, little suspecting that the girl who was giving her 'a lingering kiss' was a ruthless predator who would kick her out of her beautiful home. Like Solyony, Natasha, too, felt shy in company and like him she was vindictive. She never forgot Olga's dismay at the sight of her green belt and her words about it not suiting her and being and looking a little out of place. In the last act she told Irene that her belt did not suit her at all. 'You ought to get something bright and shiny', she added, remembering Olga's objection to her own shiny green belt four years earlier.

At the birthday party it is again Masha's disregard of convention and her great sensibility that Chekhov is careful to emphasise. At the dining-room table it is she who offends against the rules of good behaviour by striking her plate with a fork and exclaiming: 'Let's have a glass of vodka! Oh, life is sweet! What the hell!' And towards the end of the first act when the premonition she had had at its beginning that someone might turn up to dispel her 'melancholy mood' seemed to have been justified, the two magic lines from Pushkin's poem broke from her lips again and she cried 'tearfully', as though resenting the stirring of a great passion in her: 'Why do I go on saying this? Can't get these lines out of my head since morning!'

The act ends with another tête-à-tête: this time it was Andrey who told Natasha that his heart 'is full of love, of ecstasy' and that he loved her as he had never loved anyone before. The curtain falls on 'a kiss' and the two army officers, who come in at that moment, stop 'dead in amazement' at the sight of the kissing couple, as indeed the audience, who should by now have anticipated the end of that particular love affair, might well do.

Act Two

The action of the second act revolves round the fascinatingly Satanic character of Natasha. In no other play or story has Chekhov created a more terrifyingly convincing figure of evil. 'It isn't her baby who is ill,' Masha says when told that Natasha had cancelled their Shrovetide party, 'it is she herself! Here! (*Tapping her forehead.*) The stupid, selfish, trivial creature!'[1] It is Natasha with whom Chekhov opens the act. This is his stage direction: 'The scene is the same as in Act One. It is eight o'clock in the evening. Off stage, from the street, come the faint strains of an accordion. There are no lights in the house. Enter Natasha in a dressing-gown with a lighted candle.' The two lofty rooms, separated by a row of columns, which were so 'full of light' in the first act, are dark now: Natasha had decided to make it clear to the sisters – the rightful owners of the house – that she was now the mistress there, first by plunging the room into darkness as a sign that she was not going to allow the holding of a Shrovetide party in the house (she herself had arranged to go off on a sleigh ride with her lover Protopopov); secondly, by banning the traditional visit to the house of the Shrovetide masked dancers; and thirdly, by evicting Irene from her room on the pretext that her baby was ill because his room was too cold, while Irene's room was 'dry and gets the sun all day'.

In the second act, too, the Moscow theme is given a prominent place, but, again, in a way that ensures audience participation by making the spectators constantly aware of its delusive nature, or, in other words, by making them see what the characters fail to see. This occurs at the very beginning of the act when Andrey, taking advantage of Ferapont's deafness, talks of the way he had been disappointed in his expectations of an academic career and of his dream that he is a professor of Moscow University, a celebrated scholar, 'of whom the whole of Russia is proud'. If he had been in Moscow he would be sitting in a famous restaurant where no one knew him and where he would not feel

[1] The word Chekhov uses to describe Natasha is *meshchanka*, usually translated as a *petite bourgeoise* or philistine, but the word has a much more derogatory meaning.

a stranger, whereas 'here where you know everybody and everybody knows you, you are a stranger, a stranger and all alone.' The mention of Moscow jogs Ferapont's memory and he counters with a story of a Moscow businessman who choked himself to death after eating forty or fifty pancakes in a Moscow restaurant, the point – which the audience should not be slow to get – being that Moscow is no more civilised than the least cultured provincial town. Ferapont caps this story with another one of a rope being stretched 'right across the whole of Moscow', a story no less fantastic than Irene's dream of the wonderful transformation that Moscow would bring to her life. Later in the same act, in reply to Masha's remark that anyone who did not notice whether it was summer or winter was a happy man and that if she had been in Moscow she would be indifferent to the weather, Vershinin tells her of a former French Cabinet Minister who during his imprisonment watched 'with rapturous delight' the birds he could see through the prison bars, but when released lost all his interest in bird-watching. 'Neither will you', Vershinin observed, 'notice Moscow when living there.' In the same act, too, it is Irene who is counting the months before she and Olga would be leaving for Moscow, without realising that Andrey's gambling losses would make it impossible for them to go there. A little later, watching Fedotik laying out a game of patience, she cries: 'I can see it's working out: we shall be in Moscow.' But it didn't work out, which, Fedotik concluded with a laugh, 'means that you won't be in Moscow'. Finally, Chekhov exposes the delusory idea of Moscow by a news item read out by Chebutykin.

CHEBUTYKIN. Tsitsihar. A smallpox epidemic is raging here.

Tsitsihar – what an exotic place, even more remote and unattainable than Moscow, and yet it is nothing but a pest hole.

To the characters in the play that piece of news must seem utterly irrelevant (nobody comments on it), but it is not at all irrelevant as far as the audience is concerned, for it gives it a chance of knowing more than the dramatis personae: the most direct way to ensure audience participation.

The short opening scene of the second act is a masterpiece of compactness. It shows Chekhov's marvellous skill in delineating so devious a character as Natasha in a few casually uttered words. On entering the drawing-room, Natasha stops at the door of Andrey's room; she opens the door and looks in. She seems to be only interested in what he is doing. 'Reading? Never mind, I just . . .' She then opens the door of another room, looks in and shuts it again. 'Any light left burning . . .' she murmurs. But what she is really after is to arouse Andrey's curiosity and get him to come out of his room. This she does, for he does come out of his room with a book in his hand. Her explanation that she was making sure the servants had not left any candles burning in some room has nothing to do with the real purpose of her appearance. She leads up to it cautiously by asking him the time. His reply that it is a quarter past eight, provides her with an opening for explaining one of the reasons for her appearance.

NATASHA. Olga and Irene are still out. Not home yet. Hard at work, poor darlings. Olga at the staff meeting, Irene at the telegraph office. (*Sighs.*) [Hypocritically.] Only this morning I said to your sister [to Irene whom she is anxious to throw out of her room]: 'You must take more care of yourself, Irene darling.' But she won't listen to me. A quarter past eight did you say? [Now she at last broaches the subject of Irene's eviction from her room.] I'm afraid our Bobikin is not at all well. Why is he so cold? Yesterday he had a temperature, but today he's quite cold. I'm so worried.

ANDREY. Don't worry, Natasha. The boy is well enough.

But Natasha is not yet ready to come out with her plan to get Bobikin into Irene's room and make Irene share Olga's room. For the moment she suggests that 'we must be more careful about Bobikin'. She is now ready to broach the subject of the masked dancers by suggesting that they might disturb the child.

NATASHA. . . . I'm told the masked dancers are expected to come here after nine o'clock. I wish they weren't coming, Andrey dear. [Andrey realises that what Natasha wants is to challenge his sisters' authority in their own house, and having gambled away some of their money, he is afraid of a row with them.]

ANDREY. Well, I don't know. They've been invited, you see.

Natasha ignores the fact that the sisters had invited the dancers. Instead, she again changes the subject to Bobikin.

NATASHA. This morning the little darling woke up, looked at me and suddenly smiled. He must have recognised me. Good morning, Bobikin, I said, Good morning, darling! He laughed. Little children understand. Oh, they understand everything. [Then having softened Andrey up by this evidence of the prodigious intellect of his son, she reverts to the subject of the carnival dancers.] You don't mind, Andrey dear, if I tell the servants not to let the dancers in, do you?

ANDREY (*hesitantly*). But, you see, it depends on my sisters. It is their house.

NATASHA. Yes, it's their house, too. I'll tell them. They're so kind.

Having clinched the matter, she goes back to her plan to throw Irene out of her room. She begins by expressing her solicitude for Andrey's health. Then, after a pause, becomes even more solicitous about the health of their child.

NATASHA. Bobikin is cold. I'm afraid his room is too cold. We'll have to find him another room. At least till the warm weather. Now, Irene's room is just right for a baby: it is dry and it gets the sun all day long. She must be told that for the time being she should share Olga's room. She's not at home during the day, anyway. She only sleeps here. . . . [A pause, during which Natasha realises that she would never get Andrey to consent to Irene's eviction from her room, not in so many words, at any rate, unless she softened him up a little more: she usually calls him Andryusha – dear Andrey – but now she calls him by a much more affectionate name: Andryushan-chik – quite untranslatable except by the rather lame: Andrey darling.] Andrey darling, why don't you say something?

ANDREY. Oh, I was just thinking. . . . Besides, there's nothing to say, is there?

And there wasn't, for she had got what she wanted.

The third scene of this act starts immediately after Andrey returns to his room with his book. 'Enter Masha and Vershinin. While they talk a maid lights a lamp and candles.' This is all that Chekhov states as an indication of the lapse of time between the meeting of Masha and Vershinin in the first and the second act. Indeed, the two scenes seem almost to follow each other, although during the year that separates the two acts Masha and Vershinin must have met many times. There is, however, no hint of any previous meeting in this scene in which

Vershinin declares his love for Masha and in which we hear for the first time Masha's soft, happy laughter. Indeed, it is in this scene that the great argument about the meaning of happiness is conducted between Vershinin and Tusenbach. Vershinin and Masha had disagreed about the difference between civilians and army men, Masha plumping for army men, and Vershinin arguing that there was no difference between them. 'Listen to any educated person here,' Vershinin says [and here he certainly expresses Chekhov's views], 'whether civilian or army officer, and he'll tell you that he's sick and tired of his wife or his family or his estate or his horses. Why', he asks, 'does a Russian, who is so susceptible to high ideals, stoop so low in his own life? ... Why is he sick and tired of his children, sick and tired of his wife, and why are his wife and children so sick and tired of him?' When Masha merely echoes his own questions and then surmises that he must be in a bad mood, he confesses that he has had a violent quarrel with his wife.

We started quarrelling at seven o'clock and at nine I walked out, slamming the door behind me. (*Pause.*) I never talk of it to anyone [he thought it necessary to reassure her, for he must have noticed the bad impression his confession had had on her] and, strange to say, it is to you alone that I complain. (*Kisses her hand.*) Don't be angry with me. I've nobody but you – nobody.' (*Pause.*)

But she was superstitious and the howling of the wind in the chimney reminded her that before her father died the wind howled in the chimney just like that – a bad omen for their romance.

VERSHININ [commenting on her admission that she was superstitious]. That's strange. (*Kisses her hand.*) You're a magnificent, wonderful woman. Magnificent, wonderful! It's dark here, but I can see your eyes shining.

MASHA (*sits down on another chair*). There's more light here.

VERSHININ. I love you, I love you, I love you! I love your eyes, your movements. I dream about them. Magnificent, wonderful woman!

MASHA (*laughing softly*). When you talk to me like that I can't help laughing, though I'm terrified. Don't say it again, I beg you. (*In an undertone.*) Yes, yes, do. (*Covers her face with her hands.*) I don't mind. Someone's coming. Talk of something else.

It was Irene and Tusenbach who entered. Tusenbach had been trying to explain that in spite of his triple-barrelled aristocratic German name he was a genuine Russian at heart and in religion, but Irene was not interested. Her first brush with reality at the telegraph office that day had proved a very disconcerting experience: a woman had come in to send a telegram to her brother in a remote Russian town with the news of the death of her son. In her distress she could not remember his address and that annoyed Irene. 'I was rude to her. I don't know why. I'm busy, I told her.' She then sent off the telegram to the town without waiting for the woman to remember the address. The woman cried. The whole thing was 'so stupid'. She now wanted to get another job that would be more 'poetic and intellectual' than her work at the telegraph office. At that moment Chebutykin began knocking on the floor from below to find out whether anybody was in. This reminded Irene of another distressing fact: the night before Chebutykin and Andrey had again been gambling at the club, and Andrey had again lost.

IRENE. . . . They say, Andrey lost two hundred roubles.
MASHA (*with indifference*). It's a little late to do anything about it.
IRENE. Two weeks ago he lost, in December he lost. I wish he'd hurry up and lose everything he's got. Perhaps we'd leave this town then. Dear Lord, every night I'm dreaming of Moscow. I'm going off my head. (*Laughs.*) We've leaving in June, and before June there are still left – February, March, April, May – almost six months!
MASHA. We must make sure Natasha does not find out about his losses.
IRENE. I don't think she cares.

What neither Irene nor Masha knew at the time was that Natasha had a very good reason for not caring: for, as Masha reveals in the third act, Andrey had mortgaged the house without first obtaining the consent of his sisters and handed the money over to Natasha. Except for the meagre army pension the General had left them in his will, the three sisters had no income of any kind now. They could not sell the house, as Irene had suggested in the first act, and there could no longer be any question of going to Moscow.

On entering the 'ballroom', Chebutykin, who had just got up after his after-dinner nap, sat down at the table and took out his newspaper: Chekhov wanted him to supply two items to clinch the argument

K

about happiness between Vershinin and Tusenbach and to show up once again the unreality of Irene's dream of Moscow.

/ Vershinin started the discussion by wondering what life would be like in two or three hundred years. Tusenbach argued that while man might be able to fly and even 'discover and develop a sixth sense', life would remain the same: hard, full of mysteries and—happy. 'A thousand years hence,' he says, 'man will still be sighing: "Oh, life is hard!" and will be just as afraid of death and just as unwilling to die as he is now.' Vershinin did not agree: he thought everything on earth must change and 'in two hundred, three hundred or perhaps a thousand years a new and happy life will begin. We won't take part in it, of course, but we are living for it now, working for it and – well – suffering for it, creating it, and therein lies the aim and purpose of our existence and, if you like, our happiness.' Masha could not help laughing softly, and when Tusenbach asked her what she was laughing at, she replied that she did not know, adding: 'I have been laughing all day today.' / Vershinin went on to say that the one thing he was certain of was that not only was there no such thing as happiness, but that there must not be and could not be any happiness for them: for all they had to do was 'to work, work, and work. Happiness is for our distant descendants.' He paused to drive home his point, 'If not for us, then at least for the descendants of our descendants.' /

TUSENBACH. Do you mean to say that one oughtn't even to dream of happiness? But what if I am happy?

VERSHININ [who knows that Irene is not in love with Tusenbach, is quite sure about it]. You're not!

TUSENBACH (*flinging up his arms and laughing*). We quite obviously do not understand one another. How am I to convince you? (MASHA *laughs softly*.)

TUSENBACH (*shaking a finger at her teasingly.*) Laugh!

Turning to Vershinin he repeated his conviction that even in a million years life would remain the same, for it followed its own laws and would always remain a mystery to man.

Migrant birds, cranes, for instance, fly and fly, and whatever thoughts, great or small, might be drifting through their heads, they will go on flying without knowing where or why. They will go on flying, however many philosophers may be born among them. Indeed, let them philosophise as much as they like as long as they go on flying.

MASHA. But there must be some meaning, surely.

TUSENBACH. A meaning? Look, it's snowing. What meaning is there in that? (*Pause.*)

MASHA. It seems to me a man must have some faith or be searching for some faith. Otherwise, his life is empty, empty. To live and not know why cranes fly, why children are born, why there are stars in the sky . . . You must know what you live for or else nothing matters any more. It's all meaningless nonsense. (*Pause.*)

VERSHININ [looking at Masha with whom he could have been happy, bursts out]. All the same it is a pity that I'm no longer young.

MASHA [catching the meaning of Vershinin's words, adds weight to her claim that life must have some meaning by quoting the last lines of Gogol's famous story of the meaningless quarrel between Ivan Ivanovich and Ivan Nikifirovich – another literary echo!]. Gogol says: 'It's a boring world, my friends!'

TUSENBACH. And I say, it's difficult to agree with you, my friends. Let's drop the subject.

But Chekhov had not exhausted the subject; he makes Chebutykin read out a sentence from his paper:

CHEBUTYKIN. Balzac was married in Berdichev. (IRENE *hums softly*.) Balzac was married in Berdichev. I'll make a note of that. (*Writes down in his notebook.*) Balzac was married in Berdichev. (*Reads his paper.*)

IRENE (*laying out patience, reflectively*). Balzac was married in Berdichev.

Stanislavsky states in his reminiscences that the sentence 'Balzac was married in Berdichev' was not in the original script, but was sent by Chekhov from Nice, where he must have come upon a reference to Balzac's marriage in a town proverbially known as the dullest in the whole of Russia. But why repeat the sentence three times and why make Irene repeat it 'reflectively', unless the thought might have occurred to her, if only for a moment, that one need not seek happiness in Moscow seeing that one of the greatest writers of France found it in Berdichev?

Chekhov's intention in introducing this sentence seems to have been to find a conclusive connection to the rather inconclusive argument about happiness. The association of marriage with happiness is purely subjective: Chekhov certainly hoped to find happiness in his marriage to Olga Knipper (their wedding took place about four months after the first night of *The Three Sisters*); and of the chief characters of his play Tusenbach is happy because, having resigned from the army, he was now more than ever convinced that Irene would accept his proposal of marriage; and Vershinin's as well as Masha's thoughts of happiness were also concerned with their most intimate feelings for one another.

Before Fedotik had time to show his other game of patience to Irene, Anfissa put the samovar on the table and began pouring out the tea. Solyony, morose as ever, came in and sat down at the table. Natasha, who had returned earlier, also busied herself at the table. Masha pointedly refused Anfissa's invitation to have tea at the same table as Natasha and asked for her tea to be brought to the drawing-room. Natasha was not one to overlook such a snub, but for the time being she was so flushed with her success in getting Andrey's tacit agreement to cancel the Shrovetide party that she decided to overlook it. Finding no one else to talk to, she pounced on Solyony and began telling him what a wonderful child her Bobikin was.

NATASHA. Little children understand very well. [She went on to repeat the words she had used earlier with such success to Andrey.] Good morning, Bobikin, I said, good morning darling. He gave me such a knowing look. You think it's the mother in me speaking, don't you? It isn't! Believe me, it isn't! He's quite an extraordinary child!

Solyony listened to her with feigned attention, waiting patiently for the right moment to crush her.

SOLYONY. If this child had been mine [he began quietly, while Natasha beamed at him in expectation of some really nice compliment], I'd fry him in a pan [he continued slowly, enjoying the startled look in Natasha's eyes] and eat him [he finished with relish, walking off into the drawing-room with his tea].

NATASHA (*covering her face with her hands*). What a coarse, ill-bred fellow!

Indeed, he was, as Tusenbach found out when he picked up a box of chocolates from the table and found no chocolates in it.

TUSENBACH. Where are the chocolates?

IRENE. Solyony's eaten them.

TUSENBACH. All of them?

Vershinin's quick exit after receiving a letter with the news of another suicide attempt by his wife made Masha lose her composure. She shouted at Anfissa, went over to the table in the 'ballroom' with her tea, mixed up the cards on the table:

MASHA. . . . Sprawling all over the place with your cards. Why don't you drink your tea?

IRENE. You have a foul temper, Masha.

MASHA. Don't talk to me if I have a foul temper. Leave me alone!

CHEBUTYKIN (*laughing*). Leave her alone, leave her alone.

MASHA. You're sixty, but you're always talking some damned nonsense as if you were a silly little boy.

It was now Natasha's turn to pay Masha back for having been snubbed earlier by lecturing her on how a lady ought to behave in society.

NATASHA (*sighs*). My dear Masha, why must you use such language? With your attractive appearance, I promise you, you'd be simply adorable in any refined society, if it was not for your language. *Je vous prie, pardonnez-moi, Marie, mais vous avez manières un peu grossières!*

TUSENBACH (*restraining his laughter with difficulty*). Please – please – pass me. . . . There's some brandy there I think.

It was Natasha's pretensions to refinement that nearly made Tusenbach splutter with laughter. She realised herself that if she stayed any longer she might have to meet the full brunt of Masha's *manières un peu grossières*. She, therefore, decided to retire while the going was good.

NATASHA [still addressing the company in French]. *Il paraît, que mon Bobikin déjà ne dort pas* – he's awake. I'd better go and see. Excuse me. (*Goes out.*)

Tusenbach picked up the decanter of brandy and went over to Solyony, who had been skulking in a corner, with an offer to make it up.

SOLYONY. Why make it up? I haven't quarrelled with you.

TUSENBACH. You always make me feel as if something had happened between us. You're a strange character, I must say.

SOLYONY (*declaiming*). I am strange. Who is not strange! Do not be angry, Aleko!

TUSENBACH. What's Aleko got to do with it?

Aleko, the hero of Lermontov's poem 'The Gipsies', who killed his wife and her lover in a fit of jealousy, had a great deal to do with it, but, then, Tusenbach had no idea that he was dealing with a rival who was determined to kill him if he happened to be successful. They drank and again Solyony, claiming that he even looked a little like Lermontov, uttered his veiled threat: 'Do not be angry, Aleko! Forget, forget your dreams!', while producing a bottle of scent and sprinkling his hands, the hands of a murderer. Solyony then engaged in an argument with Chebutykin, the two of them usually so preoccupied with themselves that they never listened to one another. In this scene Chekhov purposely selected two outlandish words which seemingly sound alike to bring out this singular feature of their characters.

CHEBUTYKIN (*going into the drawing-room with* IRENE). And the food was genuinely Caucasian: onion soup and for a roast – *chekhartma*.

SOLYONY. *Cheremsha* isn't meat. It's a plant, something like an onion.

CHEBUTYKIN. No, my dear fellow. *Chekhartma* isn't an onion, it's roast mutton.

SOLYONY. And I'm telling you *cheremsha* is an onion.

CHEBUTYKIN. And I'm telling you, *chekhartma* is mutton.

SOLYONY. And I'm telling you *cheremsha* is an onion.

CHEBUTYKIN. What's the use of arguing with you? You've never been to the Caucasus and you've never eaten *chekhartma*.

SOLYONY. Haven't eaten it because I can't stand it. *Cheremsha* reeks like garlic.

ANDREY [who came in quietly earlier, imploringly]. Enough, gentlemen, enough!

Tusenbach then asked Irene when the Shrovetide dancers were expected, and she replied that they should be coming any moment.

Andrey, who knew perfectly well that Natasha was not going to let them in, said nothing, but started singing a traditional Russian song and dancing with Tusenbach. At the mention of Moscow University by Tusenbach, Solyony again engaged in a futile argument about whether there were one or two universities in Moscow (Chekhov had in mind the names Moscow students gave to the old and new buildings of one and the same university).

SOLYONY. Which Moscow university? There are two Moscow universities.
ANDREY. There's only one university in Moscow.
SOLYONY. And I tell you there are two.
ANDREY. Three, if you like. So much the better.
SOLYONY. There are two universities in Moscow. (*Murmurs of protest and booing.*) There are two universities in Moscow: the old and the new. But if you don't want to listen to me, if my words annoy you, I'll shut up. I can even go to another room. (*Goes out.*)

By these arguments Chekhov wished to show not only Solyony's utter ignorance, but also his resentment at the way people reacted to it. What mattered to him was his own opinion. If he said something, however absurd, it was right: he exalted his own neurosis to an article of faith.

It was after Tusenbach had called to them to start the party and had sat down at the piano, playing a waltz, Masha waltzing and singing: 'The Baron's drunk, the Baron's drunk, the Baron's drunk', that Natasha came in and, whispering something to Chebutykin, went 'quietly' out. Chebutykin touched Tusenbach on the shoulder and also said something to him in a whisper.

IRENE. What is it?
CHEBUTYKIN. Time we were going. Goodbye.
TUSENBACH. Good night. Time we were off.
IRENE. One moment. . . . What about the dancers?
ANDREY (*greatly embarrassed*). I'm sorry, but there won't be any. You see, my dear, Natasha says that Bobikin isn't well and that's why – er – in a word, I don't know. I don't care a damn.
IRENE (*shrugging*). Bobikin isn't well!
MASHA. Oh, all right. If they're chucking us out, we'd better go.

(*To Irene.*) It isn't Bobikin who's ill, it's she herself. Here! (*Taps her forehead.*) The stupid, selfish, trivial creature!

Andrey beat a hasty retreat to his room, followed by Chebutykin. Both returned stealthily after everyone had gone. Chebutykin told Andrey that he never married because he was 'madly in love with your mother', while Andrey mournfully confessed only a year after his marriage to Natasha, that he should never have married because 'it's so boring'. He could have found a more appropriate word, but Chebutykin supplied it.

CHEBUTYKIN. That may be so, but what about loneliness? Loneliness is a terrible thing.

Andrey had already discovered it, for *that* was the only reason he would have liked to go to Moscow, where, as he had told Ferapont, he thought he would never be lonely, while in a town where he knew everybody, he was 'a stranger and alone'. It was worse at home: for he was afraid of his wife.

ANDREY. Let's get out quickly.
CHEBUTYKIN. What's the hurry. Plenty of time.
ANDREY. I'm afraid my wife may stop me.
CHEBUTYKIN. Oh!

After their departure to the club 'the doorbell rings twice' and 'voices and laughter are heard'.

IRENE (*comes in*). What's that?
ANFISSA [who has been clearing the table in the 'ballroom', whispers]. The mummers!
IRENE. Tell them there's no one at home. Say we're sorry.

ANFISSA *goes out.* IRENE *paces the room pensively: she is upset.*

It was while she was so upset that Solyony came in with his unwanted and, indeed, dreaded declaration of love. He began by apologising for having been 'so indiscreet and tactless, but', he went on, 'you're high-minded and pure. You can see the truth. You alone can understand me. I love you. I love you deeply, passionately —'
Having raised her to so high a pinnacle as to be the only person in the world to understand him, Solyony quite naturally expected her to

reciprocate his feelings. Her blunt refusal to have anything to do with him made no impression on him: he didn't even seem to hear it.

SOLYONY. I can't live without you. (*Going after her.*) Oh, my joy! (*Through tears.*) Oh, my happiness! Lovely, exquisite, wonderful eyes, eyes unlike those of any woman I've ever known.
IRENE (*coldly*). Don't, please.
SOLYONY. It's the first time I've spoken to you of my love and I feel as though I'm not on earth but on another planet. (*Rubs his forehead.*) Oh well, never mind. I can't force you to love me, of course, but I shall not put up with any successful rival. I shan't. I swear to you by everything I hold sacred that I shall kill my rival! Oh, my wonderful one!

Solyony was incapable of accepting the idea that Irene might prefer someone else to him, and he left no doubt in Irene's mind that he would carry out his threat to kill the man she promised to marry. It was at that dreadful moment that Natasha entered in her dressing-gown and, as at the opening of the second act, carrying a candle: she had come to carry out her second plan, to evict Irene from the room she had lived in for over twelve years. After apologising to Solyony for coming in in her dressing-gown (she seemed to have forgotten calling him a coarse, ill-bred fellow), she watched him leave the room and then she turned to Irene, who still could not recover from the shock of Solyony's threat, and gives her an even greater shock. As usual, Natasha began by hypocritically expressing her sympathy with Irene for looking 'so tired'.

NATASHA. You look so tired, darling. Oh, you poor child! (*Kisses Irene.*) You ought to go to bed earlier. [She always kissed her victims before delivering her fatal blow: she would do it to Olga in the third act.]
IRENE [wishing to reciprocate so friendly an approach and feeling that she ought to apologise for her sarcastic remark about Bobikin's not being well, falls into the trap Natasha had so cunningly laid for her]. Is Bobikin asleep?
NATASHA. Yes, he is, but he's very restless. By the way, my dear [she begins casually as if the idea had only just occurred to her and as if what she was going to propose was of no particular importance], I've been wanting to say something to you, but you've either been out or

I've been too busy. I can't help thinking that the nursery is too cold and damp for Bobikin. Your room is just what a baby needs. Darling, don't you think you could move into Olga's room. Just for a short time.

IRENE (*not understanding*). Where?

The harness bells of a troika could be heard as it drove up to the house.

NATASHA. You and Olga will share one room, for the time being, I mean, and Bobikin will have your room. [Having made her meaning quite clear and seeing the look of amazement and horror in Irene's eyes, she quickly goes on with her patter about Bobikin.] He's such a darling. Today I said to him: Bobikin, you're mine! Mine! And he looked at me with his sweet little eyes! (*The doorbell rings.*) Must be Olga. She is late. [She knows very well who it is, but when the maid goes up to her and whispers in her ear, she pretends to be very surprised.] Protopopov? What a funny man! Protopopov [she explains to Irene, who is still too shattered by the blow of being thrown out of her room to say anything] Protopopov wants me to go for a drive with him in his troika. (*Laughs.*) Aren't men strange? (*The doorbell rings.*) Somebody's at the door. I suppose I could go for a drive for a quarter of an hour. (*To the maid.*) Tell him I shan't be long. (*The doorbell rings.*) The doorbell again. That must be Olga. (*Goes out.*)

IRENE *sits lost in thought; enter* KULYGIN *and* OLGA, *followed by* VERSHININ.

KULYGIN. How do you like that? I was told they'd be having a party.

VERSHININ. That's funny, I left not so long ago, about half an hour ago, and they were expecting the dancers.

IRENE. They've all gone.

KULYGIN. Masha gone too! What's Protopopov waiting for outside in his troika? Who is he waiting for?

IRENE [ironically]. Don't ask me: I'm tired.

They soon 'go out': Olga too tired after her staff meeting and shocked that Andrey's loss of two hundred roubles at cards should have become the talk of the town; Vershinin glad that his wife, as usual, merely threatened to commit suicide and, feeling at a loose end, inviting the husband of the wife he was in love with, to come out with him;

and, finally, Kulygin expressing his regret (fortified by a Latin tag) at not being able 'to spend an evening in pleasant company', but refusing to accept Vershinin's proposal (was he beginning to suspect that the colonel's relationship with his wife was a little too unconventional?).

Left alone and contemplating the awful consequence of Solyony's threat and the even more awful prospect of living in the same house with a woman like Natasha, it was no wonder that Irene should cry '*longingly*': 'To Moscow, to Moscow, to Moscow!'

Act Three

The action of the third act, which takes place against the background of a great fire in the town, should be conducted quietly, Chekhov insisted in a letter to Olga Knipper from Nice on 20 January 1901, so that the audience should feel that the characters are 'tired and almost asleep'. And yet it is in the third act that the climax of the play is reached and its main themes – Natasha's takeover of the house, the love affair of Masha and Vershinin, Irene's decision to marry Tusenbach despite Solyony's threat to kill him, and Andrey's final collapse – reach the point which quite inevitably leads to its dramatic conclusion in the fourth act.

Over a year has passed between the second and third acts. Natasha has had her second child, a girl, this time by Protopopov whose relationship with her had become, as Irene declares, the talk of the town; Andrey has reached the apogee of his career by becoming a member of the Agricultural Board of which his wife's lover was the chairman; Irene has been thrown out of her room and forced to share Olga's bedroom, she has given up her job at the telegraph office and is working for the town council. It is, in fact, in Olga's and Irene's room, with its screened-off beds 'on the right and on the left', that the action of the third act takes place. It is past two o'clock in the morning. From behind the scenes comes the ringing of a fire alarm. No one in the house has yet gone to bed. Masha is lying on a sofa, 'dressed, as usual, in black', when Olga and Anfissa come in. Olga at once begins taking out clothes from the wardrobe and handing them to Anfissa for distribution among the people made homeless by the fire who had sought shelter in the house. As she opens the door to call Ferapont to take the clothes downstairs, the red glow of the fire can be glimpsed through a window and a fire engine can be heard passing the house. On Ferapont's departure with the clothes, the 82-year-old Anfissa appeals to Olga not to turn her out of the house. Olga is surprised at such a request, but Anfissa, who has no doubts about Natasha's intention to have her thrown out, repeats it. Olga, like any other naturally good person, never realises how far an evil woman like Natasha will go once she is given enough elbow room to assert herself. Convinced that the old nurse was 'talking nonsense', she makes her sit down and have a rest, but Natasha, who enters at that moment, soon proves that Anfissa's fears were fully justified. Natasha begins by a show of hypocritical concern for the homeless. She next tries to win Olga over by a show of motherly love: 'Bobikin and Sophie are peacefully asleep, the little darlings, as if nothing had happened. . . .' But immediately she makes clear her disapproval of permitting so many homeless people to take shelter in the house: 'There's an influenza epidemic in town. I'm afraid the children might catch it.' She starts preening herself in front of the mirror, repeating her usual remark about her 'looking an awful sight', but denying strongly that she was growing fat 'as people say'. She then casts a commiserating glance at Masha, who pretends to be asleep: 'She looks so tired, poor girl!' Finally – and this is why she had come into the room and what she had been so laboriously leading up to – she casts a glance at the seated Anfissa, and explodes:

NATASHA (*to* ANFISSA, *with cold fury*). . . . Don't you dare sit down in my presence! Get up! Get out of here! (ANFISSA *goes out; pause.*)

Noticing Olga's embarrassment and the look of horror on her face, she expresses her genuine surprise that anybody should want to keep an old useless woman in the house: 'I simply don't understand why you keep the old woman!'

OLGA (*struck dumb with surprise*). I'm sorry, but I—I don't understand —

NATASHA. She's quite useless in the house. She's a peasant and she must live in a village. You're spoiling her, aren't you? I like order in a house. There should be no unwanted people in a house.

As Olga is still too stupefied to say anything, Natasha begins stroking her cheek, as if she (Olga) were too tired to appreciate the nonsense she was talking.

NATASHA. Oh, you poor thing! You're tired! [She goes on trying to mollify her by throwing out the hint of her coming appointment as headmistress.] Our headmistress is tired! When my Sophie grows up and goes to school I shall be afraid of you.

OLGA [brought out of her stupor by the news of her appointment]. I shan't be a headmistress.

NATASHA [glad at the change of subject]. They're going to appoint you, darling. It's settled.

OLGA. I'll refuse. I couldn't. . . . I haven't got the strength. . . . (*Takes a drink of water.*) You treated Nanny so abominably just now. I'm sorry, but I can't bear it. It made me feel quite faint.

NATASHA [it had only just occurred to her that she had gone too far and she is anxious to propitiate Olga by apologising excitedly]. I'm sorry, darling, I'm sorry.

The whole scene was certainly too much for Masha: she gets up, picks up a cushion and goes out angrily. Olga tries to argue with Natasha but to little effect.

OLGA. Please understand, my dear. We may have been brought up in a peculiar way, but I can't bear this sort of thing. It upsets me, it makes me ill. It makes me lose heart.

Natasha did not doubt for a moment that the upbringing of the three sisters had been very peculiar indeed, but she also realises that another show of contrition is called for.

NATASHA. I'm sorry. I'm sorry. (*Kisses her.*)

OLGA. Any rudeness, however slight, any harshly uttered word upsets me.

NATASHA. I admit I often say things I shouldn't, but, my dear, you must agree that there's no reason why she shouldn't live in the country.

OLGA. She's been with us for thirty years.

Natasha looks absolutely appalled at such a ludicrous attitude towards servants.

NATASHA. But she can't do any work now! Either I don't understand you or you don't want to understand me. She's incapable of doing any work. All she does is sleep or sit about.

OLGA. Well, let her sit about.

NATASHA (*amazed*). Let her sit about? But she's a servant, isn't she? (*Through tears.*) I don't understand you, Olga. I have a nanny, a wet-

nurse, a parlour maid, a cook. What do we want that woman for?
What for?

Fire alarm offstage.

[Chekhov put in the sound effect as a forewarning to the audience of
the terrifying outburst that must quite inevitably result when anyone
tries to thwart Natasha.]

OLGA [tries, unsuccessfully, to change the subject]. I've aged ten years
tonight.

NATASHA. We must come to an understanding, Olga. You're at
school, I'm at home. You've got your teaching, I've got the running
of the house. And if I talk about servants, I know what I'm talking
about. I know what I am talk-ing a-bout! By tomorrow I want that
old thief, that old hag out of the house! (*Stamping her feet.*) The old
witch! Don't you dare exasperate me! Don't you dare! (*Recollecting
herself.*) Really, Olga, if you don't move downstairs we shall always
be bickering. This is dreadful!

It was dreadful, and the threat to send the sisters down to the base-
ment to share rooms with Chebutykin was meant in good earnest as a
foretaste of what was to come if Natasha's plans were balked. Fortunately, Kulygin appears at that moment and helps to relieve the tension.

Kulygin had been worried about Masha for some time. Her involvement with Vershinin could not have escaped him and he foresaw clearly
enough that it might result in a public scandal that must be avoided at all
cost. His marriage to Masha, even he must have realised, had been a
failure and, as he told Olga as soon as he had sat down, if it had not
been for Masha he would have married her because *she* was 'so good'—
an admission that amounted to a wish that he *had* married her instead.
At that moment, though, he is preoccupied with the condition of
Chebutykin whom he hears coming up from below and who, as he
informs Olga and Natasha, is 'on one of his drinking sprees'. To escape
a scene with the drunken army doctor, Olga and Natasha 'retire to the
back of the room' and a few moments later go out, while Kulygin hides
behind the wardrobe.

Like Astrov in *Uncle Vanya*, Chebutykin was upset because a
patient of his had died, but, unlike Astrov, it was entirely his own fault

that she had died. 'They think I am a doctor,' he mumbles 'morosely', washing his hands at Olga's washstand, 'that I can treat any illness, but I know nothing, absolutely nothing.' But he did remember that a few days earlier he had been responsible for the death of a woman patient because of his incompetence and that made him feel 'dirty, nasty, loathsome' and he got drunk. But he went a step further: 'Perhaps', he says, 'I am not a human being at all, but merely imagine that I have hands and feet and a head. Perhaps I don't exist at all, but merely imagine that I walk, eat and sleep. (*Weeps.*) Oh, if only I did not exist!' But he does exist and he has been a human being once capable of devoted and selfless love for a woman. His final degradation, his final dehumanisation is made apparent when he drops and smashes the porcelain clock, one of the treasured possessions of the woman he loved, after the entry of Irene, Vershinin and Tusenbach, the last one, typically enough, 'in a fashionable suit'. Chebutykin, resenting Irene's remark that he should go to bed, picks up the porcelain clock and begins examining it. Vershinin announces that his artillery brigade will probably have to leave for Poland or even the Far East. Tusenbach, too, had heard about it.

IRENE. We shall be leaving too.

CHEBUTYKIN (*drops the clock, which breaks*). Smashed to smithereens!

Pause; everyone looks upset and embarrassed.

KULYGIN (*picking up the pieces*). Break an expensive thing like that!
    Oh, doctor, doctor, zero minus for conduct.

IRENE. It was Mother's clock!

CHEBUTYKIN. Possibly. So it was your mother's clock. Perhaps I
    didn't smash it, but it just seems as though I did. Perhaps we only
    imagine that we exist, but we really don't exist at all. I don't know
    anything. Nobody knows anything.

But the smashing of the clock awakened memories of his now wasted life and, as he is about to leave the room, he stops at the door and shouts furiously at them: 'What are you staring at? Natasha is having a disgusting affair[1] with Protopopov and you don't see it. You're just sitting here and don't see anything, while Natasha is having her

---

[1] The word Chebutykin uses is 'romanchik', a derogatory diminutive of *roman*, a love affair.

disgusting affair with Protopopov. (*Sings.*) Won't you accept this little present from me?[1] (*Goes out.*)

Since they all know of Protopopov's affair with Natasha, Chebutykin's 'present' does not produce the sensation he expected. Vershinin's laughing comment: 'Well, well.... As a matter of fact, the whole thing is rather odd!' about summed up the situation. Vershinin goes on to relate his experiences of the fire. He found his two little daughters standing at the front door in their night clothes (their mother seemed to have abandoned them) and he could not help thinking what other frightful things the girls would have to experience during a long life. 'I snatched them up, started running and all the time I could not help thinking: What else would they have to experience in this world?' Vershinin might well have wondered, but neither he nor even Chekhov could have imagined that had the little girls lived long enough, they would have experienced two revolutions as well as two world wars and the terrible devastation and human suffering left in their wake. But the fire alarm and the pause that followed immediately after Vershinin's rhetorical question was as good a prognosis as Chekhov could have given of the events of the next fifty years at the time.

It was at the conclusion of Vershinin's account of arriving at the Prozorov's house and being met by an angry and screaming wife that Masha entered, still clutching her cushion, and sat down on the sofa.

A little earlier, shortly before the smashing of the clock, Tusenbach had proposed that Masha should give a concert in aid of the homeless. Masha was an accomplished pianist, a fact Kulygin was quick to confirm, though Irene thought that she must have forgotten how to play because she had not played for three or four years.

TUSENBACH. . . . I assure you Masha plays wonderfully, almost like a concert pianist.

KULYGIN. You're quite right, Baron. I love Masha very much. She's a dear.

Tusenbach, piqued by Kulygin's rather lukewarm endorsement of

---

[1] In a letter to Stanislavsky from Nice on 15 January 1901, Chekhov points out that the sentence Chebutykin sings was from some operetta, but that he could not remember which. Its literal translation is: 'Won't you accept this date (*finik*) from me', the word *finik* also having in old Russians the meaning of 'a marginal note'. The sentence Englished would be: Put that in your pipe and smoke it!

his proposal, observes that it is a pity that no one seems to appreciate how well she plays. This immediately makes Kulygin admit that the reason why he does not want his wife to take part in a concert is that his headmaster might object to it. 'It is true it is none of the headmaster's business,' he quickly adds after a pause, noticing the unfortunate impression his objection has produced, 'but all the same, if you like, I might perhaps have a talk to him.'

Masha re-entered the room just in time to hear Vershinin once more express his belief that in two or three hundred years

> people will look back upon our present life with horror and con-tempt, and everything we accept so unquestioningly today will seem clumsy and wretched, extremely uncomfortable and strange. Oh, I'm sure of it. What a wonderful life it will be, what a life! (*Laughs.*) I'm sorry, I'm afraid I've got carried away again, but, please, let me go on. I would so much like to go on philosophising. I'm in the mood for it now.

There was no response: they all seemed to be asleep. But he just would not be deterred from expressing his conviction of a better life in the future even if it meant repeating what he had already said when he first met the three sisters:

> There are only three like you in the town now, but in generations to come there will be more and more and more, and the time will come when everything will change as you would have it, people will live as you do now, and later you, too, will become outdated – people will be born who will be better than you. (*Laughs.*) I'm in a sort of peculiar mood today. Damn it, I want to live and live! (*Sings.*) To love all ages are in thrall, her impulses are good for all[1]. . . . (*Laughs.*)

Masha found Vershinin's vitality and affirmation of life so infec-tious that she responded to it with a wonderfully rousing musical flourish:

MASHA. Trum-tum-tum!
VERSHININ [echoing her]. Tum-tum!
MASHA [more dramatically zestful]. Tra-ra-ra!
VERSHININ. Tra-ta-ta! (*Laughs.*)

[1] Prince Gremin's aria from *Eugene Onegin*.

They understood each other without words. The entry of Fedotik with the news that he had lost all his possessions in the fire merely emphasised the challenge of Masha's defiant call. They were so wrapped up in one another that they completely disregarded the menacing tone of Solyony's protest at not being allowed into the room by Irene and his strange action of sprinkling himself with perfume to suppress the smell of putrefaction he exuded. They went on with their musical exchanges, this time in the form of question and answer.

Chekhov gives a clear indication of the meaning of this wordless dialogue in a letter to Olga Knipper from Nice on 20 January 1901. Chekhov wrote: 'Vershinin pronounces "Trum-tum-tum" in the form of a question, while you [Olga Knipper played the part of Masha in the first production of *The Three Sisters*] reply in the form of an answer, and you think it is such an original idea that you pronounce this "trum-tum" with a grin. . . . You utter "trum-tum" and burst out laughing, not loudly, but barely audibly. . . . Remember, you are easily amused and angry.'

What Vershinin asked was: 'Do you love me?' and Masha's reply was 'Yes'—a declaration of love which took place in the hearing of everybody, but which only Vershinin and Masha understood.

Vershinin laughed and, noticing Solyony's grim expression, asked him to go down to the ballroom with him.

SOLYONY. Very well. We'll make a note of that [meaning he would repay Irene for her snub]. 'I could make my tale more clear, but that might annoy the geese, I fear.'[1] [He gives Tusenbach, who had fallen asleep, a look of hatred and expresses his contempt for him in his usual way:] Cluck-cluck-cluck.

After the departure of Vershinin, Fedotik and Solyony, Irene wakened Tusenbach who pleaded with her to go away with him. He reminded her how 'bright and cheerful' she had looked at her birthday party and how sad and dissatisfied she was with life now. Masha tells him to go away, which he reluctantly does.

The next scene is given up entirely to the relationship between Masha and her husband. Masha asks him why he doesn't go home. Kulygin, obviously anxious to come to some kind of an understanding with his wife, goes about it, as usual, in a way that only exasperates her.

[1] A quotation from Krylov's fable *Geese*.

MASHA (*lying down on the sofa*). Are you asleep, Fyodor?
KULYGIN. Eh?
MASHA. Why don't you go home?
KULYGIN. My dear Masha, my darling Masha —
IRENE [noticing Masha's mounting anger]. She's tired, let her have a rest.
KULYGIN. I'll be going in a minute. My wife's a good, nice woman. I love you, my only one.

It was certainly the wrong thing to say to a wife who had fallen desperately in love with another man. Masha flares up angrily and derides his kind of love by sarcastically conjugating the present tense of *amare*. But her sarcasm is completely lost on the slow-witted Latin master, who takes it as a huge joke.

KULYGIN (*laughs*). Isn't she wonderful? I've been married to you for seven years, but it seems as if we left the church only yesterday. On my word of honour! You really are a wonderful woman. I'm content, content, content.
MASHA. I'm fed up, fed up, fed up![1] [She sits up and goes on speaking: the violence of her outburst at last breaks through his facile assumption that by pretending that nothing has really happened the whole thing will blow over without involving him in a public scandal which his headmaster would certainly not stomach. For a moment the expression of contentment on his face changes to anguish and Masha quickly switches the conversation to Andrey.] I can't get it out of my head. It's disgraceful. It preys on my mind. I can't keep silent. I'm talking about Andrey. He's mortgaged the house and his wife's grabbed all the money, but the house doesn't belong to him alone, does it? It belongs to all of us. He should have realised it if he's an honest man.
KULYGIN [assuming again his expression of feigned contentment]. Why should you worry, Masha? What do you care? Andrey is up to his neck in debt. Well, let him do what he likes.

---

[1] Masha's outburst is usually translated by 'I'm bored, bored, bored', which rather diminishes the violence of her reaction to Kulygin's decision to ignore what has just passed between her and Vershinin by pretending to be asleep. The Russian colloquial word Chekhov uses is: *nadoyelo* which corresponds *literally* to the English 'fed up'.

MASHA [satisfied with the alacrity with which her husband covered up his dismay, seems ready to accept his curious excuse for Andrey's action in robbing his sisters]. It's disgraceful, however you look at it. (*Lies down again.*)

KULYGIN [quick to respond to her consent to accept his way of dealing with their unhappy marital situation by ignoring it]. You and I aren't poor. I work, I teach at our grammar school, I give private lessons, I'm an honest man. A plain man. *Omnia mea mecum porto*, as they say.

MASHA. I don't want anything, but I can't bear injustice. [*A pause, during which both of them contemplate the advantages of Kulygin's peace offering.*] Go home, Fyodor.

KULYGIN (*kisses her*). You're tired. Rest for half an hour. I'll wait for you downstairs. Try to sleep. (*Going.*) I'm content, content, content. [Having reached this tacit understanding with his wife, he goes out.]

Andrey's fiddling while everything goes up in flames around him brings home to Irene her own desperate situation.

IRENE. . . . (*Distractedly.*) Oh, it's awful, awful, awful! (*Weeps.*) I can't bear it any longer, I can't, I can't. (OLGA *comes in and starts tidying things up on her bedside table.* IRENE *sobs loudly.*) Throw me out! Throw me out! I can't bear it any longer!

OLGA (*frightened*). What's the matter? What is it, darling?

IRENE (*sobbing*). Where, where has it all gone? Oh, God, oh God! . . . I've forgotten everything, and life's passing and will never return, never! We'll never go to Moscow. . . .

Olga tries to quieten her, but to no avail. She hated her new job at the town council, she was losing her looks, and there was nothing she could look forward to. Her dream of 'a beautiful life' was receding further and further, she was in despair and thought she was heading for some 'horrible disaster'. Indeed, she wondered why she had not killed herself 'before now'.

Olga's only advice to her was to marry Tusenbach, which brought the admission from Irene that the reason why she wished to go to Moscow was that it was in Moscow she hoped 'to meet the right man', the man she dreamed of, the man she already loved. 'But, as it turned out,' she had at last to admit mournfully, 'it was all nonsense, all non-sense.'

OLGA (*embracing her sister*). My dear, my sweet sister, I understand, I understand everything. When the Baron left the army and came to see us in his civilian clothes, I thought he looked so unprepossessing that I couldn't help crying. He asked me why I was crying, but I couldn't tell him, could I? But I'd be very happy if he married you. That's quite a different matter, quite different.

Irene had no time to reply, for at that moment, '*Natasha, carrying a lighted candle* [according to Chekhov's stage direction] *walks across the stage in silence from the door on the right to the door on the left.*'

That Chekhov considered this stage direction of the utmost import-ance is made clear in a letter he wrote to Stanislavsky from Nice on 2 January 1901: 'You write[1] that in the third act Natasha, as she walks through the house at night, blows out the lights and looks for thieves under the furniture. It seems to me, though, that it would be much better if she walked with a lighted candle across the stage in a straight line without looking at anyone or anything, *à la* Lady Macbeth—that would be much shorter and much more terrifying.'

It would also explain Masha's comment: 'She walks as if she had set the town on fire herself.'

What was so 'terrifying', however, was not the impression that Natasha had set the town on fire, but that she had set the house of the three sisters on fire. Their house might as well have been burnt down to the ground, for it no longer belonged to them. They had given shelter to people who had been made homeless, but they were now as homeless as the people whose houses had burnt down.

Another note by Chekhov, written this time to Olga Knipper from Nice on 21 January 1901, concerns the important scene of Masha's 'confession' immediately after Natasha's exit with the candle. 'Masha's confession in the third act', Chekhov wrote, 'is not a confession at all, but merely a frank conversation. Your acting must be nervous but not hysterical, don't shout, smile even if occasionally, and, most of all, in your acting you must convey the fact that it is very late and that you are tired. The audience must also feel that you are more intelligent

---

[1] Stanislavsky wrote to Chekhov on 23 December, that is, a week before the first night of *The Three Sisters*.

than your sisters, at least that you consider yourself to be more intelligent.' It is obvious that what Chekhov meant was merely to indicate the general feeling, the mood, pervading the scene of Masha's 'confession', but left it to the actress to decide at which point in her dialogue to smile. For the translator the dialogue of this scene is particularly difficult since it abounds in words and locutions which, if translated literally, may distort Chekhov's intention. A more relaxed, if not entirely free, translation may help to convey the mood of the whole scene as Chekhov intended it.

MASHA. I have a confession to make to you, dear sisters. It's been on my mind a long time. I'll confess to you and not say another word to anyone—ever. Now I'll tell you. (*Softly.*) You see, it is my secret, but I want you to know it. I can't keep it to myself. . . . (*Pause.*) I love him, I love him. I love that man. Well, I may as well say it outright: I love Vershinin.

OLGA (*goes behind the screen*). Don't go on. I'm not listening to you, anyway.

MASHA. I'm afraid it can't be helped. (*She clasps her head.*) At first I thought him strange, then I began to pity him, and then I fell in love with him. I fell in love with his voice, his talk, his misfortunes, his two little girls. . . .

OLGA (*behind the screen*). I'm not listening all the same. Say any foolish thing you like, I'm just not listening.

MASHA. Oh, it is you who are foolish, darling. I love him. It's happened. It's fate. I have to accept it. He loves me too. Terrible, isn't it? Not nice, is it? (*She draws* IRENE *by the hand and puts her arm round her.*) Oh, my dear, what's to become of us? What's our life going to be like? When you read some novel all this sounds so old-fashioned, so obvious, but when you fall in love yourself you realise that no one knows anything and that everyone must decide for himself. Oh, my dear, dear sisters . . . I've made a clean breast of it. I shall be silent. I shall be like Gogol's madman—silence . . . silence. . . .

The entry of Andrey, followed by Ferapont, puts an end to the scene. Andrey had come to have it out with his sisters. He had robbed them of their property and, while he felt bad about it, his first impulse was to try to justify his action. Ferapont, unwittingly, comes to his aid by being too familiar with him. He tells him sternly to address him as 'sir', and later apologises to his sisters for having said 'something silly'. He pretends to have come to ask Olga for the key to a cupboard. Olga hands him the key in silence, while Irene demonstratively retires behind her screen. He challenges Olga to tell him why she is 'so silent'. He wishes they would drop 'all this nonsense' and stop 'sulking'. Since they are all there, he wants to have 'a frank talk' with them. He wants to know what they have got against him.

OLGA. Leave it alone, Andrey. We'll have our talk tomorrow. (*Agitatedly.*) What an awful night!

ANDREY (*looking very embarrassed*). Don't get excited. I'm perfectly calm and I'm asking you what you've got against me. Tell me straight.

At this point Vershinin can be heard off stage repeating Masha's earlier rousing call: 'Trum-tum-tum!' as a signal that he was waiting for her. It is also Masha's cue to get out before Andrey makes a complete ass of himself.

MASHA (*gets up; loudly*). Tra-ta-ta! (*To* OLGA.) Goodbye, darling. God bless. (*Goes behind the screen and kisses* IRENE.) Sleep well. . . . Goodbye, Andrey. Go away now. They're tired. Talk it over tomorrow. (*Goes out.*)

But Andrey refused to put it off, although Olga had gone behind her screen and left him alone in the room. He embarks on a long 'explanation' of why his sisters were sulking and what they had against him and his wife. His excuse for Natasha's behaviour is that she is 'an honest and decent' person whom he loves and respects. The reason why his sisters resented her was that they were 'so eager to find fault with her'. As for the way his sisters behaved towards him, that was because they were angry with him for giving up his studies and for not having become a professor of Moscow University. But he was a member of the Agricultural Board and he regards his service as honourable and important as service to science. As his sisters still refuse to say anything, he comes to the real purpose of his visit: 'Thirdly . . . there's one more thing I'd like to say. I've mortgaged the house without your consent. It was wrong of me—yes. I'm sorry. I was driven to it by my debts—thirty-five thousand. I've given up gambling for some time

now, but the only thing I can say to justify myself is that you girls, you
get Father's pension while I have nothing, no income, I mean.'
    Olga and Irene still refuse to say anything. Fortunately, Kulygin
enters at that moment. He stops in the doorway, looking distraught: he
has been waiting for Masha downstairs but she seems to have gone.

KULYGIN (*at the door*). Isn't Masha here? (*Anxiously.*) Where could
    she be? Strange! ... (*Goes out.*)

Andrey, too, at last decides to make a clean breast of it.

ANDREY. They're not listening. [He tries his bluff again, though rather
    undecidedly.] Natasha's an excellent, honest person. (*Paces the stage
    in silence and then stops dead.*) When I got married I thought that
    we'd be happy, all of us. But, my God! (*Weeps.*) My dear sisters, my
    darling sisters, don't believe me, don't believe. ... (*Goes out.*)

Kulygin – the other unhappy husband – again appears at the door.

KULYGIN (*upset*). Where's Masha? Isn't Masha here? Extraordinary
    business! (*Goes out.*)

The last short scene begins with the sound of the fire alarm. The
stage is empty: then the doctor's knocking on the floor from below
starts Olga and Irene talking and ends in Irene's consent to marry
Tusenbach.

IRENE. ... I respect the Baron. I think highly of him. He's a fine man.
    I will marry him. I agree. Only, let's go to Moscow. Please, let's go.
    There's no place like Moscow in the whole world! Let's go, Olga.
    Let's go!

There was, indeed, no place like Moscow, for there Tusenbach
would be safe from Solyony's bullet. Irene knew that. 'I knew it, I
knew it!' she was to say at the end of the last act after the news of
Tusenbach's death at Solyony's hand.

Act Four

While Chekhov was particularly anxious that the third act should be
played 'quietly', the action of the fourth act is full of mounting tension.
Indeed, unlike his usual practice, it is in the fourth act that Chekhov
lets the dramatic action reach the maximum of tension as well as the
maximum of audience participation. The tense atmosphere of the
fourth act, which takes place on a day in late autumn about a year after
the third act, becomes manifest with the rise of the curtain: the empty
champagne glasses, the farewell embraces, the two young army officers
in field dress. The mention of Solyony's delayed departure by one of
the officers should at once ensure audience participation, for by now
the audience know about Irene's consent to marry Tusenbach and
Solyony's threat to kill his successful rival. Moreover, the first words
Irene addresses to Fedotik and Rodé give an insight into the future
which neither they nor, for that matter, Chekhov could have possibly
foreseen, thus ensuring the first prerequisite of audience participation,
namely, that they know more of what the future holds for the characters than the characters themselves.

IRENE. Au revoir.
FEDOTIK. Not au revoir. It's goodbye. We shall never meet again.
KULYGIN. Who knows? (*Wipes his eyes, smiles.*) Look at me—crying.
IRENE. We shall meet one day.
FEDOTIK. In ten or fifteen years? . . .
RODÉ (*embracing* TUSENBACH). We shan't meet again.

Rodé must certainly have known of Tusenbach's impending duel
with Solyony and must also have guessed what its outcome would be.
But Fedotik could not have known what the audience know or should
know – that the First World War would break out in thirteen years and
that the likelihood of the two young officers surviving it was very
slight. Indeed, they might have been killed three years later in the
Russo–Japanese war.

But quite apart from this look into the not too distant future, the
audience's participation in the action is engaged at once after the

departure of the two officers. It is, indeed, directly involved in the duel between Tusenbach and Solyony. After a few bantering exchanges between Chebutykin and Kulygin apropos of Kulygin's shaved-off moustache, Irene tells Chebutykin in the presence of Tusenbach that she is worried about the quarrel between Tusenbach and Solyony on the boulevard the day before.

IRENE. Dear doctor, I'm terribly worried. You were out on the boulevard yesterday. Be a darling and tell me what happened there.
CHEBUTYKIN. What happened? Nothing at all. (*Reads his paper.*) Makes no difference.
KULYGIN. From what I gather Solyony and the Baron met yesterday on the boulevard near the theatre —
TUSENBACH. Do shut up! Really.... (*Waves his hand and goes into the house.*)

Tusenbach waved his hand to signify that nothing could be done to stop the duel. Why didn't he say so? Why run off into the house? Did he hope that if he, an officer and a gentleman, could do nothing to avoid fighting Solyony, Irene might stop the duel if she learnt of it betimes?

KULYGIN. ... near the theatre. Solyony began picking a quarrel with the Baron, who lost his temper and made some offensive remark.
CHEBUTYKIN. Don't know. It's all nonsense.

It is then that Kulygin tells his amusing story about a seminary student whose essay the teacher marked with the word 'nonsense', which the student, thinking that it was written in Roman and not in Russian characters, read as 'renyxa'.[1]

Chebutykin repeated the nonsense word 'renyxa' after Irene had told him that she and Tusenbach were planning to leave immediately after their wedding the next day to start their 'new life'—he at the brickworks and she at the school; she was longing to start work once more for after she had decided to accept Tusenbach, who was quite 'an extraordinarily good man', her soul 'grew a pair of wings' and she felt 'cheerful and lighthearted' again, but something had happened the day before and now 'some kind of awful uncertainty' seemed 'to hang' over her. The word 'renyxa' struck Chebutykin as the quintessence of

[1] The Russian word for nonsense 'chepukha' can be mistaken for a Latin word because all its letters are identical with the Roman alphabet.

nonsense, but it conveyed nothing to Irene, for the old doctor used it subjectively in the sense that nothing mattered to him any more or, to quote the expression he uses throughout the play, 'it makes no difference'. He repeated the phrase after he had given a full account of the quarrel on the boulevard a little later to Masha and Andrey and had told them that the duel would take place at half past twelve (half an hour after the beginning of the fourth act) in a copse on the other side of the river. 'Bang-bang!' he laughed as he pointed to the river at the end of the garden. But, he corrected himself, it was no laughing matter, for it was Solyony's third duel, implying that Solyony had already killed two men. When Masha said that the duel must be stopped, for, she added naïvely, the Baron might be wounded or even killed, Chebutykin replied that the Baron was an excellent fellow but 'one baron more or less—what difference does it make?' When Andrey interjected that to be present at a duel even as a doctor was 'simply immoral', Chebutykin replied that it only seemed so, for 'we don't exist, nothing exists in the world. Besides, what difference does it make?' While sitting in an easy chair waiting to be summoned to the duel, Chebutykin, Chekhov points out in the stage direction of the fourth act, is 'in a good humour which does not desert him throughout the whole of the act'. It is the good humour of a man who, in Chebutykin's own words, is 'not a human being' any more and so regards the calamity that he knows will soon befall his favourite, Irene, with complete indifference.

Chebutykin is not the only one to be in a good humour: curiously enough, Kulygin, too, does not allow anything to interfere with his 'contentment'. A firm believer in the *modus vivendi*, he shaved off his moustache when he became second master because his headmaster had shaved off his. 'No one likes it,' he tells Irene and Chebutykin, 'but I don't care. I am content. Whether with or without a moustache, I am content.' Tusenbach remarked to Irene in a later scene that Kulygin was the only man in the town who was 'content' that the military were leaving. Kulygin was not ashamed to admit it: 'The soldiers will be gone today and everything will go on as before', he tells Chebutykin and Irene. 'Whatever people may be saying, Masha is a good, honest woman. I love her very much and I am thankful.' He follows up this concealed avowal of his knowledge of his wife's affair with Vershinin by another characteristic story about an old schoolmate of his who could not master the intricacies of the *ut consecutivum*. 'He's terribly hard up now and in poor health. Every time I meet him I say to him "How are you, *ut consecutivum?*" "Yes, indeed," he replies, "that's just it: *consecutivum.*" and starts coughing. But I've been lucky all my life. I am happy. Why, I've even been awarded the order of Stanislav, second class, and am now teaching others the *ut consecutivum.* Of course, I'm an intelligent man, much more intelligent than most people, but', he admits a little ruefully, 'that's no guarantee of happiness.' It isn't, indeed, but Kulygin seems to be able to make the best of the unfortunate situation between Masha and Vershinin, and he certainly shaved off his moustache (or rather Chekhov made him shave it off) at the right time to make it possible for him to put on a false moustache and beard at the end of the play to relieve the tension of the scene that follows immediately after Masha's parting from Vershinin.

Kulygin is little impressed by Irene's hopes of a 'new life'. He has had sufficient experience of teaching to regard them as 'just fine ideas, nothing very serious', but that does not prevent him from expressing the rather doubtful hope that after Vershinin's departure 'everything will go on as before'. He was a little too simple-minded to see the irony of such a hope. Actually, the only thing that was quite certain to go on 'as before' was Natasha's playing 'The Maiden's Prayer' on the piano. 'Thank goodness', Irene exclaimed before going into the house with Kulygin to meet Olga, 'I shan't have to listen to "The Maiden's Prayer" tomorrow night nor have to meet Protopopov again!' She left behind Chebutykin sitting in his easy chair, reading his paper and humming ta-ra-ra-boom-di-ay, and Andrey wheeling the pram with his little son in the background. Masha had been fuming with rage as she kept walking round the garden, waiting for Vershinin to come to say goodbye to her (he had been detained at a luncheon given by the mayor in honour of the departing troops). The thought that her only great love, which, she felt, came to her 'piecemeal and in little bits', was to have such an abrupt and inevitable end filled her with a blind fury, which spilled over as she eyed contemptuously the contented figure of the doctor, her mother's old lover, reading a paper and humming a tune as if nothing in the world mattered.

MASHA. There he sits, enjoying himself.
CHEBUTYKIN. And why not?
MASHA (*sits down*). Oh, nothing. (*Pause.*) Did you love my mother?

CHEBUTYKIN. Very much.

MASHA. And did she love you?

CHEBUTYKIN (*after a pause*). That, I'm afraid, I can't remember.

MASHA. Is my man here? That's what our cook Marfa used to call her policeman: 'my man'. Is *my* man here?

CHEBUTYKIN. No, not yet.

MASHA. When you have to snatch your happiness piecemeal, in little bits, and then lose it as I've lost it, you gradually coarsen and go mad with fury. . . . (*Pointing at her breast.*) I feel it seething here inside me. (*Looking at* ANDREY *who is wheeling the pram.*) There's old Andrey, our dear brother. All our hopes have perished. Thousands of people were raising a bell, much money and labour was spent on it, and then suddenly it fell and got smashed. So did Andrey.

Andrey must have heard her mention his name, for he came up and, after a few remarks about the departure of the artillery brigade, asked Chebutykin what had happened on the boulevard near the theatre the day before. This time Chebutykin gave his full account of the quarrel engineered by Solyony on the eve of Tusenbach's marriage to Irene. Chebutykin's exposition of his 'philosophy of life', which was so different from Masha's own deeply-held conviction that life must have an aim, filled her with disgust and diverted her attention from the duel.

MASHA. People talk and talk all day long. (*Walking away.*) You live in a climate where it might start snowing any moment and here they just go on talking. (*Stopping.*) I won't go into the house. I can't go in there. [As she walks along the avenue of firs, she looks up at the sky. Catching sight of flocks of migrating birds, her longing to go away with Vershinin finds expression in the words she addresses to them.] The birds are already flying away. Swans or geese. . . . Oh, my dear ones, my lucky ones. . . . (*Goes out.*)

Left with Chebutykin, Andrey is overcome with panic at being left alone in the house with Natasha.

ANDREY. There will be no one left in the house. The army officers will be gone, you will go, my sisters will get married, and I'll be left alone.

CHEBUTYKIN. What about your wife?

ANDREY. A wife's a wife.[1] She is an honest, decent woman, well, yes!—
a kind woman, but for all that there's something in her that brings
her down to the level of a mean, blind animal, a sort of horrible:
rough-skinned animal. At any rate, she's not a human being. I'm
telling you this as a friend, as the only person to whom I can open up
my heart. I love Natasha, that's true, but sometimes she strikes me as
extraordinarily vulgar and then I feel lost. I don't understand why,
for that reason, I love her so much or, anyway, did love her.

Chebutykin who knows all about not being a human being, for once
gives Andrey a sound, though hardly practical, piece of advice.

CHEBUTYKIN (*getting up*). Well, my dear fellow, I'm going away
tomorrow, and we may never meet again, so here's my advice to
you: put on your hat, take your walking stick in your hand, and go
away—go away and go on walking without looking back. And the
further you go, the better.

At that moment Solyony walks across the back of the stage accompanied by two army officers, his seconds – all three in field dress: a slow
and macabre procession heralding the approaching murder of an innocent man. Seeing Chebutykin, Solyony turns towards him, while the
two officers walk slowly on.

SOLYONY. It's time, Doctor. Half past twelve already. (*Exchanges
greetings with* ANDREY.)
CHEBUTYKIN. One moment please. [Overcome with sudden disgust
at what amounts to the public execution of Solyony's rival.] Oh, I'm
sick of the lot of you! (*To* ANDREY.) I say, my dear fellow, if anyone should ask for me tell them I'll be back presently. (*Sighs.*) Dear,
oh dear!
SOLYONY [quoting the line from Krylov's fable but this time anticipating with unconcealed delight the death of Tusenbach]. He had

---

[1] Stanislavsky writes in his reminiscences: 'In the fourth act of *The Three Sisters*
Andrey gives his conception of a wife from the point of view of a person who has
gone to seed. It was a wonderful monologue of two pages. Suddenly we get a note
in which he tells us to delete the whole monologue and put in its place four short
words: "A wife's a wife" . . . This is very characteristic of Chekhov, whose work
is always compact and meaningful.' But is it not much more likely that Chekhov
had cut out Andrey's long monologue of two pages because he had given him
another long and much more important monologue in the next scene?

barely time to catch his breath / Before the bear was hugging him to death.' [Chebutykin, who has got up from his chair, joins Solyony and walks along with him.] What are you groaning about, old man?

CHEBUTYKIN [still in his contrite mood]. Well!

SOLYONY. Feeling all right?

CHEBUTYKIN (*angrily*). Fit as a fiddle!

SOLYONY [a little surprised at Chebutykin's taking it so hard and anxious to placate him for fear that he might at the last moment thwart his plan]. There's nothing to be upset about, old man. I shan't go too far. Just wing him like a woodcock. (*Takes out perfume bottle and sprinkles his hands.*) Emptied a whole bottle on my hands today and they still smell – smell like a corpse. (*Pause.*) Yes. . . . Remember Lermontov's lines? 'And he, the rebel, the raging tempest seeks / As though peace in tempests could be found. . . .'

CHEBUTYKIN [who is not fooled, sarcastically]. Yes. 'He had barely time to catch his breath / Before the bear was hugging him to death.' (*Goes out with* SOLYONY.)

Chebutykin found Solyony's obsession with Lermontov more than ridiculous. Solyony, he had told Masha with a laugh earlier, imagined that he was 'a second Lermontov. He even writes poetry.' Lermontov had become a cult among young army officers after the poet's early death in a duel. The members of this cult identified themselves with Pechorin, the hero of Lermontov's novel *A Hero of Our Time*, whom they regarded as a proud man who wished to cut a figure in society but, hurt by its indifference and spurned by the woman he loved, vowed to vent his spite on his rival.

The exit of Chebutykin and Solyony is followed by the retirement of Andrey and his constant shadow Ferapont to the back of the stage, far enough to be out of earshot and out of sight. The scene is now set for the last meeting between Irene and Tusenbach. The poignancy of this farewell scene depends to a large extent on the fullest audience participation. The audience now possess all the prerequisites of such a participation: they know that Solyony is determined to kill Tusenbach and has arranged the duel to take place on the eve of Tusenbach's wedding to the girl who spurned his love. They know therefore that Irene and Tusenbach will never meet again. The poignancy of this scene is still further heightened for the audience by the knowledge that the relationship between Tusenbach and Irene is none too happy but that both of them are eager to make their marriage a success in spite of it.

TUSENBACH [doing his best to conceal the fact of the duel and trying to sound reassuring]. Darling I'll be back presently.

IRENE [who does not believe him]. Where are you going?

TUSENBACH [unable to make his white lies sound convincing]. I've something to see to in town and – er – afterwards I must go and see off my fellow officers.

IRENE. It's not true, Nicholas. Why are you so preoccupied today? (*Pause.*) [Both are addressing each other in the second person singular, which makes their relationship appear much closer than it is.] What happened outside the theatre yesterday?

TUSENBACH [making an impatient movement tantamount to confessing the truth]. I shall be back in an hour and I shall be with you again. (*Kisses her hand.*) My dearest darling. . . . (*Gazes into her eyes.*) It's five years since I fell in love with you, and I still can't get used to it. You seem more and more beautiful to me. What lovely, wonderful hair! What lovely eyes! I'm going to take you away tomorrow. We shall work. We shall be rich. My dreams will come true. You will be happy, darling. Only one thing, one thing only worries me: you don't love me!

IRENE. I can't help that. I shall be your wife, your true and faithful wife, but I don't love you. We can't do anything about that. (*Weeps.*) I've never been in love and, oh, how I dreamed of love, dreamed of it for years and years, night and day, but my heart is like an expensive grand piano that is locked and the key is lost. (*Pause.*) You look troubled.

TUSENBACH. I didn't sleep last night. There's nothing in my life I'm afraid of. It is only the lost key I'm worried about. Say something to me.

IRENE. What? What do you want me to say? What?

TUSENBACH. Just something.

IRENE. Don't fret, dear. Don't, please. (*Pause.*)

TUSENBACH [making up his mind at last not to torture her any longer by letting her see how inevitable it was that he should do what had to be done]. It is strange how sometimes little things, mere stupid trifles, suddenly, without rhyme or reason, become important in life.

M

You laugh at them, as one always does, you consider them of no importance, but you go on all the same, and you haven't got the strength to stop. Oh, don't let's talk about it! I feel fine! I feel as though I were seeing those firs, maples, and birch trees for the first time in my life, as though they were all looking curiously at me and . . . waiting. How beautiful these trees are and how beautiful life near them really ought to be. (*There is a shout* [from his second] '*Coo-ee! Hullo!*') I must go. It's time. This tree here is dead, but it goes on swaying in the wind with the others. So I, too, can't help feeling that if I should die, I'd go on taking part in life one way or another. Good bye, darling. (*Kisses her hands.*) The papers you gave me are on my desk under the calendar.

IRENE. I'm coming with you.

TUSENBACH (*uneasily*). No, no! (*Walks away quickly but stops in the avenue.*) Irene!

IRENE. What?

TUSENBACH (*not knowing what to say*)). I haven't had my coffee today. Please, tell them to have it ready for me. (*Goes off quickly.*)

Irene stands lost in thought [she knew, as she was to admit later, that the prospect of Tusenbach's return to her was black, but she was still not giving up hope], then she walks off to the back of the stage and sits down on a swing. Andrey enters with the pram, followed by Ferapont.

Andrey's long soliloquy, when at last it comes, certainly expresses Chekhov's own views, and is more in the nature of a comment: it is not Andrey addressing deaf Ferapont, but Chekhov addressing the audience on provincial society.

ANDREY. Oh, where's my past? Where has it gone to? Where is the time when I was young, gay, clever, when my dreams and thoughts were so exquisite, when the present and the future were so bright with hope? Why is it that before we even begin to live, we become dull, drab, uninteresting, lazy, indifferent, useless, unhappy? Our town's been in existence for two hundred years, it has a hundred thousand inhabitants, and yet not one of them is different from the rest. Not one saint – now or in the past – not one scholar, not one artist. Not one fairly outstanding personality who could arouse envy or a passionate desire to emulate him. They just eat, drink, sleep, then die. Others are born and they, too, eat, drink, sleep, or, to avoid lapsing into complete idiocy out of sheer boredom, try to introduce some variety into their lives by nasty gossip, drink, cards or malicious litigation. The wives deceive their husbands; the husbands tell lies, pretend not to see anything, not to hear anything; and their profoundly vulgar influence has so crushing an effect on their children that the divine spark in them is extinguished and they too become pitiful, lifeless creatures as like to one another as their fathers and mothers.

Andrey then turns to Ferapont and asks him crossly (as though he didn't know) what he wants. While signing the official papers, he listens to Ferapont's interminable tales of woe – this time about a rumour that there was a frost of two thousand degrees in Petersburg. This again gives Chekhov the opportunity of commenting that while the present was hateful, he could discern a glimmer of light in the future: 'I can see freedom, I can see my children becoming free from idleness, from kvass, from goose with cabbage stuffing, from after-dinner naps, from a life of low-down sponging.' Ferapont's further bloodchilling tale of two thousand people frozen to death in Moscow or Petersburg (he could not remember which), makes Andrey think of his sisters and, particularly, of Masha who, he suspects, will quite soon have to suffer a terrible blow.

ANDREY (overcome with tenderness). My dear sisters! My wonderful sisters! (Through tears.) Masha, my sister. . . .

It was the hectoring voice of Natasha who, looking out of the window, asked crossly who was talking 'so loudly', that brought him down to earth: 'Is it you, Andrey dear? You'll wake little Sophie. Il ne faut pas faire de bruit, la Sophie est dormée déjà. Vous êtes un ours. (Getting angry.) If you must talk, give the pram with the child to someone else. Ferapont, take the pram from the master.'

Ferapont takes the pram, while Andrey, abashed, remonstrates timidly and goes into the house to sign the papers Ferapont has brought, while Natasha goes on drooling over her child.

Chekhov arranges a short musical interlude before the even more poignant farewell scene between Masha and Vershinin. Vershinin, Olga and Anfissa come out of the house and, joined by Irene, listen in silence

to the street musicians playing a violin and a harp. At Olga's suggestion, Anfissa, the only happy and contented member of the Prozorov
family, gives some money to the musicians and then follows Irene who
has gone off in search of Masha. The dialogue between Olga and Vershinin is rather inconsequential, Vershinin asking Olga to keep an eye
on his wife and children, whom he has to leave behind for a month or
two, and Olga remarking that things never turned out as one wanted.
'I didn't want to be a headmistress and yet I'm one now. So,' she
finally dismisses their obsession with Moscow, 'we shan't be in
Moscow.' While admitting that he had been talking 'a lot', Vershinin
embarks on another attempt at 'philosophising' but gets rather repeti-
tive and muddled towards the end. At last Masha appears. The farewell
scene, charged with emotion, is very short.

VERSHININ. I've come to say goodbye.

OLGA *walks away a little so as not to interfere with their leave-taking.*

MASHA (*gazing at his face*). Goodbye.

A prolonged kiss.

OLGA. Enough, enough. . . .

MASHA *sobs bitterly.*

VERSHININ. Write to me. . . . Don't forget me! Let me go now – it's
time. Olga, take her please. I have to go. . . . I'm late as it is. (*Deeply
moved, he kisses* OLGA's *hands, then embraces* MASHA *again and goes
out quickly.*)

OLGA. There, there, Masha. Don't, darling, don't. . . .

Kulygin, looking embarrassed, as well he might, enters and, as usual,
says the wrong things: whatever may have happened, Masha is his wife,
he is happy, he is not complaining, he will never let her hear a single
word of reproach from him – and he calls Olga to witness that he
means what he says. Masha pays no attention to him. Brokenhearted,
she tries to suppress her sobs and repeats the two lines from Pushkin's
poem, but this time they have lost their magic, the words of the poem
convey nothing to her, she falters and cries despairingly: 'I'm going
mad!' Olga tries to calm her and asks Kulygin to give her some water.

MASHA. I'm not crying any more.

KULYGIN. She's not crying. . . . She's good. . . .

A dull report of a distant shot is heard.

No one on the stage reacts to the shot: Olga and Kulygin are too busy looking after Masha, who goes on trying desperately to remember the lines of the poem and getting more and more muddled. Even Irene, who enters presently, does not seem to have heard it. The audience alone has heard it and it is only the audience who realise that Tusenbach is dead. In this way Chekhov again ensures the fullest audience participation during the next two scenes until the entry of Chebutykin before the end of the play.

Meanwhile Olga goes on begging Masha to compose herself and suggests that they should go indoors.

MASHA (*angrily*). I am not going into that house. (*Sobs but stops immediately.*) I won't go into that house again – never again!

Her anger brings her some relief and for once Kulygin does something to amuse her by putting on the false moustache and beard he has confiscated from one of his schoolboys.

KULYGIN. . . . . I look like our German master, don't I? (*Laughs.*) Those boys are funny beggars.

MASHA. You do look like your German.

OLGA (*laughs*). Yes.

MASHA *cries*.

IRENE. Stop it, Masha.

KULYGIN. Yes. I certainly look like him.

It is the entry of Natasha rather than Irene's plea, that makes Masha dry her tears. Natasha is accompanied by her maid. In two short speeches Chekhov lays bare Natasha's truly devilish character. Protopopov and Andrey are to take charge of their respective children, the first nursing his little girl in the house and the second wheeling his little boy in the garden. 'Children are such a bother!' Then she turns to Irene to commiserate with her for having to leave what was her house and to suggest hypocritically that she should stay at least for another week. She had got used to her and wouldn't find it easy to part from her. She is going to install Andrey in Irene's room: 'Let him scrape

away with his fiddle there!' Little Sophie is to have Andrey's room:
'What a lovely child! Such a darling. Today she looked at me with such
big eyes and said "mama!"' She ignores Kulygin's compliment to her
'lovely child', and sums up the position in one short sentence: 'So I
shall be alone here tomorrow', following up her triumphant remark
with a hypocritical sigh. It is then that she turns to her future plans:
'First of all I shall have this avenue of firs cut down, then that maple –
it's so unsightly in the evenings.' Full mistress of the house and garden
at last, she is destroying beauty everywhere (a little earlier Tusenbach
was praising the beauty of the trees Natasha is now going to cut down),
and even the flowers, which Vershinin admired so much in the drawing-room in Act One, become an abomination in her mouth: 'I shall
have flowers, flowers, flowers everywhere and there'll be such a lovely
scent!' Her wonderful plans, however, are met with icy silence, and that
infuriates her. It is then that she notices the fork on the garden seat and
asks 'severely': 'Why is the fork left lying about on the seat?' But her
question is completely ignored, and as she walks off into the house,
she vents her spite on the maid: 'Why's the fork left lying about on the
seat, I ask you? (*Screams.*) Don't answer me back!' The only comment
comes from Kulygin: 'There she goes again!' Deep down Natasha feels
her inferiority to the three sisters, and her last scream of rage is her
acknowledgement of the fact that, though she had driven them out of
their house, they are still her superiors.

It is then that a military march is heard off stage: the brigade is leaving
the town. 'They are going away', Olga remarks as Chebutykin returns
from the duel looking uncomfortable. By now Masha has completely
recovered.

MASHA. Our friends are going away. Well, happy journey to them.
    (*To her husband.*) We'd better go home. Where's my cloak and hat?
KULYGIN. I left them in the house. I'll go and fetch them.
OLGA. Yes, we can go home now. It is time.

Curiously enough, in their preoccupation with Masha's grief, they
seem to have forgotten all about Tusenbach, but Chebutykin was there
to remind them.

CHEBUTYKIN. I say, Olga.
OLGA. What is it? (*Pause.*) What?

CHEBUTYKIN. Oh, nothing. I don't know how to tell you. (*Whispers in her ear.*)

OLGA (*aghast*). It can't be!

CHEBUTYKIN. Yes. . . . Too bad. . . . I'm awfully tired—exhausted. I'm not going to say another word. (*Vexed.*) Still, it makes no difference.

IRENE. What's happened?

OLGA (*embracing* IRENE). What a dreadful day! I don't know how to tell you, my dear.

IRENE. What's happened? Tell me quickly: what? (*Cries.*)

CHEBUTYKIN. The Baron has just been killed in a duel.

IRENE (*cries softly*). I knew it. I knew it.

Chebutykin sits down on a bench at the back of the stage and takes out his newspaper. The only advice he offers to Irene is to have a good cry. He then starts humming Tara-ra-boom-di-ay, stopping only to comment: 'What difference does it make?'

The three sisters have lost everything: love, husband, home, but it is on a note of hope and courage that they join in a chorus expressing their affirmation of life to the accompaniment of the rousing march of the military band of the departing artillery brigade:

MASHA. Oh, how gay the music sounds! They're going away from us – one has gone already, gone forever – and we shall be left alone to start our lives anew. We must live. . . . We must live.

IRENE (*lays her head on* OLGA'S *breast*). The time will come when there will be no more secrets, when all that is now hidden will be made plain, and when all will know what these sufferings are for. Till then we must live. We must work, only work! Tomorrow I shall go away alone; I shall teach in a school, and I shall give my life to those who may need it. . . . It is autumn now. It will be winter soon, and everything will be covered with snow. But I shall be working. . . . I shall be working. . . .

OLGA (*embraces her two sisters*). The music is so cheerful and gay, and I want to live. Dear God! The time will pass and we shall be gone forever. We shall be forgotten, and people will no longer remember our voices or our faces or how many of us there were. But our sufferings will pass into joy for those who live after us. . . . Peace and happiness will reign on earth, and we who live now will be remembered with gratitude and will be blessed. Oh, my dear, dear sisters, our lives are not finished yet. Let us live! The music is so gay, so joyful, and it almost seems that in a little while we shall know why we live and why we suffer. Oh, if only we knew . . . if only we knew!

The music is growing fainter and fainter; Kulygin, looking happy and smiling, comes in carrying Masha's hat and cape. Andrey is wheeling the pram, in which Bobikin is sitting.

CHEBUTYKIN (*sings softly*). Tara-ra-boom-di-ay . . . I'm sitting in a room-di-ay. . . . (*Reads his newspaper.*) It makes no difference! It makes no difference!

OLGA. If only we knew . . . if only we knew!

THE CHERRY ORCHARD

Introduction

Chekhov spent about ten months in writing *The Cherry Orchard*, his last great masterpiece, which he had been carefully turning over in his mind for three years. He had constantly to interrupt his writing because of ill-health. The following extracts from his letters show the great difficulties Chekhov experienced in writing the play, constantly battling against his worsening health and the harassing requests made by the two directors of the Moscow Art Theatre *and* his wife, Olga Knipper, to finish the play before the new season. But (which is more important) they also show the indomitable spirit with which he persisted in completing his 'gay and lighthearted' comedy, in which he condensed the social history not only of Russia, but also of the whole Western world: the landowning nobility, their serfs, the business tycoons, and the revolutionaries, without stripping them of their humanity or their individuality, and he did it all with the fun and panache of genius.

1 January 1903 (to Stanislavsky). I shall start writing the play in February.

3 January (to Olga Knipper). I really should like to write *The Cherry Orchard* in three long acts, but I could also make it into four acts.

27 January (to Vera Kommissarzhevskaya, a famous actress, who ran her own theatre. She asked Chekhov for the play, but Chekhov was very reluctant to let her have it because he had already promised it to the Moscow Art Theatre). The central role in this play is an old woman – to the great regret of the author.

5 February (to Stanislavsky). I was ill, but am recovered now, my health has improved, and if I do not work as I ought to, it is because of the cold (in my study it is only eleven degrees), lack of company and, probably, laziness, which was born in 1859, that is, one year before me. Nevertheless, I'm planning to sit down to the play after the 20th and finish on March 20th. I've already got it all worked out in my head. Its title is *The Cherry Orchard*, four acts, in the first act the blossoming cherry trees can be seen through the windows, the whole orchard a mass of white. And the ladies wear white dresses . . .

11 February (to Stanislavsky's wife, Maria Lilina). I'm starting writing the play after February 20th. . . .

22 February (to Olga Knipper). I still can't tell you anything about the play. I shall tell you soon. Your part is that of a perfect fool. Would you like to play a fool? A kind fool [Varya]. [In the final casting of the play Olga Knipper was given the part of Mrs Ranevsky, but it is obvious that Chekhov thought his wife too young to play the part of 'an old woman'.]

1 March (to Olga Knipper). I've already put out the paper for my play on my desk and written the title.

[Olga Knipper did not seem to realise how serious his illness was and scolded him for being 'lazy' and threatened to 'take him in hand'.]

4 March (to Olga Knipper). You have probably forgotten that since the days of Noah I have been telling all and sundry that I would set to work on the play at the end of February or the beginning of March. My laziness does not come into it at all. I am not my own enemy and if I had the strength I would write not one but twenty-five plays.

5 March (to Olga Knipper). In *The Cherry Orchard* you will be playing Varvara or Varya, an adopted daughter, aged twenty-two.

6 March (to Olga Knipper). If my play does not turn out as I have conceived it, you may hit me on the head with your fist. Stanislavsky has a comic part and so have you.

18 March (to Olga Knipper). I am afraid I'm having trouble with my play. One of the characters is not sufficiently thought out, but I hope that by Easter it will be quite clear to me and I shall have got rid of my difficulties.

21 March (to Olga Knipper). *The Cherry Orchard* will be written. I'm trying to have as few characters as possible. That will make it more intimate.

11 April (to Olga Knipper). I find it quite impossible to write a play here – no end of visitors. . . . Will you have an actress for the part of the elderly woman in *The Cherry Orchard*? If not, there won't be any play.

15 April (to Olga Knipper). I have no desire to write for your theatre, chiefly because you have no old woman. They will be making you play the part of the old woman, though there is another part for you, and besides, you have already been acting an old woman in *The Seagull*. [Chekhov's work was interrupted in April by his journey to Moscow and Petersburg and was resumed only after his return to Yalta in July.]

28 July (to Stanislavsky). My play is not ready. It is progressing rather slowly, which I explain by laziness, the wonderful weather and the difficulty of the plot. When the play is ready, or before that, I shall write to you or better still telegraph. Your role [Lopakhin[1]] has turned out quite well, but I am no judge for I understand very little about plays in general, when I read them. I'm not going to read my play to you because I'm a very bad reader.

22 August (to Nemirovich-Danchenko). . . . As for my own play, *The Cherry Orchard*, so far everything is all right. My work is progressing slowly. If I am a little late, it is no great matter. I have reduced the decor of the play to a minimum, there won't be any need for special scenery, and you won't have to concoct anything of your own. While my health is good, I don't wish for anything better, so long as I can get on with my work.

2 September (to Nemirovich-Danchenko). It is important that the author should be felt in a play. . . . My play will be finished soon. I found it difficult, very difficult, to write the second act, but it seems to have turned out all right. I shall call my play a comedy.

13 September (to Mikhail Chlenov, a neurologist). I've almost finished a play and was just about to start making a fair copy when a week ago I fell ill and now I can't do a thing. I find it difficult to dictate.

15 September (to Lilina). I've almost finished the play, but about eight or ten days ago I fell ill, started coughing, grew weak, in a word, it's last year's story all over again. Now, that is today, it is warm and my health seems to have improved, but still I can't write, for my head aches. . . . I shall send all the four acts as soon as I am able to sit down to work again for a whole day. . . . What I got was not a drama but a comedy and in places even a farce. For you I wrote not at all a pious but a very sweet young girl. [Chekhov wanted her to play Varya.]

20 September (to Olga Knipper). Today I'm feeling much better . . . I'm no longer eyeing my manuscript angrily, I'm writing now and, when I finish it, I'll send you a telegram at once. The last act will be very

[1] Stanislavsky played Gayev, to Chekhov's great disgust.

gay and the whole play is gay and lighthearted. Sanin [a producer of The Moscow Art Theatre] will not like it. He will say that I am no longer profound.

23 September (to Olga Knipper). Compared to the other acts, the fourth act will be rather meagre in content, but effective.

25 September (to Olga Knipper). I found it easy to write the fourth act and it seems to be well constructed. I did not finish it sooner because I was not too well. I can't help thinking that there's something new in my play however boring it may be. There is not a single shot in the whole of the play, incidentally [nor a love triangle, nor – a doctor!].

27 September (to Olga Knipper). I have already telegraphed you that the play is finished, all the four acts have been written. I am now making a fair copy. The characters are all alive, that is true, but what the play itself is like I don't know. I'll send it to you, you will read it and you will find out for yourself. . . . I have been writing on the paper Nemirovich gave me; with the gold nibs I also got from him. Whether this will make any difference I don't know.

29 September (to Olga Knipper). The play is now finished, but I am copying it out slowly because I have to correct and reconsider all sorts of things. One or two passages I will send on uncorrected, I am leaving it for later. . . . Oh, if only you'd play the governess in my play! It is the best part. I don't like the others.

2 October (to Olga Knipper). I am writing every day, though only a little, but still I am writing. I'll send you the play, you will read it and realise what could have been made of the subject in more favourable circumstances, that is to say, had I been well. But, as things are, it couldn't be worse: you write about two lines a day, try to absorb what you've written, etc., etc.

3 October (to Olga Knipper). Do not be angry with me about the play, my darling, I'm copying it out slowly, because I can't write quickly. Some passages I do not like, I rewrite them and then copy them out again. But soon, soon, darling, I shall finish and send it off. As soon as I have sent it off, I shall telegraph you. You see, I am not as stingy as you, a rich actress: I never received *your* telegram . . .

Darling, forgive me for the play! Forgive me! I promise you I have finished it and am now copying it out.

7 October (to Olga Knipper). The play has not been copied out yet. I have just about got up to the middle of the third act. I'm dragging it out, and because I am dragging it out I can't help feeling that my play is immensely long.

9 October (to Olga Knipper). I am copying out my play and shall soon finish it. I promise you every additional day is of benefit, for my play is getting better and better and already the characters are clear. The trouble is there are pieces which the censorship might cut and this would be terrible [as appears from another letter Chekhov was referring to Trofimov's dialogue].

10 October (to Stanislavsky). Don't be angry! I am copying out the play a second time and that is why I am so late. I shall send it in three days!

12 October (to Olga Knipper). And so, darling, long live your long-suffering and mine! The play is finished, finally finished, and to-morrow evening or on the morning of the fourteenth at the latest it will be sent off to Moscow. At the same time I shall send you some notes. If any corrections should be necessary then, it seems to me, they will be very small ones. The worst thing in the play is that I did not write it at one go, but took a long time over it, so that I am afraid a certain sluggishness may be felt. Anyway we shall see . . . Darling, I found it so difficult to write this play!

14 October (to Olga Knipper). Telegram: Play sent off. I am well. Kisses. Regards. *Antonio.*

[*21 October: Stanislavsky's telegram to Chekhov.* The reading of your play to the cast has taken place. Exceptional, brilliant success. Listeners enthralled from the first act. Every subtlety appraised. All wept after last act. . . . No play ever received such acclaim. *Alexeyev.*[1]]

23 October (to Olga Knipper). Nemirovich writes that there are too many tears and some coarseness. Write to tell me whether you think there is something not quite right and I'll correct it. It isn't too late and I could still rewrite a whole act.

7 November (to Nemirovich-Danchenko). For the last three years I have been planning to write *The Cherry Orchard* and for three years I have

---

[1] This is the origin of Stanislavsky's distortion of the play by treating it as a 'weepy', a distortion that spread to theatres throughout the world. Chekhov did not comment on Stanislavsky's telegram in his letter to him on 30 October, except to thank him for sending it. But he was absolutely flabbergasted that his 'gay and lighthearted' comedy should have produced such a flood of tears. As he had no high opinion of Alexeyev's judgement he only referred to the 'weeping' in his letters to Olga Knipper and Nemirovich on 23 October.

been telling you that you should get an actress for the part of Lyubov Andreyevna. Well, now lay out your patience, which is not working out however much you try.

23 November (to Olga Knipper). Stanislavsky wants to have a train going past in the second act. He has to be stopped. He also wants to have frogs and landrails.

23 November (to Stanislavsky). Haymaking usually takes place between 20th and 25th of June and I don't think you can hear the call of landrails at that time, and the frogs too have grown silent; it's only the oreole that is still singing. There is no cemetery [in the second act]. It was there a long time ago. One or two gravestones still lie about here and there. That is all that remains of the cemetery. If it is possible to show a train without a noise, without the slightest sound, then by all means have it. I am not against having one and the same setting for the third and fourth acts provided that it is possible to go in and out comfortably in the fourth act.

18 March 1904 (to Olga Knipper). Tell Nemirovich that the sound effect in the second and fourth acts[1] must be shorter, much shorter, and one must feel that it comes from a long distance away. What a trivial thing it is and yet they can't even get a trifling thing like that right although in the play the nature of the sound is made quite clear.

29 March (to Olga Knipper). Stanislavsky is acting abominably in the fourth act by dragging it out so terribly. This is dreadful! An act which should last at most twelve minutes lasts forty minutes.[2] One thing I can say: Stanislavsky has ruined my play. Oh well, I don't suppose anything can be done about it.

In his letters Chekhov also gave the following descriptions of the characters:

LYUBOV (LYUBA) RANEVSKAYA

14 October (to Olga Knipper). Not too smartly dressed but with great taste. Intelligent, very warm-hearted, inattentive; she is very loving towards everybody, always a smile on her face.

---

[1] Chekhov refers to the sound of a breaking string towards the end of Act II and at the very end of Act IV.

[2] Stanislavsky was quite deliberately piling on the non-existent agony, which most directors, who fancy themselves as 'creative' artists, have been doing ever since.

25 October (to Olga Knipper). No, I never wanted to make Lyubov lose her zest for life. The only thing that would make a woman like her lose it would be death. . . . It is not difficult to play the part of Lyubov provided you get the right tone from the very beginning; one has to find the right kind of smile and manner of laughing and one must know how to dress.

ANYA

14 October (to Olga Knipper). Anya is seventeen-eighteen, a slim girl, must be played by a very young actress. Above all, she is a child, gay to the very end, who does not know life and who does not cry even once except in the second act where it is only tears in her eyes.

23 October (to Nemirovich-Danchenko). I'm very much afraid that Anya might have a weepy tone or that she might not be played by a very young actress. Anya does not cry once in my play and she never talks in a weepy voice except that in the second act there are tears in her eyes, but her tone of voice is still gay and lively.

2 November (to Nemirovich-Danchenko). Anyone can play Anya, even a totally unknown actress, provided she is young and looks like a young girl and her voice is young and fresh.

VARYA

14 October (to Olga Knipper). Varya is a little rude and a little silly, but very good-natured. She is not at all like Sonia and Natasha. A figure in a black dress, nun-like, rather silly, tearful, etc., etc. Black dress, wide belt . . .

23 October (to Nemirovich-Danchenko). Why do you say in your telegram [the telegram has not been preserved] that there are many weeping characters in my play? Where are they? It is only Varya who weeps, but that is because Varya is a crybaby by nature and her tears must not arouse any feeling of gloom in the spectator. You will often find in my plays the expression 'through tears', but that merely indicates the mood of the characters and not tears. There is no graveyard in the second act.

30 October (to Stanislavsky). It must be borne in mind that Varya is in love with Lopakhin and that she is a serious-minded and religious young woman: she would not have fallen in love with some vulgar money-grubber.

N

LOPAKHIN

30 October (to Stanislavsky). It is true Lopakhin is a merchant, but he is a decent fellow in every respect, and he must behave with the utmost decorum like a cultured person and without any vulgarity or tricks.

2 November (to Nemirovich-Danchenko). A white waistcoat and brown shoes, walks about waving his arms and taking large steps; thinking during his walk and walking along a straight line; his hair is not short and that is why he tosses back his head; when thinking, he combs his beard from underneath with his fingers, that is to say, from his neck to his mouth.

10 November (to Stanislavsky). In Lopakhin's presence Dunya and Yepikhodov stand and do not sit down. Lopakhin behaves like a gentleman, addresses the servants in the second person singular, while they always address him in the second person plural. . . . Lopakhin's role is central in the play.

30 October (to Olga Knipper). Lopakhin must not be played as a loud-voiced and noisy man, nor must he be played as a typical merchant – he is a gentle person.

2 November (to Nemirovich-Danchenko). If Lopakhin is made colourless and is played by a colourless actor then his role and the play will be ruined.

CHARLOTTA

14 October (to Olga Knipper). Charlotta must be played by an actress who has a sense of humour. In the fourth act she performs a trick with Trofimov's galoshes.

2 November (to Nemirovich-Danchenko). Charlotta doesn't speak Russian with an accent; only occasionally does she mispronounce the ending of a word and makes mistakes in the masculine and feminine endings of adjectives.

9 November (to Olga Knipper). Tell the actress that she must be funny in the part of Charlotta. That is the most important thing.

2 November (to Olga Knipper). You must remember that Charlotta's part is a very important one.

TROFIMOV

19 October (to Olga Knipper). You must remember that Trofimov very often lives in exile [that is, exiled as a revolutionary by the authorities, to some remote town, where he is kept under police surveillance], that he is frequently expelled from university; how is one to depict all these things?

PISHCHIK

2 November (to Nemirovich-Danchenko). Pishchik is a typical Russian landowner, suffering from chronic gout, old age and good living, portly, wearing the traditional Russian long-waisted coat, top boots without heels.

GAYEV

Not realising the tragic figure Stanislavsky would make of Lyubov's ghastly flaneur of a brother, Chekhov did not think it necessary to give any description of so well known a type of person. He did, however, ask the actor whom he suggested for the part to try to listen to billiard players and note down the different terms they were using. 'I never played billiards,' he wrote to Olga Knipper on 14 October 1903, 'or if I ever did play it, it was a very long time ago and I have forgotten everything. I just put down any terms I happened to think of.'

THE STATION MASTER

2 November (to Nemirovich-Danchenko). The Station Master who recites *The Fallen Woman* should be an actor with a bass voice.

Chekhov, finally, provided the following description of the country house in the play:

14 October (to Olga Knipper). The country house is a very old mansion. At one time the people living in it were very rich and that must be felt in the interior. Rich and comfortable.

5 November (to Stanislavsky). The country house in the play is a large two-storied building. In the third act a staircase is mentioned going up to the second floor. It is a solidly constructed timber or brick building, it makes no difference which. It is a very large and very old house. Holiday-makers do not rent such a house. As a rule, such houses are pulled down and the material is used for the building of country cottages. . . . People buying such a house, usually think that it is much cheaper and easier to build a smaller house than to convert the old house. The furniture is antique and very solid. The impoverishment and indebtedness of the owners is not evident from the furniture.

The action of *The Cherry Orchard* covers just over four months, from the beginning of May to the beginning of September.

As for the ages of the chief characters, Lyubov would be in her early forties, her daughter Anya is seventeen, her adopted daughter Varya is twenty-four (two years older than Chekhov first gave her age in his letters), her brother Gayev is fifty-one (he gives his age in the first act). Lopakhin would be in his mid-thirties, Trofimov about twenty-eight, Charlotta would be in her late thirties, Pishchik in his late sixties, Firs is eighty-seven, Dunyasha and Yasha in their late teens.

Act One

The first act of *The Cherry Orchard* takes place in the former nursery of the country house shortly before the arrival of its owner, Lyubov Ranevsky, from Paris with her teenage daughter Anya and her daughter's governess Charlotta. It is a cold early May morning. Through the closed windows of the nursery one can glimpse the vast cherry orchard in front of the house. Lyubov has been away for five years. She had left for Paris six years after the death of her husband and five months after the death of her seven-year-old son Grisha. Like Arkadina in *The Seagull*, Lyubov is a noblewoman who married a commoner. 'I've always been throwing money about like a madwoman,' she says of herself in the second act, 'and I married a man who did nothing but pile up debts. My husband died of champagne – he drank like a fish – and to my misfortune I fell in love with another man and became his mistress. It was at that very time – my first punishment, a straight blow to the heart – that my boy was drowned in the river here. I went abroad, never to return, never to see that river again, I was beside myself with grief. I shut my eyes and ran. My lover followed me— pitilessly, brutally. I bought a villa near Menton because he fell ill. For the next three years I knew no rest, nursing him day and night. I was worn out. Everything inside me was dead. Then, last year, I had to sell the villa to pay my debts. I left for Paris, where he robbed me, deserted me and went to live with another woman. I tried to poison myself. It was all so stupid, so shameful. It was then that I suddenly felt a longing to go back to Russia, to my homeland, to my daughter. . . .' It was her daughter who had gone with her governess to fetch Lyubov home. By that time she had spent all the money she could raise on her estate, which was to be sold at a public auction on 22 August, two and a half months after her arrival back home.

Anya gives this brief, but very illuminating, account of her mother's life in Paris. She and Charlotta had left for Paris in February. When she arrived there it was cold and snowing. She found her mother living on the fourth floor. 'When I got there,' Anya tells Lyubov's adopted daughter Varya in the first act, "Mother had some French visitors, a few ladies and a Catholic priest with a book. The place was full of tobacco smoke and terribly uncomfortable. She had already sold her villa at Menton. She had nothing left. I hadn't any money, either. There was hardly enough for the journey. Mother just won't understand!' She 'won't understand' because, as Trofimov tried to explain to Anya at the end of the second act, 'your mother, you yourself and your uncle no longer realise that you have been living at other people's expense, at the expense of those you won't admit further than your entrance hall . . .'

The only man who did understand was the son of their former serf, a rich, self-made man, 'a decent fellow in every respect', as Chekhov described him, who had a sentimental admiration for the mistress of the cherry orchard. 'She's such a nice person', he tells the maid Dunyasha at the opening of the play. 'So simple and easygoing.' He could never forget how kind she had been to him when, as a boy of fifteen, his drunken father, the village shopkeeper, had punched him in the face and made his nose bleed. 'We'd gone into the yard to fetch something and your mistress – I remember it as if it happened yesterday – she was such a young girl then and so slim – took me to the washstand in this very room, the nursery. "Don't cry, little peasant," she said, "you'll be all right by the time you wed."' The memory of the kindness shown to him by the young mistress of the estate lingered all through the years and now, he felt, the time had come for him to repay it. He had a plan which would not only save her estate from being sold, but would make her a rich woman. It seemed so simple and so reasonable to him that he had no doubt that she would not hesitate to accept it. That was why he had come specially to the old house so as to be in time to meet the train, help her with the luggage, see whether she had greatly changed, and, above all, tell her that she need not worry any more. The thought that he would save her made him so excited that he could not forgive himself for having fallen asleep and missed the train. It is this excitement with which he is looking forward to being able 'to say something nice and cheerful' to her and to assure her that 'there was no need for her to worry about the sale of the estate', that must be conveyed immediately to the audience in order to assure their fullest participation in the development of the action of the play. It must be conveyed the moment Lopakhin comes into the nursery with the maid Dunyasha; it must be conveyed in his account of how Lyubov had been kind to him in this very nursery when he was only a boy of fifteen; it must even be conveyed in the few words he exchanges with 'twenty-two calamities' Yepikhodov, the 'highbrow' book-keeper on the estate. It was Yepikhodov that Chekhov had chiefly in mind when he described his play as 'almost a farce'. Yepikhodov, unlike Medvedenko in *The Seagull* whom he resembles, is a typical figure from a farce. What Medvedenko says about the highbrow books he has read makes sense, but when Yepikhodov, who claims to be 'a man of some education', starts talking about 'the remarkable books' he has read, it is impossible to make sense of anything he says. 'It sounds all right,' Dunyasha tells Lopkahin, 'only you can't make head or tail of it.' Lopakhin's tremendous excitement must, above all, be conveyed in the short scene between Anya and Varya in which they are lamenting the impending, and seemingly inevitable, sale of the estate with its cherry orchard.

ANYA. Well, what's been happening? Have you paid the interest on the mortgage?

VARYA. Heavens, no.

ANYA. Oh dear, oh dear . . .

VARYA. The estate will be up for sale in August.

ANYA. Oh dear! . . .

LOPAKHIN (*pokes his head through the door and bleats*). Bah-h-h!

Overhearing the two girls talking, he could not contain his excitement any longer: it was he, he alone, who knew how the estate could be saved! This gesture of utter contempt for the inexperience of the two silly girls must be made absolutely clear to the audience. Moreover, the spectators have by now been able to form a sufficient picture of both Lopakhin and – from her brief appearance on the stage and Anya's account of her life in France – of Lyubov also, to make them realise that their attitudes towards the essential things that make life tolerable were so irreconcilable that, however reasonable Lopakhin's plan might be, it was bound to be rejected. A successful and prosperous business-man, like Lopakhin, must therefore in the end be proved to be even sillier than the two young girls—a truly comic situation!

The audience should have no difficulty in anticipating this clash between two irreconcilable attitudes to life at the very beginning of the play and in this way take an active part in its action. This clash, in fact,

takes place immediately after the commotion of the homecoming has
died down and they have all sat down to cups of coffee dispensed by the
ancient, deaf and muttering butler Firs. Lopakhin found it no longer
possible to keep the glad tidings to himself. He had to leave for
Kharkov at five o'clock, but first he had to have a good talk with
Lyubov who, he could not help declaring, was 'as magnificent as
ever'.

PISHCHIK (*breathing heavily*). Lovelier, I'd say. Dressed in the latest
    Paris fashion. Now, if I'd been twenty years younger—ho-ho-ho!
LOPAKHIN [disregarding the old lecher's youthful memories]. This
    brother of yours says that I'm an ignorant oaf, a tightfisted peasant
    but . . . let him talk. All I want is that you should believe in me as you
    used to, that you should look at me with those wonderful eyes of
    yours. Merciful heavens! My father was a serf of your father and
    your grandfather, but you, you alone, did so much for me in the past
    that I forgot everything, and love you as if you were my own flesh
    and blood.

But the effect of this careful approach to revealing his plan to save the
estate was completely lost in the ecstatic cries Lyubov uttered as she
jumped up and began pacing the room 'in great agitation', admiring
everything in it: an ominous sign, if Lopakhin could only have
realised it, for the success of his plan, which would have involved the
pulling down of the house and the destruction of everything dear to
her in it. Gayev somewhat dampened her excitement by his news of the
death of two old retainers and the defection of 'boss-eyed Peter' for
a more lucrative post. Taking a box of fruitdrops from his pocket, he
puts one into his mouth, for sucking fruitdrops and popping imaginary
billiard balls into pockets were his instant reactions to any distressful
occurrence in his life. But when Pishchik began delivering his usual
regards from his darling daughter Dáshenka, Lopakhin, who was getting
more and more impatient, made up his mind to put an end to all these
sentimental exchanges and make them face the bitter facts which were
staring them in the face, but which they so determinedly ignored.

LOPAKHIN. I'd like to say something very nice and cheerful to you.
    (*Glancing at his watch.*) I shall have to be going in a moment and
    there isn't much time to talk. Well, I'll be brief. As you know, your

cherry orchard is being sold to pay your debts. The auction has been fixed for the twenty-second of August. But there is no need to worry, my dear. You can sleep soundly. There's a way out. Here's my plan. Listen carefully. Your estate is only about twelve miles from town, and the railway is not very far away. Now, all you have to do is to divide up your cherry orchard and the land along the river into building plots and lease them out for country cottages. You'll then have an income of at least twenty-five thousand a year.

The hostile reaction to Lopakhin's plan was immediate:

GAYEV. I'm sorry, but what utter nonsense!
LYUBOV. I don't quite understand you, Lopakhin.

But Lopakhin was not to be discouraged: there was really nothing to understand. The advantages of his plan were so obvious that all that was left for him to do was to congratulate her: she was saved. It was true the place would have to be 'tidied up' a little first: the old buildings would have to be pulled down, including the old country house, and —'the old cherry orchard will have to be cut down'.

Lopakhin should not have mentioned the cherry orchard for it gave Lyubov and Gayev an excellent opportunity to evade the issue altogether. Except for its sentimental value, there was nothing remarkable about their country house: there were thousands of similar country houses throughout Russia. But the cherry orchard was unique, although, as even Firs was not slow in pointing out, while quite useful and profitable fifty years before, it was quite useless and unprofitable now.

LYUBOV. Cut down [the cherry orchard]? I'm very sorry but I don't think you know what you are talking about. If there is anything of interest, anything quite remarkable, in fact, in the whole of our province, it is our cherry orchard.
LOPAKHIN. The only remarkable thing about the orchard is that it is very large. It only produces a crop of cherries every other year and even then you don't know what to do with them. Nobody wants to buy them.
GAYEV. Why, you'll find our cherry orchard mentioned in the encyclopaedia.

It was not an argument to impress a businessman like Lopakhin, who quite rightly argued that if they could not make up their minds about the cherry orchard their whole estate would be sold at the auction. But his insistence that there was no other solution was completely ignored by Lyubov. Her interest was only aroused by Firs's mention of some miraculous but, alas, forgotten, recipe which had made the cherries such a valuable merchandise forty or fifty years earlier and by Pishchik's inquiry as to whether she had eaten frogs in Paris. Lopakhin's attempt to paint a rather rosy picture of the 'happy, prosperous and thriving' place the cherry orchard would become after the invasion of the holiday-makers was not likely to arouse any enthusiasm from its owners, either. It merely produced Gayev's indignant exclamation: 'What nonsense!'

Lyubov tore up unread the two telegrams from her lover in Paris which Varya had produced from the old bookcase. 'I have finished with Paris', was her curt though unconvincing remark. Gayev made no comment on her dramatic gesture, his whole attention being taken up by the bookcase which Lyubov had kissed earlier in her transport of joy at being back home. Gayev had discovered earlier that the bookcase was over a hundred years old, and this prompted him to address an emotional invocation to this 'inanimate object, but still a bookcase', in which he 'saluted' it for having devoted itself for over a hundred years 'to the glorious ideals of goodness and justice' and for having 'sustained for several generations of our family the courage and faith in a better future' and for having 'fostered in us the ideals of goodness and social consciousness.'

Lopakhin's ironic 'Aye!' seemed a fair comment on Gayev's 'liberal' effusion as, indeed, was Lyubov's comment: 'You haven't changed a bit, have you, Leonid darling?' Gayev, as usual, tried to conceal his uneasiness by popping an imaginary billiard ball into an equally imaginary pocket, but it was hardly noticed in the laughter that followed the two even more farcical scenes: Pishchik swallowing all Lyubov's pills and Charlotta snatching away her hand from Lopakhin, who was going to kiss it, and his comment: 'It's not my lucky day!' They all begged Charlotta to show them 'a trick', but she refused and went off to bed. Before going off, too, Lopakhin asked Lyubov again to let him know as soon as she had made up her mind about the country cottages. 'If you decide to go ahead,' he told her, 'I'll get you a loan of fifty thousand. Think it over seriously!'

VARYA (*angrily*). For goodness' sake, go!

LOPAKHIN. I'm going. I'm going. (*Goes out.*)

GAYEV. The oaf!

Gayev knew how to express all the contempt and hatred felt by a down-at-the-heel nobleman for the prosperous son of a former serf in one short monosyllable; but he apologised to Varya for insulting her 'intended', though making that word sound no less scornful than 'oaf'. But Varya knew her 'dear uncle' too well to be put out by anything he said.

VARYA. Don't say things you'll be sorry for, Uncle.

LYUBOV [coming to her brother's rescue]. But why not, Varya? I should be only too glad. He's a good man.

Pishchik, who had been digesting Lyubov's pills in silence, backed up her view of Lopakhin as 'a most honourable man', dropped off and snored, then woke up with a start: he suddenly remembered the real reason for his visit: 'By the way, my dear lady,' he addressed Lyubov, 'you will lend me two hundred and forty roubles, won't you. Must pay the interest on my mortgage tomorrow.'

VARYA (*terrified*) [she knew how easy it was to get money out of her 'mother', whose habit of throwing money about regardless had landed them in their present difficulties]. We have no money! We haven't!

But although Lyubov assured him that they really had no money, Pishchik was quite certain that if she had 'a good look round', she would find it. A habitual scrounger, he never lost hope. 'Sometimes I think I'm done for, then – lo and behold – they build a railway over my land and pay me for it. Something's bound to turn up, if not today then tomorrow. . . . Dáshenka [his daughter] might win two hundred thousand. She's got a lottery ticket, you know. . . .'. But he had to wait for his loan.

All through the act the dialogue assumes a desultory character, for everybody is tired from the journey and their attention continually wanders from one subject to another. At that moment Varya and Gayev opened the windows and called Lyubov to admire the 'lovely trees' and the long avenue that ran on and on 'as straight as an arrow'.

LYUBOV (*looking through the window at the orchard*). Oh, my child-hood, oh, my innocence! I slept in this nursery. I used to look at our orchard from here. Every morning happiness used to wake with me. The orchard is just the same, nothing has changed. (*Laughs happily.*) White, all white! Oh, my orchard! After the dark, rainswept autumn and the cold winter, you're young again, full of happiness. The heavenly angels haven't forsaken you. If only this heavy load could be lifted from my heart! If only I could forget my past!

She was, of course, referring to her unhappy entanglement with the man who had left her for another woman in Paris, but whom she still loved; but all that Gayev, who resented his sister's 'immoral' affair, could think of was the – to him – even more extraordinary fact that their creditors might actually sell their orchard to pay their debts.

GAYEV. Well, and now they're going to sell the orchard to pay our debts. Funny, isn't it?

Lyubov, who was suppressing her secret dread of the inevitable calamity of the sale of her estate and the cherry orchard, had immersed herself so deeply into her past, where there was no cloud on the horizon threatening her happiness, that she imagined she could see her mother walking in the orchard.

LYUBOV. Look! Mother's walking in the orchard. (*Laughs happily.*) It *is* Mother!
GAYEV. Where?
VARYA. Really, Mother dear, what are you saying?
LYUBOV. There's no one there. I just imagined it. Over there, on the right, near the turning to the summer-house, a little white tree is leaning over. It looks like a woman.

It was while she was still immersed in admiration of her wonderful orchard and the masses of white blossom and the blue sky that Trofi-mov, the former tutor of her little son Grisha, made his appearance, shattering her momentary peace of mind by bringing back to her the greatest tragedy of her life—the death of her boy. At first she did not recognise him: the vicissitudes of his life as a revolutionary had changed him so much. When she did, she was violently brought back to earth and embraced Trofimov 'weeping quietly'.

LYUBOV. My little boy died, drowned. Why, why my friend? (*More quietly.*) Anya's asleep and here I'm shouting, making a noise. Well, Peter? You're not as good-looking as you were, are you? Why not? Why have you aged so much?

She was certainly not a person with whom Trofimov could discuss his revolutionary activities: he made a somewhat sour joke: 'A peasant in a railway carriage called me "a moth-eaten gentleman".' Lyubov, who remembered him as 'a charming young student', wondered whether he was still a student.

TROFIMOV. I expect I shall be an eternal student.

Another hint at his 'extra-mural' activities, for 'eternal' students were the revolutionary students who were prevented from taking their examinations because of the special attention the police paid to them, but Lyubov was not interested in politics.

LYUBOV (*kisses her brother and then* VARYA). Well, to bed now. You, Leonid, have aged, too.

The indomitable Pishchik, who had been keeping quiet all the time, thought the moment opportune for repeating his request for two hundred and forty roubles 'early tomorrow morning'.

GAYEV. He does keep on, doesn't he?
PISHCHIK. Two hundred and forty roubles – to pay the interest on my mortgage.
LYUBOV. But I have no money, my dear.
PISHCHIK. I'll pay you back, dear lady. Such a trifling sum.
LYUBOV. Oh, all right. Leonid will let you have it. Let him have it, Leonid.
GAYEV. Let him have it? Like hell I will.
LYUBOV. What else can we do? Let him have it. He needs it. He'll pay us back.

'My sister', Gayev remarked gloomily to Varya, after Lyubov, followed by Firs, Trofimov and Pishchik, had gone out, 'hasn't got out of her habit of throwing money about.'

Annoyed, he told Lyubov's valet Yasha to get out of his way, adding: 'You reek of the henhouse.' But Yasha, a typical lackey who knew how to exploit his mistress's weaknesses, was not afraid to show his contempt for her weakling of a brother by disregarding his insults.

YASHA (*grins*). And you, sir, are the same as ever.
GAYEV. I beg your pardon? (*To* VARYA.) What did he say?

But Varya ignored Gayev's attempt to overlook Yasha's impudent remark by pretending not to have heard it and went on to talk to Yasha in a language he understood by calling him 'a shameless bounder' and ordering him to go and see his mother who 'has been sitting in the servants' quarters since yesterday'.

Having got rid of Yasha, Varya mournfully echoed Gayev's earlier remark about her 'mother' not having changed by declaring that 'if you let her, she'd give away everything'. This led Gayev to the even more melancholy reflection that 'when a lot of remedies are suggested for an illness it means that the illness is incurable.' He then went on to enumerate the 'remedies' for saving the estate and the cherry orchard: 'It would be marvellous if someone left us a lot of money, it would be marvellous if we found a rich husband for Anya, it would be marvellous if one of us went to try our luck with our great aunt, the Countess, who is very rich.'

VARYA (*crying*). If only God would help us.

After telling Varya not to 'howl', Gayev goes on with his enumeration of the reasons why the very rich great-aunt is not likely to give them any money: first, because his sister did not marry a nobleman, secondly, because his sister had not been leading 'an exactly blameless life'. Without noticing Anya who at that moment appeared in the doorway, he went on: 'She's a good, kind, lovable person and I'm very fond of her, but whatever extenuating circumstances you may think of, you must admit that she is immoral. You can sense it in her slightest movement.'

VARYA (*in a whisper*). Anya's in the room.
GAYEV [taken aback]. Beg your pardon. [Realising that he has made a *faux pas*, he makes the farcical excuse that he didn't notice Anya because there was something in his eye and he couldn't see her.]

Funny thing, something's got into my right eye. . . . Can't see properly.

He tried to propitiate Anya by lavishing endearments on her, but that only brought the two girls down on him for talking too much.

VARYA. . . . You oughtn't to talk so much. Just don't talk, that's all.
ANYA. If you stopped talking, you'd feel much happier yourself.
GAYEV. Not another word. (*Kisses* ANYA'*s and* VARYA'*s hands.*) Not another word.

Having given his solemn promise, he at once broke it by embarking on another of his remedies for saving the cherry orchard. He had been at the county court, met a lot of people, started talking about 'this and that' and it seemed that 'we might manage to raise some money on a promissory note and pay the interest to the bank.' He would be there again 'on Tuesday' and have another talk. Then their mother would have another talk with Lopakhin and Anya would go to Yaroslavl to have a talk with the Countess. He was sure that by 'tackling the problem from three different directions, we'll get it settled.' And popping a fruit drop into his mouth, he swore 'by anything you like' that the estate would not be sold.

GAYEV. . . . (*Excitedly.*) Why, I'll stake my life on it! Here's my hand. Call me a rotten scoundrel if I permit the auction to take place. I stake my life on it!

His staking his life 'on it' twice seemed to have quite reassured Anya, who embraced her uncle and declared that she was no longer worried and was happy. Gayev was by now so bucked himself by the brilliant prospects of saving the estate that he told Firs, who came in to help his master go to bed, that this time he would undress himself. This generous gesture to his former slave made him expatiate again on his 'liberal' convictions. 'I am a man of the eighties', he declared, the eighties being well known for the brief efflorescence of liberalism in Russia. 'People don't think much of that time, but let me tell you I've suffered a great deal for my convictions during my life. It's not for nothing that the peasants love me. You have to know the peasants, you have to know how to —
His nieces, who did not seem to think much of his knowing the

peasants, told him to shut up, while Firs reminded him 'angrily' that he was waiting to take him to bed.

GAYEV. Coming! Coming! You, too, go to bed. Off two cushions into the middle. Pot the white! (*Goes out,* FIRS *shuffling off after him.*)

Anya, who, as Chekhov described her, 'does not know life,' was no longer worried and felt that she ought to be grateful to her uncle for putting her mind at rest, while Varya began telling her a long story of her battles with the old servants, who had spread the story that she was feeding them on dried peas. Anya fell asleep before she could finish it.

VARYA. . . . (*Looks at* ANYA.) Darling! (*Pause.*) Asleep. . . . (*Takes* ANYA *by the arm.*) Come to bed, dear. Come along. . . . (*Leads her by the arm.*) My darling has fallen asleep. Come along. (*They go towards the door.*)

A shepherd's pipe can be heard playing from afar on the other side of the orchard. TROFIMOV *walks across the stage and, catching sight of* VARYA *and* ANYA, *stops.*

VARYA. Sh-sh! She's asleep. Come along, my sweet.

ANYA (*softly, half asleep*). I'm so tired. . . . I keep hearing harness bells. . . . Uncle . . . dear . . . Mother and Uncle. . . .

VARYA. Come, my sweet, come. . . .

They go into ANYA's *room.*

TROFIMOV (*deeply moved*). My sunshine! My spring!

A wonderful curtain, which loses most of its splendour in translation.

Act Two

The second act forms a quiet interlude before the storm finally breaks over the heads of the owners of the cherry orchard and the Gayev estate. Its approach is sensed by Lyubov who is haunted by the fear that something awful is going to happen, just as though, she tells Lopakhin at the beginning of the act, 'our house was going to collapse on top of us'. Lyubov's growing apprehension of the coming catastrophe is further aroused at the end of the act by the mysterious sound, resembling the snapping of a violin string, which seems to be coming out of the sky (one of Chekhov's early memories of a mining disaster when he was spending his summer holidays on a farm in the Ukraine not far from the mining district and heard the sound of a bucket falling down a mineshaft). There is, besides, Lopakhin's hint, completely lost on Lyubov and Gayev, that he might himself be forced to join the bidding at the public sale of the estate on 22 August, because another rich businessman was so interested in its purchase that he planned to be present at the auction. But these ominous forebodings and anticipations do not disturb the peace of the warm evening in June (or July— Chekhov, as usual, is vague about the exact date) at the start of the second act.

In the afternoon of that day Lyubov and Gayev had had lunch at one of the best restaurants in town. 'That disgusting restaurant of yours', as Lyubov describes it, 'with its stupid band and its tablecloths smelling of soap', quite unlike, in fact, the Paris restaurants where she used to order the most expensive dishes and dispense generous tips to the waiters. To Lyubov's disgust, Gayev ate a lot, drank a lot and talked a lot, this time haranguing the waiters on the rosy prospects of liberalism in Russia in the seventies (a short time after the liberation of the serfs) and, of all things, on the 'decadents' of the nineties. At home Lyubov was still receiving telegrams from her lover in Paris, asking her to forgive him and imploring her to return.

The only change that has taken place during the intervening weeks among the servants is that Dunyasha, who had been so excited by Yepikhodov's proposal of marriage, has fallen in love with Yasha.

As the curtain rises on the second act, Charlotta, Dunyasha and Yasha are discovered sitting on the old bench of the abandoned grave-yard at the back of the cherry orchard, while Yepikhodov is standing beside it strumming on his guitar. Besides the bench, the graveyard has an old well, a few broken and scattered gravestones and a tumbledown chapel. In the distance a row of poplars, hiding the cherry orchard, stand out dark against the setting sun and, on the other side of the road, leading to the Gayev estate, a row of telegraph poles, and far away on the horizon the silhouette of a large town 'which can be seen on a clear day'.

Charlotta, modelled by Chekhov on an English governess he had met at the country house of some friends and taken a liking to, finding her 'a very jolly girl', is the first to speak. While mending the strap of her shotgun, she gives a brief sketch of her life. Yepikhodov is singing appropriately a melancholy love song, accompanying himself on his guitar. Dunyasha is looking at herself in her hand mirror and powder-ing her face, stopping only to point out to Yepikhodov that it is not a mandoline he is playing but a guitar. But all Yepikhodov has to say in reply is that 'to a madman who is in love, it is a mandoline'. When she further remarks enviously on the 'happiness' Yasha must have experienced during his travels abroad, Yepikhodov, the farcical counterpart of the 'grave and solemn' intellectuals who 'just chatter about science and know nothing about art' whom Chekhov was to satirise later in one of Trofimov's speeches, declares that it goes without saying since 'everything abroad has long been of the fullest complexity'.

YASHA [impressed by Yepikhodov's 'learned' word]. Naturally.
YEPIKHODOV. I'm an intellectual. I read all sorts of remarkable books, but I just can't understand my orientation, I mean what I really want to do, whether to go on living or whether, strictly speaking, I ought to blow my brains out. Nevertheless, I always carry a revolver about me. Here it is. (*Shows his revolver.*)
CHARLOTTA [who has finished mending the strap on her shotgun]. Thank goodness that's done. Now I can go. (*Puts shotgun over her shoulder.*) You, Yepikhodov, are a very clever and fearsome fellow. Women must fall madly in love with you. Brrr! (*Walking away.*) These clever fellows are so stupid. I've no one to talk to. Always

alone, alone. I've no one and goodness only knows who I am and what I am for. . . .' (*Walks off slowly.*)

YEPIKHODOV [continuing without paying any attention to Charlotta]. Strictly speaking and without touching upon any other subject I must, incidentally, say that as regards myself Fate has been treating me without any mercy, like a storm treats a small boat. If, assuming I am mistaken, then why, by way of illustration, should I wake up this morning and behold a spider of enormous size on my chest. (*Shows spider's size with both hands.*) And, another thing, I pick up a jug of kvass to have a drink and there's something outrageously indecent, like a cockroach, inside it. (*Pause.*) Have you read Buckle's *History of Civilisation?* (*Pause.*) I desire to have a talk with you, Dunyasha. Just a word or two.

Dunyasha makes no attempt to conceal the fact that she is no longer interested in Yepikhodov, who goes off threatening to shoot himself. Dunyasha, too, threatens that she wouldn't be responsible for what happened to her 'nerves' if Yasha deceived her, and this farcical tri-angular situation (the only one in the whole of the play) resolves itself with the appearance of their masters and Lopakhin, though not before Yasha has snatched a kiss from her and lit a cigar ('It's pleasant to smoke a cigar in the open air.') and sent her off home by a circuitous route: he didn't want anyone to imagine that he had arranged a ren-dezvous with her ('Can't stand that sort of thing!').

Immediately on his entrance, Lopakhin demands a reply to his 'simple question': 'Do you agree to lease your land for country cot-tages: yes or no?' To Lyubov and Gayev the question seems too absurd to require any answer:

GAYEV (*yawning*). Beg your pardon?

LYUBOV [more pertinently even if not helpfully]. Yesterday I had a lot of money, but today there's hardly any left. Poor Varya tries to economise by feeding everybody on milk soup and the old servants in the kitchen on peas and I am just throwing money about senseless-ly. (*Drops her purse, scattering some gold coins.*) Goodness, all over the place!

Yasha picks up the coins, while his mistress reflects dolefully on the wretched lunch they had had in town and on Gayev's ridiculous speeches to the waiters. Gayev has his ridiculous bickering match with

Yasha, who does his best not to burst out laughing in his face, ending with the melodramatic ultimatum: 'Either he or I.' On Lyubov's orders, Yasha walks off and Lopakhin tries again to pin them down to an answer, this time hinting that 'the rich merchant Deriganov' who is thinking of buying the estate, might raise the bidding to a figure that they could not match, but, not realising the full significance of the hint, they ignore it. Gayev, however, comes forward with the news that 'the Yaroslavl' aunt promised to send them money, but when and how much they did not know.

LOPAKHIN. How much will she send? A hundred thousand? Two hundred?

LYUBOV. Well. . . . Ten or fifteen thousand at most, and we must be thankful for that.

LOPAKHIN. I'm sorry, but such improvident people as you, such un-businesslike, strange people, I've never met in my life. I'm telling you in plain language that your estate's going to be sold, and you don't seem to understand.

To Lopakhin's astonishment, Lyubov asks, with quite staggering guilelessness, what she has to do, although, as he was not slow in pointing out, he had been telling them 'every day' that they had only to agree to let their cherry orchard and their land for country cottages and they would be able to raise as much money as they liked.

Lyubov's reply was typical of a woman who could not conceive of being deprived of a way of life she considered to be her inalienable right to enjoy.

LYUBOV. Country cottages, holiday-makers—I'm sorry, but it's so vulgar.

GAYEV. I'm of your opinion entirely.

Lopakhin could not contain himself any longer.

LOPAKHIN. I shall burst into tears or scream or have a fit. I can't stand it. You've worn me out. (*To* GAYEV.) You're a silly old woman.

GAYEV. I beg your pardon?

LOPAKHIN. A silly old woman! (*He gets up to go.*)

LYUBOV (*in dismay*). No, don't go. Please stay, my dear. I beg you. Perhaps we'll think of something.

LOPAKHIN. What is there to think of?

LYUBOV. Don't go, I beg you. Somehow, I feel much more cheerful with you here. (*Pause.*)

Contemplating the black prospect ahead, she did at last confess that she sometimes felt as though the house would collapse on top of them, a remark that made Gayev, who was, as Chekhov's direction has it, 'deep in thought', perhaps at the prospect of the house collapsing on top of him, put his usual defence mechanism in motion, this time by not only popping a ball into a pocket but also making a cannon. Lyubov thought at last of an explanation for their troubles. They were caused by her 'sins'. She was not referring to the way she and her ancestors (as Trofimov tells Anya at the end of the act) had been living, that is to say, at the expense of people who had laboured to keep them in comfort and had supplied them with the money they had been squandering. She was thinking of her adulterous affair for which she had been immediately 'punished' by the death of her little boy. She had run away to France, but had resumed her relationship with her lover who had joined her there and later left her for another woman. He was now bombarding her with requests to come back to him which she found difficult to resist. 'Lord, O Lord,' she at last appealed to heaven, 'be merciful, forgive my sins, don't punish me any more!'

Producing a telegram from her lover in Paris, which, loath to part with it, she had been carrying in her pocket, she proceeded to tear it up, no doubt as a demonstration to heaven that she really did mean to mend her ways. Then, distracted by some distant music, she inquired where it came from.

GAYEV. That's our famous Jewish band. Remember? Four fiddles, a flute, and a double bass.

LYUBOV. Does it still exist? We ought to arrange a little party and have them all over to the house.

The word Chekhov uses is *vecherok*, a rather flippant diminutive of *vecher* – literally 'an evening', but also meaning 'a party', to show the flippant way in which Lyubov quite suddenly passed from her terrible 'sins' to the party, which was eventually to take place on the day of the sale of the cherry orchard, in the hope, no doubt, that it would turn out to be an occasion for gaiety rather than despair. Lopakhin's announcement that he had been to see a play the night before leads Lyubov to remark (voicing Chekhov's views) that 'you shouldn't be watching plays, but more often yourselves: what dull lives you live, what a lot of nonsense you talk!' This, in turn, leads Lopakhin to his own shortcomings, his handwriting, in particular, being so bad that it makes him feel ashamed to let people see it. Lyubov, who must have been looking for some excuse to introduce the subject of Lopakhin's marriage to Varya, which everybody seems to be talking about, thought this the right moment to do so.

LYUBOV. You ought to get married, my friend.
LOPAKHIN. Yes. . . . That's true.
LYUBOV. To our Varya. She's a nice girl.
LOPAKHIN [not over-enthusiastically]. Yes.
LYUBOV. She's of peasant stock. She's a hard-working girl, and she loves you. That's the important thing. Why, you've been attracted to her for a long time yourself.
LOPAKHIN. Well, why not? I've no objection. She is a good girl.

The pause that followed this practically arranged match was interrupted by Gayev, who suddenly announced that he'd been offered a job in a bank at six thousand a year, but Lyubov was not impressed.

LYUBOV. You in a bank? You'd better stay where you are.

The way her brother depended on the aged Firs, who came in carrying a warm overcoat for his master, seemed to confirm her doubts about his career as 'a financier'.

LYUBOV. How you've aged, Firs!
FIRS. What's that, ma'am?
LOPAKHIN. Your mistress says you've aged a lot.
FIRS. I've been alive a long time. They was going to marry me off before your dad was born. (Laughs.) By the time the freedom came I was chief valet. I didn't agree to accept freedom and stayed on with my master. (Pause.) I well remember how glad they all was, but what they was glad about, they didn't know themselves.
LOPAKHIN [who had been regarding the old retainer with a quizzical look, couldn't restrain himself from pulling the man's leg]. It wasn't such a bad life before, was it? At least, they flogged you.

FIRS (*not hearing him*). I should say so. The peasants were attached to their masters and the masters to their peasants. Now they're all at sixes and sevens. You can't understand nothing.

GAYEV. Shut up, Firs. I've got to go to town tomorrow. I've been promised an introduction to a general who might lend us money on a promissory note.

LOPAKHIN. Nothing will come of it. And you won't be able to pay the interest. You may be sure of that.

LYUBOV. He's imagining it all. There aren't any generals.

The painful subject of the sale of the cherry orchard and the estate was changed at the entrance of Trofimov and the two girls. Lopakhin and Trofimov could not help liking each other. They addressed each other in the second person singular like two old friends, and yet they were constantly quarrelling.

LOPAKHIN. Our eternal student is always walking about with the young ladies.

TROFIMOV. Mind your own business.

LOPAKHIN. He'll soon be fifty and he's still a student.

TROFIMOV. Drop your idiotic jokes.

LOPAKHIN. Why are you angry, you funny fellow?

TROFIMOV. Well, stop pestering me.

LOPAKHIN (*laughs*). Let me ask you, sir, what do you think of me?

TROFIMOV. Simply this: you're a rich man and you'll soon be a millionaire. Now, just as a wild beast devours everything in its path and so helps to preserve the balance of nature, so you, too, perform a similar function.

They all laugh.

The dialogue then switched to the more serious problems of human pride and human destiny, Chekhov using Trofimov as his mouthpiece, though never out of character, but this time the two subjects were certainly not strictly in context. Pride seemed to Chekhov to be rather a senseless quality since 'looked at simply, without being too clever about it, man is far from perfect physiologically and, in the vast majority of cases, is coarse, stupid and profoundly unhappy. Man ought to stop admiring himself. He ought (Chekhov is never tired of repeating) just to work!'

To Gayev's objection that man must die all the same, Chekhov had no answer, except that man, being part of mankind, must work 'to assist those who are looking for the truth' and, as Vershinin put it in *The Three Sisters*, must make life happy 'for the descendants of our descendants'. However, he lets Trofimov, in his reply to Gayev's objection: 'We're going to die all the same', speak in character: 'Who knows? And what do you mean by "we're going to die all the same"? For all you know, a man may possess a hundred senses and only the five we know of are lost at his death and the other ninety-five live on.'

LYUBOV. How clever you are, Peter!
LOPAKHIN (*ironically*). Oh, terribly!

But what Chekhov makes Trofimov say about the prospect of civilisation and the way the intellectuals were betraying their own ideals, is much more pertinent than what he made Vershinin say in *The Three Sisters*:

TROFIMOV. Mankind marches on, perfecting its powers. Everything that is incomprehensible to us now, will one day become familiar and comprehensible. All we have to do is to work and to do our best to assist those who are looking for the truth. Here in Russia . . . the vast majority of the educated people I know . . . are quite incapable of doing any work. They call themselves intellectuals, but speak to their servants as inferiors and treat the peasants like animals. They're not particularly keen on their studies, they don't do any serious reading, they are bone idle, they merely talk about science, and they understand very little about art. They are all so solemn, they look so very grave, they talk only of important matters, they philosophise. . . . I dislike and I'm frightened of all these solemn countenances, just as I'm frightened of all serious conversations. Why not shut up for once?

In his dislike and fear 'of all these solemn countenances' Chekhov seemed to anticipate what they would do to his plays not only in his own time and in his own country, but also throughout the world during the seventy years after his death.

As for Lopakhin, Chekhov also uses him to give the audience an insight into his own mind: 'One has only to start doing something', Lopakhin says, 'to realise how few honest, decent people there are about. Sometimes when I lie awake, I keep thinking, Lord, you've given us vast forests, boundless plains, immense horizons, and living here, we ourselves ought really to be giants —' an opinion which is as applicable today to any country in the world as it was in Chekhov's day to Russia.

But there is also a great deal of good sense in Lyubov's comment (no wonder Chekhov regarded her as an intelligent woman): 'You want giants, do you? They're all right in fairy tales. Elsewhere they frighten me.'

Yepikhodov crosses the stage in the background, playing his guitar. The brief scene beginning with his entrance is a prelude to one of the finest sound effects to be found in a Chekhov play. To get the greatest thrill from it, Chekhov had gradually to get all his characters on the stage into a state of suspended animation. This he achieves by the silent figure of Yepikhodov slowly crossing the stage in the background playing his guitar, which seems to have an almost hallucinatory effect on Lyubov and Anya, who utter the same three words as though in a trance:

LYUBOV.... (*Pensively.*) There goes Yepikhodov.
ANYA (*pensively*). There goes Yepikhodov.
GAYEV [very quietly]. The sun's set, ladies and gentlemen.
TROFIMOV. Yes.

For once Gayev's empty rhetoric is used by Chekhov to heighten the trance-like effect of the scene.

GAYEV (*softly, as though declaiming*). Oh nature, glorious nature! Glowing with eternal radiance, beautiful and indifferent, you, whom we call Mother, uniting in yourself life and death, you—the life-giver and the destroyer...
VARYA (*imploringly*). Darling uncle!
ANYA. Uncle, again!
TROFIMOV. You'd better cannon off the red into the middle pocket.
GAYEV. I'm silent, silent.

All sit silently, lost in thought. Everything is still. The dead silence is broken only by the muttering of Firs. Suddenly a distant sound is heard. It seems to come from the sky, the sound of a string snapping, dying away, melancholy

The effect of the snapping violin string, for which Chekhov made such elaborate preparation, must, as he pointed out, be of short duration and could be very effectively reproduced by modern methods: it symbolises the passing of a social class that had been exerting its domination over all the other classes throughout Europe for centuries. It is no wonder that Lyubov, the representative of that class, should react to it with a 'shudder', that it should give her an 'unpleasant' feeling and bring tears to Anya's eyes. Firs's reaction to it is, of course, typical of a serf who resents the 'freedom' he refused to accept.

FIRS. Same thing happened before the misfortune: the owl hooted and the samovar kept hissing.
GAYEV. Before what misfortune?
FIRS. Before the freedom.

The scene with the 'passer-by' that follows merely accentuates the fecklessness of a ruling class on the eve of its disappearance. Dressed in his battered peak cap and overcoat, the tramp, for that is what he is, mumbles the well-known slogans of those who volunteered to live among the Russian peasants to alleviate their 'sufferings'. Varya's threat to 'go away' after Lyubov had given a gold coin to the tramp at a time when 'there was no food for the servants in the house', and Lyubov's promise to give her all the money she had, followed by a characteristic request to Lopakhin to lend her some money, merely emphasised the parlous state of the finances of the owner of the cherry orchard. But it also gives Lyubov the chance 'to congratulate' Varya on her coming engagement to Lopakhin, who teasingly advises her, after her remark that 'it is no joking matter', to go into a nunnery. Lopakhin only quotes Hamlet's line to Ophelia (whose name he mispronounces), but it shows that he has little respect for her, a clear indication of what turned out to be the failure of Lyubov's 'matchmaking'. The scene ends with Lopakhin's warning: 'Let me remind you, my friends: the cherry orchard will be up for sale on the twenty-second of August. Think about it! Think!'

The last scene of this act shows Anya as very young and inexperienced and Trofimov as a starry-eyed idealist – two innocents who can be safely counted on to bring a lump to the throat of the spectator. Anya laughs happily to have got rid of Varya's supervision. Trofimov is indignant that Varya should be afraid lest they should fall in love, not being able to grasp 'with her narrow mind' that they were 'above love'. To him the sole aim and meaning of life is the avoidance of 'everything petty and illusory', everything that prevents people from being 'free and happy'.

TROFIMOV. . . . Forward! Let us march on irresistibly to the bright star which is shining there in the distance! Forward! Don't lag behind, friends!

ANYA (*clapping her hands*). How splendidly you talk! It's so heavenly here today!

TROFIMOV [preoccupied with much higher things than the weather, agrees with a singular lack of enthusiasm]. Yes, the weather is wonderful.

To Anya's surprised admission that because of him she was no longer as fond of the cherry orchard as when she used to think that there was no lovelier place on earth, Trofimov delivers his famous speech in which Chekhov, himself the son of a former serf, uses the young student to express not only his views of events in Russia in his own day, but of the passing of the old order throughout the world.

TROFIMOV. The whole of Russia is our orchard. The earth is great and beautiful. There are very many lovely places on it. (*Pause.*) Think, Anya: your grandfather, your great-grandfather, and all your ancestors owned serfs. They owned living souls. Can't you see human beings looking at you from every cherry tree in your orchard, from every leaf and every tree trunk? Don't you hear their voices? To own living souls—that's what has changed you all so much, you who are living now and those who lived before you. That's why your mother, you yourself, and your uncle no longer realise that you are living on borrowed capital, at other people's expense, at the expense of those whom you don't admit farther than your entrance hall. We are at least two hundred years behind the times. We haven't got anything at all. We have no definite attitudes towards our past. We just philosophise, complain of depression, or drink vodka. Isn't it abundantly clear that before we start living in the present, we must atone for our past, make an end of it? And atone for it we can only by suffering, by extraordinary, unceasing labour. Understand that, Anya.

Even in this speech Chekhov never allows himself to forget that his character must always be true to himself. In his advice to Anya, who assures him that she is quite ready to leave the house that has never really been theirs for a long time, Trofimov speaks fully in character:

TROFIMOV. If you have the keys of the house, throw them into the well and go away. Be free as the wind.

ANYA (*rapturously*). How well you put it!

TROFIMOV [now fully in character]. Believe me, Anya, believe me! I'm not yet thirty, I'm young, I'm still a student, but I've been through hell more than once. I'm driven from pillar to post. In winter I'm half starved, I'm ill, worried, poor as a beggar. You can't imagine the terrible places I've been to! And yet, always, every moment of the day and night, my heart is full of ineffable visions of the future. I feel, I'm quite sure, that happiness is coming, Anya. I can see it coming already.

ANYA (*pensively*) [looking up at the sky]. The moon is rising.

Chekhov, as earlier in this act, brings on Yepikhodov with his guitar to create a scene full of magic.

YEPIKHODOV *can be heard playing the same sad tune as before on his guitar. The moon rises. Somewhere near the poplars* VARYA *is looking for* ANYA *and calling, 'Anya, where are you?'*

TROFIMOV. Yes, the moon is rising. (*Pause.*) There it is—happiness! It's coming nearer and nearer. Already I can hear its footsteps, and [echoing Vershinin] if we never see it, if we never know it, what does that matter? Others will see it.

VARYA (*off stage*). Anya, where are you?

[Varya's second call brings Trofimov and Anya back to earth.]

TROFIMOV. That Varya again! (*Angrily.*) Disgusting!

ANYA. Never mind, let's go to the river. It's lovely there.

TROFIMOV. Yes, let's. (*They go off.*)

VARYA (*off stage*). Anya! Anya!

Act Three

The incongruity between reality as it is and as it is imagined to be, between fact and wishful thinking, which lies at the very heart of every comedy, is best illustrated in the climactic third act of *The Cherry Orchard*. 'Such a calamity [that is to say, the sale of the estate and the cherry orchard] seems so inconceivable to me', Lyubov tells Trofimov at the beginning of the act, 'that I don't know what to think [that is to say, about Gayev's being so late turning up from the public auction]. I'm completely at a loss.' The 'little party' on the day of the auction was, therefore, not an accident. It had been arranged, as suggested earlier, to celebrate the retention of the estate by its owners. How could such a misconception have arisen? Quite apart from the sale of her ancestral estate being 'so inconceivable', Lyubov has some practical reason for hoping that the 'calamity' might be averted.

LYUBOV. Still no Leonid. I can't understand what he can be doing in town all this time. . . . Either the estate has been sold or the auction has not taken place. Why keep us in suspense so long?

VARYA (*trying to comfort her*). I'm certain Uncle must have bought it.

TROFIMOV (*sarcastically*). Oh, to be sure!

VARYA. Our great-aunt sent him power of attorney to buy the estate in her name and transfer the mortgage to her. She's done it for Anya's sake. I'm sure God will help us and Uncle will buy it.

LYUBOV. Your great-aunt sent fifteen thousand to buy the estate in her name. She doesn't trust us, but the money wouldn't even pay the interest. (*Covering her face with her hands.*) My whole future is being decided today. . . .

She knew, therefore, that the money the Countess had sent, would not be enough to save the estate and with it her 'whole future'. What, then, was she hoping for? Unlike Varya, she had no faith in miracles. She simply did not believe (as she said) that such a calamity as the loss of the estate could happen. She would not believe it even when Lopakhin tried to explain the situation to her, even when he tried to make her understand that a man like the rich merchant Deriganov would not hesitate to acquire a property bringing in fifty thousand a year, or that Lopakhin himself would not hesitate, now that it seemed certain that Gayev stood no chance of buying the estate, to outbid Deriganov.

On her first appearance in the third act Lyubov shows no signs of worrying about the auction. She is humming a popular dance tune, telling Varya to offer the dance-band tea, gaily applauding Charlotta's conjuring tricks. She is annoyed with Gayev for being so late, which rather spoils her enjoyment of the party, but deep inside her she is convinced – she *knows*! – that the estate with its cherry orchard will remain hers. It is important that this conviction should be conveyed to the audience to ensure its participation in the action, for by now the audience should have no doubts as to the result of the auction: it knows what no one of the characters on the stage knows, a *sine qua non* of audience participation.

The set of the third act is almost identical with the set of the first and second acts of *The Three Sisters*. As the curtain goes up, the party is in full swing. The Jewish band, mentioned in the second act, is playing off stage. In the ballroom people are dancing The Grande Ronde. Pishchik, the master of ceremonies, calling out *Promenade à une paire*, appears in the drawing-room with Charlotta in the first couple, Trofimov and Lyubov in the second, Anya and a post office clerk in the third, Varya and the station master in the fourth. The last two gentlemen elicit the scornful comment from Firs: 'We used to have generals, barons and admirals at our dances before, but now we send for the post office clerk and the station master.' Dunyasha is in the last couple with an anonymous 'partner'. Pishchik, an expert on high society dances, is calling out the sequences and, as he tells Trofimov, he finds it very hard work, suffering from high blood pressure as he does. Actually, he confides to Trofimov, he is as strong as a horse, a simile which leads Chekhov to have a dig at the noble families with their ancient pedigrees: 'My father', he makes Pishchik go on, 'used to say that the ancient line of Simeonov-Pishchiks derives its origin from the horse that Caligula made a senator.'

TROFIMOV. There really is something horsy about you.

PISHCHIK. Well, a horse is a good beast. You can sell a horse.

Pishchik is hard up again: 'The day after tomorrow', he tells

Trofimov, 'I've got to pay three hundred and ten roubles. I've got one hundred and thirty. (*Feels his pockets, in alarm.*) My money's gone, I've lost my money! (*Through tears.*) Where is it? (*Happily.*) Ah, here it is, in the lining!' He had forgotten about the holes in his pocket, but, as Trofimov sagely remarks, if he had spent the energy he wasted on trying to raise the money to pay the interest on his debts on something else, he'd probably have succeeded in turning the world upside down.

PISHCHIK [mentioning the German philosopher who was very popular in Russia at the time]. Nietzsche,[1] the German philosopher – a great man, a man of tremendous intellect – says in his works that there's nothing wrong with forging bank-notes.

TROFIMOV. Have you read Nietzsche?

PISHCHIK. Well, no, Dáshenka told me. In my present position I shouldn't mind forging bank-notes myself.

Trofimov's attitude towards Pishchik wavers between goodnatured contempt and warmhearted sympathy for a man who was struggling helplessly against economic forces he did not understand; there was no contempt in Trofimov's attitude towards Lopakhin, the 'wild beast', whom he could not help liking and even admiring; but he was both contemptuous and malevolent towards Varya who had quite unwittingly exposed the fundamental dishonesty of his repeated assertions that he was 'above love', belied by his apostrophe to Anya at the very end of the first act. Varya, he told her mother, was a little too 'zealous'. She poked her nose into other people's affairs. She wouldn't leave him and Anya alone all through the summer, afraid that they might have an affair. What business was that of hers? He was so furious with Varya that he kept taunting her all through the third act by calling her 'Mrs Lopakhin' and scoffing at her wish to retire to a convent. Their first clash occurred at the very beginning of the act when, in reply to his calling her 'Mrs Lopakhin! Mrs Lopakhin!', she retorted by calling him 'a moth-eaten gentleman', which brought the unexpected reply that he was 'proud' of being a moth-eaten gentleman. Varya was too

[1] Chekhov referred to Nietzsche's popularity in Russia in a letter to his publisher Alexey Suvorin on 25 February 1895: 'I should have liked to meet a philosopher like Nietzsche in a railway carriage or on a boat', he wrote, 'and spent a whole night talking to him. However, I do not think the influence of his philosophy will last. It is not so much convincing as spectacular'.

worried about where to find the money to pay the band to pursue her feud with Trofimov. Charlotta's conjuring tricks, for a while, relieved the growing tenseness of the atmosphere. Pishchik, carried away by his enthusiastic admiration of Charlotta's skill, declared that he was 'simply in love with her', to which the ever-ready female conjurer expressed her doubts of his prowess as a lover: '*Ein guter Mensch, aber schlechter Musikant*'—an excellent fellow, but a bad musician! At the end of her show, after Charlotta had disappeared pursued by Pishchik, the feud between Varya and Trofimov was resumed, Trofimov unable to conceal his contempt for Varya's facile assumption that Gayev would succeed, 'with God's help', in buying the estate and again calling her 'Mrs Lopakhin'.

VARYA (*getting cross*). Eternal student! Expelled twice from the university, weren't you?

Lyubov tried to avoid the rather dangerous subject of the reason for Trofimov's expulsion, by asking her why she shouldn't marry 'a nice, interesting' man like Lopakhin. Varya admitted that she liked Lopakhin, but she could not very well propose to him.

VARYA. Everyone's been talking to me about him for the last two years ... But he either says nothing or makes jokes ... If I had any money, just a little, a hundred roubles, I'd give up everything and go right away as far as possible. I'd have gone into a convent.
TROFIMOV [jeering at her oft-repeated description of life in a convent]. Wonderful!
VARYA (*to* TROFIMOV). A student ought to be intelligent! (*In a gentle voice, through tears.*) How unattractive you have become, Peter! How you've aged! (*To* LYUBOV, *no longer crying.*) I can't live without having something to do, Mother! I must be doing something all the time!

The opportunity to do something presented itself at once. Already, at the very start of the act, Chekhov had introduced the billiard theme, which was to play such an important part later on in the act, though only in a stage direction: 'From an adjoining room comes the sound of people playing billiards.' Varya had been too preoccupied with the need to find the money for the musicians to pay any attention to it. Besides, she was immediately engaged in the feud with Trofimov. As though in reply to the declaration that she must be doing something all the time, Yasha entered, and, 'hardly able to restrain his laughter', announced that 'Yepikhodov has broken a billiard cue!'

VARYA. What's Yepikhodov doing here? Who gave him permission to play billiards? Can't understand these people! (*Goes out.*)

These two short and seemingly unimportant bits of dialogue were to develop and grow in intensity and reach a climax on the return of the triumphant Lopakhin from the auction.

Varya's exit is followed by the clash between Lyubov and Trofimov, whose repeated declaration that he was 'above love' is shown to be ludicrous after Lyubov's shattering analysis of the absurdity of the so-called 'generation gap', that is to say, the idea that it is only the young who 'can look truth straight in the face' and provide the right solution to all the important problems.

LYUBOV. . . . You boldly solve all the important problems, but tell me, isn't it because you're young, isn't it because you haven't experienced the suffering of living through even one of your problems? You look ahead boldly, but isn't it because you neither see nor expect anything terrible to happen to you because life is still hidden from your own young eyes? You're bolder, you're more honest, you see much more deeply than any of us, but think carefully, try to be generous just a tiny bit, spare me. . . .

But her appeal to spare her, to try to understand that life had no meaning for her without the cherry orchard and that, if it had to be sold, then let her be sold with it, only brought the cold reply:

TROFIMOV. You know I sympathise with you with all my heart.
LYUBOV. You should have put it differently. . . .

As she takes out a handkerchief to wipe her tears, a telegram falls on the floor. She does not notice it and goes on appealing to Trofimov not to 'condemn' her. She even assures him that she would 'gladly' let Anya marry him, if only he'd finish his course at the university, that is, give up his political work or, as she puts it, stop drifting from place to place. And, she adds, he must do something about his beard. 'Make it grow somehow. (*Laughs.*) You do look funny!'

TROFIMOV (*coldly as he picks up the telegram from the floor*). I have no desire to be handsome.

The telegram is, of course, from her 'wild man' in Paris, who begs her to come back to him, and she was really beginning to think that she ought to go back to Paris because he was ill and in trouble again. 'You're looking very stern, Peter, but what's to be done, what am I to do? He's ill, he's lonely, he's unhappy. Who'll look after him there? Who'll stop him from doing something silly, who'll give him his medicine at the right time? And' – the true reason at last – 'why hide it? I love him. . . . He's a millstone round my neck and he's dragging me down to the bottom with him, but I love the millstone, I can't live without it. Don't think badly of me, Peter. Don't say anything. Don't speak.'

But that Trofimov could not do. He *had* to tell her 'the truth', however painful it might be and however reluctant he might feel about doing so.

TROFIMOV (*through tears*). For God's sake, I'm sorry to be so frank, but he's left you penniless.

LYUBOV. No, no, no! You mustn't say that! (*Puts her hands over her ears.*)

TROFIMOV [not suspecting that in another moment he was going to hear the truth about himself]. Why, he's a scoundrel, and you are the only one who doesn't seem to know it. He's a contemptible scoundrel, a nonentity.

LYUBOV (*angry but restraining herself*). You're twenty-six or twenty-seven, but you're still a schoolboy, a sixth-form schoolboy.

TROFIMOV. What does that matter?

LYUBOV. You ought to be a man. At your age you ought to understand people who are in love. You ought to be in love yourself. You ought to fall in love. (*Angrily.*) Yes, yes! And you're not so pure, either. You're simply a prig, a ridiculous crank, a freak!

TROFIMOV (*horrified*). What is she saying?

LYUBOV. 'I am above love!' You're not above love, you're simply what Firs calls a nincompoop. Not to have a mistress at your age!

TROFIMOV (*horrified*). This is terrible! What is she saying? (*Walks quickly into the ballroom, clutching his head.*) It's dreadful! I can't! I'll go away! (*Goes out but immediately comes back.*) All is at an end between us! (*Goes out into the hall.*)

LYUBOV (*shouting after him*). Peter, wait! You funny fellow, I was only joking. Peter!

Someone can be heard running rapidly up the stairs and then suddenly falling down with a crash. Anya and Varya scream, but immediately laughter is heard.

LYUBOV. What's happened?

ANYA (*runs in, laughing*). Peter's fallen down the stairs.

LYUBOV. What an eccentric!

The dramatic action gathers momentum between Trofimov's precipitous fall on the stairs and Varya's unpremeditated attack on Lopakhin —two examples of poetic justice meted out on the idealist without a heart and on the business tycoon at the moment of his return from his latest financial coup. But between these two comic events Lyubov apologised to Trofimov and joined him in the general dancing; she asked the overworked and overconscientious old butler, worried about Gayev, his fifty-year-old 'youngster', who had gone to the auction wearing a light overcoat, where he would go if the estate were sold, and received his loyal answer that he would go where she told him; she listened to Yasha's plea to take him back to Paris with her as he could no longer put up with living in an 'uncivilised' country; and she went off with Pishchik, who was still insisting on getting a loan from her, to the ballroom where Charlotta was performing another of her conjuring tricks. Dunyasha, left alone powdering her face in the sitting-room, told Firs that the post office clerk had said that she was 'like a flower', which 'quite took her breath away', but it only made Yasha yawn and walk out, and Firs thought it necessary to warn her that she would come 'to a bad end'. At that moment Yepikhodov made his appearance and, reminding Dunyasha that she had given him her word, appealed to her not to treat him 'like an insect'. His complaint of being overtaken by some calamity every day was immediately proved to be true by the entry of Varya, who ordered Dunyasha to be off and turned angrily on Yepikhodov for disobeying her order to leave the house.

The scene between Varya and Yepikhodov has been most carefully, even craftily (Chekhov greatly admired Tolstoy for his 'craftiness' in working out his plots) worked out by Chekhov to account for Varya's attack on Lopakhin at the moment of his triumphant return. Varya was furious with Yepikhodov not so much because he had broken a billiard cue as because he had turned up at the party without her permission. She had told him to leave the house, but now he had turned up again.

VARYA. Are you still here, Simon? What an ill-mannered fellow you are! First you go and play billiards and break a cue and now you wander about the drawing-room as if you were a guest.

YEPIKHODOV [displaying quite an unusual access of independence]. You have no right to reprimand me, if you don't mind my saying so.

VARYA. I'm not reprimanding you, I'm telling you. All you do is to drift about from place to place without ever doing a stroke of work. We keep a clerk, but goodness only knows why.

YEPIKHODOV (offended). Whether I work or drift about, whether I eat or play billiards is something on which only people who are older than you, who know what they are talking about, are entitled to pass an opinion.

VARYA (flaring up). How dare you talk to me like that? How dare you? So you think I don't know what I'm talking about, do you? Get out of here! This instant!

YEPIKHODOV (cowed) [disquieted, but still standing his ground]. Express yourself with more delicacy, please.

VARYA (beside herself). Get out of here this minute! Out! (He goes towards the door, she follows him.) Twenty-two calamities! Never set foot here again! Don't let me see you here again! (YEPIKHODOV goes out. He can be heard saying behind the door: 'I shall lodge a complaint against you.') Oh, so you're coming back, are you? (Picks up the stick which FIRS has left near the door.) Come on, come on, come on, I'll show you! Coming, are you? Coming? Well, take that! (Swings the stick as LOPAKHIN comes in.)

LOPAKHIN [reminded of the stick with which his drunken father, the serf, always used to beat him, sarcastically]. Thank you very much.

Unable to suppress her annoyance with Lopakhin for never coming to the point of proposing to her, Varya is, in a way, enjoying the situation.

VARYA (*angrily and ironically*). I'm so sorry!

LOPAKHIN. It's all right, ma'am. Thank you very much for your kind reception.

VARYA. Don't mention it. (*Walks away, then turns round and asks gently.*) I didn't hurt you, did I?

LOPAKHIN [still unappeased]. Oh no, not at all. There's going to be an enormous lump on my head for all that.

The arrival of Lopakhin was greeted by excited cries of 'Lopakhin's arrived' in the ballroom; by a hug from Pishchik, who guessed the sensational news from the half-embarrassed, half-joyful expression on Lopakhin's face and the strong smell of brandy on his breath, and was only waiting for an opportune moment to touch him for a loan; and, lastly, by the anxious Lyubov, who wanted to know why he had been so long and where Leonid was. But all Lopakhin would say was that Gayev had returned with him and would be coming along presently. He refused to say anything more than that the auction was over by four o'clock and that they had missed their train. At that moment Gayev came in, carrying parcels and wiping away his tears. He did not reply to Lyubov's frantic questions but just waved his hand at her. As he handed the anchovies and the Kerch herrings – which he must have bought in town before the auction – to Firs, he looked completely shattered by what he had been through that day. All he could bring himself to say was that he had had nothing to eat all day. It was then that the dramatic effect of the billiard theme, which Chekhov had been leading up to throughout the play, came off brilliantly. The stage direction makes it quite clear: '*The door of the billiard room is open: the clicking of billiard balls can be heard and Yasha's voice saying: "Seven and eighteen!" Gayev's expression changes. He is no longer crying.*'

Who opened the door of the billiard room? Why was it opened just at the moment Gayev had come into the sitting-room? It was Chekhov himself who opened it to show that it needed only the click of a billiard ball to make Gayev forget all the terrible disappointments of that day and, indeed, reconcile him to the loss of the estate and the cherry orchard 'mentioned in the encyclopaedia'. He didn't even stop to tell his sister what had happened at the auction. After saying that he was 'awfully tired', and asking Firs to come and help him change, he walked through the ballroom to his own room.

Bewildered, Pishchik and Lyubov turned to Lopakhin.

PISHCHIK. Well, what happened at the auction? Come, tell us.
LYUBOV. Has the cherry orchard been sold?
LOPAKHIN. It has.
LYUBOV. Who bought it?
LOPAKHIN. I bought it. (*Pause.*)

A perfect climax achieved by only three short words and resulting in the most effective pause in all Chekhov's plays, a pause that is full of dramatic action as is shown by Chekhov's concise stage direction: 'LYUBOV *is crushed; she would have collapsed on the floor had she not been standing near an armchair.* VARYA *takes off the keys from her belt, throws them on the floor in the centre of the drawing-room and goes out.*' For a moment Lopakhin felt too dazed to speak. He could only repeat the three words: 'I bought it.' But his account of the sale was as dramatic as it was short. The thought of how he had defeated his rival Deriganov made him laugh. He went on:

> Deriganov was already there when we got to the auction. Gayev had only fifteen thousand, and Deriganov began his bidding at once with thirty thousand over and above the mortgage. I realised the position at once and took up his challenge. I bid forty. He bid forty-five. He kept raising the bid by five thousand and I by adding another ten thousand. Well, it was soon over. I bid ninety thousand on top of the arrears and the cherry orchard was knocked down to me. Now the cherry orchard is mine! Mine! (*Laughs loudly.*) Merciful heavens, the cherry orchard is mine! Come on, tell me I'm drunk. Tell me I'm out of my mind. Tell me I'm imagining it all. (*Stamps his feet.*) Don't laugh at me! . . .

Nobody was laughing at him. He was not the man anyone would dare to laugh at at the moment when he became the owner of the estate where his father and grandfather had not even been allowed inside the kitchen. He picked up the keys Varya had thrown down, 'smiling affectionately': 'Wants to show she's no longer mistress here.' At his command the band struck up and he invited them all 'to come and watch Yermolay Lopakhin take an axe to the cherry orchard and watch the trees come crashing down' in preparation for the building of the country cottages so that 'our grandchildren and great-grandchildren' might see 'a new life springing up here'. His dream of a new life turned out to be, in his words, 'a figment of the imagination shrouded in a mystery', for it was a dream that was not destined to last and, for a brief moment, he seemed to be aware of it himself. For as he turned to Lyubov, who had sunk into a chair and was weeping bitterly, he asked her 'reproachfully' why she had not listened to him, for she would never get her cherry orchard back, and he added 'with tears': 'Oh if only all this could be over soon, if only our futile and unhappy life could somehow be changed soon.' But that moment of regret and tenderness was shortlived. His past, which had come back to him in a flash when Varya had hit him with the stick, reasserted itself more violently now that the whole significance of his ownership of the ancestral home had sunk in, when, perhaps for the first time, he realised that he, the beaten and semi-literate Yermolay, the son of flogged and illiterate serfs, who used to run about barefoot in winter, had bought 'the most beautiful estate in the world'. Indeed, the moment Pishchik had led him away from the grieving figure of Lyubov, the coarse peasant in him came to the fore and submerged his better nature. He was no longer afraid 'to betray his joy', he shouted to the band to play up. 'Let's have everything as I want it now. (*Ironically.*) Here comes the new landowner, the owner of the cherry orchard!'

In the intoxication of his triumph over the gentry, waving his arms about and staggering towards the ballroom, he brushed against a small table and nearly knocked over the candelabra (a foretaste of what he was going to do to the cherry orchard) and made the all too familiar remark of the poor peasant turned millionaire: 'I can pay for everything.'

He went out with Pishchik, leaving both the drawing-room and the ballroom deserted except for Lyubov 'sitting in a chair', Chekhov's stage direction runs, '*hunched up and crying bitterly. The band plays quietly.* [All the intensely emotional scenes in this play are accompanied by soft music.] ANYA *and* TROFIMOV *come in quietly.* ANYA *goes up to her mother and kneels in front of her.* TROFIMOV *remains standing by the entrance to the ballroom.*'

What Anya says to her mother is merely a repetition of what Trofimov has told her. It is the way she says it – the touching innocence of her faith in a bright future and, most of all, the loving tenderness with which she appeals to her mother to stop crying because she still has her life ahead of her and her 'kind and pure heart' – that is so touching: 'Come with me, darling Mother. Come, let's go away from here. We shall plant a new orchard, an orchard more splendid than this one. You will see it, you will understand, and joy, deep, serene joy, will steal into your heart, sink into it like the sun in the evening, and you will smile, Mother. Come, darling, come.'

Act Four

In the fourth act of *The Cherry Orchard* (more so than in any act of this
or any other of his last plays) Chekhov makes magnificent use of such
undramatic things as the weather, walls and ceilings, windows, a bottle
of champagne, a pair of old galoshes, an umbrella, to disclose the inner-
most feelings of his characters with greater dramatic force than the conventional use of the soliloquy which he completely dispenses with in
his last play.

The fourth act opens on a cold and sunny October morning in the
nursery, a little over a month after the sale of the cherry orchard and
about half an hour before the departure of its former owners. 'Might
just as well be summer', Lopakhin observed, adding in a gratified voice:
'Good building weather.' It was not the weather Lyubov was thinking
of as she looked at the bare walls of the nursery, from which the
curtains and the pictures had been removed. 'The things these walls
have seen', she murmured after bidding goodbye to 'the dear old
house' which, when next spring came, 'won't be here any more'. What
was she thinking of when uttering those words? Was she by any
chance thinking of the fifteen-year-old barefoot peasant boy, beaten
up by his father, she had brought into the nursery, wiping the blood from
his face and telling him it would get better by the time he wed?
(Chekhov does not tell us what was passing through Lyubov's mind
while wondering what things those walls had seen, but in keeping that
'event' firmly in her mind an actress would have something tangible to
hold on to, instead of indulging in some sentimental moan about walls
and ceilings, something that every actress could convey to the audience
in her own individual way and thus ensure its active participation.
Such a definite clear-cut picture in her mind would also lend added
poignancy to her remark shortly before leaving her ancestral home for
good: 'I feel as though I had never seen the walls and ceilings of this
house before: I look at them with such eagerness, with such tender
emotion. . . .' It was her tenderness that had made Lopakhin remember
that scene in the nursery so many years later.)

Gayev, too, as he looked through the window at the bare skeletons of the cherry trees soon to be felled by the axe, goes back forty-six years in time: 'I remember when I was six years old', he says, 'sitting on this window-sill on Trinity Sunday and watching father going to church. . . .' A hot July day,[1] the ripening red cherries gleaming through the green leaves of the trees: no thought of destruction hanging over the cherry orchard: they knew 'the recipe' then, as Firs had said.

Lopakhin had bought a bottle of champagne at the railway station on a sudden impulse in the hope that a toast to the happiness of the brother and sister would make Lyubov's departure less painful. 'This isn't real champagne', Yasha, who had drunk 'real' champagne at Lyubov's house in Menton, disillusions him. 'Take it from me, sir.' Lopakhin's reply is in character: 'Paid eight roubles for the bottle.' Nobody, not even Lopakhin himself, shows any inclination for his cheap champagne, no one, that is, except Yasha who, when left alone with Dunyasha, empties one glass of champagne after another (Dunyasha is too immersed in crying over Yasha's fickleness and then powdering her face to notice anything). It is the audience alone who knows it, which ensures its full participation when Lopakhin, accepting Lyubov's suggestion to propose to Varya, tries to draw Lyubov's attention to his champagne which, he declares, 'is appropriate to the occasion', only to discover that Yasha had drunk it ('lapped it up') – hardly a good omen for the 'occasion'.

Trofimov's search for his galoshes provided a good insight into Varya's mind before and after her meeting with Lopakhin. At the beginning of the act when she was still wondering whether, even with Lyubov's assistance, Lopakhin would come up to scratch and pop the question, her nerves were on edge with worry: she throws a pair of galoshes through the open door with words that clearly show her state of mind: 'Oh, take your filthy things!' But after her hopes had been dashed, she quickly recovered.

LYUBOV [comes through the door cautiously and, glancing at the quietly sobbing Varya, realises at once that her attempt to persuade Lopakhin to propose to her adopted daughter has failed]. Well? (*Pause.*) We must go.

[1] Trinity Sunday, a week after Whitsun, usually some time in June, falls about a fornight later in the Greek Orthodox church.

VARYA (*no longer crying, dries her eyes*). Yes, it's time, Mother. I'd like to get to the Ragulins' today. I only hope we don't miss the train.

A few minutes later she shows that she harbours no ill feelings even against Lopakhin and his heartless jokes: 'Varya pulls an umbrella out of a bundle of clothes with such force, that it looks as if she were going to hit someone with it; Lopakhin pretends to be frightened.'

VARYA. Good heavens, you did not think that —

She does not finish the sentence: there is no longer any anger in her heart against him as there certainly was after she had hit him with Firs's stick by mistake in the third act and expressed her regret 'angrily and derisively'.

Then, finally, as she hands his galoshes to Peter, she shows no trace of her earlier irascibility.

VARYA. There are your galoshes, Peter. By that suitcase. (*Tearfully.*) Oh, how dirty they are, how old. . . .

When the curtain goes up on the fourth act only Lopakhin and Yasha are in the nursery. Lyubov and Gayev can be heard through the open entrance door saying goodbye to the peasants. Gayev, a 'liberal' to the bitter end, can be heard addressing them as 'my dear fellows'. (He forgets his 'liberal' ideas later on, his aristocratic nostrils reacting haughtily to the presence of his sister's valet: 'Smells of salt herrings here', salt herrings being the staple food of the Russian lower orders.) On emerging into the nursery Lyubov looks upset. 'She is not crying', Chekhov's stage direction states, 'but she is pale, her face is twitching, she cannot speak.' Gayev is angry with her for having given her purse away to the peasants.

GAYEV. You gave them your purse, Lyuba. You shouldn't. You really shouldn't.

LYUBOV. I – I couldn't help it. I just couldn't help it.

They completely ignore Lopakhin's invitation 'to take a glass of champagne; one glass each before we leave'. Both go out. Trofimov comes in from outside, wearing an overcoat and looking for his galoshes. When Lopakhin tells him that he has been wasting his time with them long enough and that he could not live without work, Trofimov remarks drily that he supposed he (Lopakhin) would soon resume his 'useful labours'. Lopakhin ignores the taunt and asks him to have some champagne, but Trofimov refuses.

LOPAKHIN. Off to Moscow, are you?

TROFIMOV. Yes. I'll see them off to town and I shall be going off to Moscow tomorrow.

LOPAKHIN. I see. Well, I suppose the professors have stopped lecturing while you've been away—all waiting for you to come back.

TROFIMOV [who never could take a joke]. Mind your own business.

LOPAKHIN. How many years have you been studying at the university?

TROFIMOV [again rising to the bait]. Why don't you think of something more original for a change? This is old and stale.

But he could not help liking the property tycoon in spite of disagreeing with the ethics of his business deals. 'You have', he tells Lopakhin, 'such fine, sensitive fingers, the fingers of an artist, and such a fine, sensitive soul.' He then proceeds to give Lopakhin his friendly advice 'to stop throwing his arms about', which, he explains, also means trying to make a packet by persuading holiday-makers to turn themselves into smallholders by buying plots on his newly-acquired estate—an all too justified warning, for, as it turned out, it took only sixteen years after Lopakhin's first appearance on the stage in his white waistcoat and his brown shoes for Trofimov's warning to take effect.

Lopakhin would not be denied the pleasure of getting the awkward idealist to accept some money from him. He had sown about three hundred acres of poppyseeds in the spring, he told Trofimov, and made a clear profit of forty thousand. 'When my poppies were in bloom', he added, as though justifying Trofimov's words about his being an artist at heart, 'what a wonderful picture they made!' But Trofimov refused to accept any money from him in spite of his profit of forty thousand and in spite of his plea not to turn up his nose at his offer of a loan, for he was a peasant and did not stand on ceremony.

TROFIMOV. Your father was a peasant, my father was a pharmacist, all of which proves exactly nothing. (LOPAKHIN takes out his wallet.) Put it back! Put it back! If you offered me two hundred thousand I wouldn't accept it. I'm a free man. Everything you prize so highly, everything that means so much to all of you – rich and poor – has no more power over me than a bit of fluff blown about in the air. I can manage, thank you. I can pass you by. I'm strong and proud. [So far he had expressed the view of our 'modern *avant-garde* thinkers' perfectly, but he was no 'drop-out' or whatever the followers of the latest trends call themselves, for he had an aim in life.] Mankind is marching towards the highest truths, towards the greatest happiness possible on earth, and I'm in the front rank!

LOPAKHIN. Will you get there?

TROFIMOV. I will. (*Pause.*) I will get there or show others the way to get there.

Lopakhin could not help being impressed by Trofimov's determination to 'get there', and he confessed ruefully that it was only when he worked long and without stopping that he seemed to think that he, too, knew what he lived for. But 'how many people in Russia exist for goodness only knows what?'

His question remained unanswered, for at that moment Anya appeared in the doorway with a message from her mother to stop the cutting down of the cherry trees until she had gone. It was a bad oversight on the part of Lopakhin and he did not want Trofimov to be reminded of his lack of tact.

LOPAKHIN. I'll see to it at once, at once!...

The most comic incident in the fourth act concerns the way in which the aged Firs was left locked up in the deserted house by the people who cared greatly for one of their most loyal servants. Lyubov was first made aware of Firs's condition in the third act. 'You look awful', she had said to him. 'Are you ill? You'd better go to bed.' But as Firs pointed out, he was the only man capable of looking after things in the whole house. When Lyubov asked him where he would like to go if they had to leave, he replied that he would go wherever she told him to. It was decided that Firs should be sent to hospital. When Anya asked Yasha whether Firs had been sent off to the hospital, Yasha replied that he thought he had because he mentioned it to one of the servants.

ANYA (*to* YEPIKHODOV). Please find out whether Firs has been taken to the hospital.

YASHA (*offended*). I told Yegor this morning. I haven't got to tell him a dozen times, have I?

YEPIKHODOV [accepting Yasha's explanation, but thinking it necessary to add a philosophic *aperçu* of the Great Leveller]. Old man Firs, if you want my final opinion, is beyond repair, and it's high time he was gathered to his fathers. So far as I'm concerned, I can only envy him. (*Puts a suitcase on a hatbox and squashes it.*) There, you see? I knew it.

YASHA (*sneeringly*). Twenty-two calamities!

VARYA (*from behind the door*). Has Firs been taken to the hospital?

ANYA. He has.

VARYA. Why then didn't they take the letter for the doctor?

ANYA. We'd better send it on after him. (*Goes out.*)

And there the matter rested, nobody bothering to go and look for Firs in his room, where he was all the time.

The question of Firs cropped up again shortly before they all left the house. Lyubov said she was worried about Firs because he looked so ill, but Anya reassured her: 'Firs was taken to hospital this morning', she said. 'Yasha sent him off.' But Yasha had only said that he thought that Firs had been sent off to the hospital because he had told someone to see to it. It must have been the dead silence in the locked-up house that alarmed Firs and made him leave his room at the end of the play.

When Lyubov appeared again (after the brief scene between Dunyasha and Yasha, which put an end to the farcical love triangle in the play), she showed no signs of her emotional upset when taking leave of the peasants. She seemed reconciled to the fact that by the next spring nothing would be left of it. Kissing Anya 'warmly', she remarked on how radiant she looked. 'Your eyes sparkle like diamonds', she said. 'Are you happy? Very happy?'

ANYA. Oh yes, very! A new life is beginning, Mother!

GAYEV (*gaily*). Indeed, everything is all right now. We were all so worried and upset before the sale of the cherry orchard, but afterwards, when everything had been finally and irrevocably settled, we all calmed down and even cheered up. I'm a bank official now, a financier. . . . Pot the red in the middle . . . and you, Lyuba, say what you like, are looking a lot better. No doubt about it.

LYUBOV. Yes, my nerves are much better, that's quite true. (*Someone helps her on with her hat and coat.*) I sleep well. Take my things out, Yasha. It's time. (*To* ANYA.) We'll soon be seeing each other again, darling. I'm going to Paris. I shall live there on the money your great-aunt sent to buy the estate – three cheers for Auntie! – though I don't expect the money will last long.

It wouldn't indeed. But what is so remarkable is that neither Lyubov nor anyone else mentioned the fact that their great-aunt had sent the money to buy the estate for Anya. The money was, therefore, Anya's, whom her mother was leaving behind without a penny and without even wondering how Anya was going to manage while she was wasting her daughter's money on her lover in Paris. Anya herself did not seem to worry about how she was going to live after her mother's departure. Nothing is so touching as her lack of experience of life, which Chekhov stressed so much in analysing her character in his letters and which comes out so clearly in her reply to her mother.

ANYA. You'll come back soon, Mother, very soon. Won't you? I'm going to get on with my studies, pass my school exams and after that I'll work and help you. We shall read all sorts of books together, won't we, Mother? (*Kisses her mother's hands.*) We shall read them during the autumn evenings, we'll read lots and lots of books, and a new wonderful world will open up to us. Oh, do come back, Mother!

The entry of Lopakhin and Charlotta, who, after performing one of her conjuring tricks, asked the new owner of the estate to obtain for her a job as governess with another country family, brought a breath of reality into Anya's world of dreams. Pishchik, the 'nine-days'-wonder', as Lopakhin greeted him, next surprised everybody by repaying part of his debts and more especially by his 'most extraordinary' story of some Englishmen who had discovered a kind of 'white clay' on his land and had offered him money for a twenty-four years' lease of it. He soon 'galloped off' to surprise his other creditors with the good news, but not before reflecting sadly, as he surveyed the preparations for their departure, that everything in the world must come to an end.

'When you hear that my end has come', he declared, kissing Lyubov's hand, 'remember the old horse and say, "Once upon a time there lived a man called Simeonov-Pishchik, God rest his soul. . . ."'

Admirable weather we've been having. . . . Yes. (*Goes out in great embarrassment, but immediately comes back and stands in the doorway.*) My Dáshenka sends her regards.' (*Goes out.*)

Before leaving, Lyubov had two things to settle: one of them, concerning Firs, had already been 'settled' for her, while the other, concerning Varya, she begged Lopakhin to settle. Lopakhin admitted that the relationship between Varya and himself was 'rather odd', but said that he was not averse from proposing to her, adding the rather unhopeful admission that but for Lyubov he would never have proposed to her. Lyubov, for her part, also made the distinction between their feelings for one another: Varya loved him, but he only liked her. One is left wondering whether, having let Lyubov down by dispossessing her, he was not trying to put things right by agreeing to propose to her adopted daughter. There was, in fact, a rather deceptive air about the way he responded to Lyubov's assumption that it shouldn't take more than a minute 'to settle it at once'.

LYUBOV (*excitedly*). Fine. We'll go out. Yasha, *allez*! I'll call her. (*Through the door.*) Varya, leave what you're doing and come here for a moment. (*Goes out with* YASHA.)

Lyubov's excitement and, in fact, the whole thing was not right somehow. Lopakhin as well as Varya realised it only too well.

LOPAKHIN (*glancing at his watch*). Aye. . . .

Pause. Behind the door there was suppressed laughter and whispering. Enter VARYA.

Varya was, of course, waiting for Lopakhin to propose to her or at least say something, but he remained silent, for *a long time* while Varya was pretending to be examining the luggage.

VARYA. Funny, can't find it.

At last the cue came for Lopakhin to say something.

LOPAKHIN. What are you looking for?
VARYA [realising now that the proposal would never come]. Packed it myself and can't remember.

Another longish pause during which no progress at all was made, Varya stupidly unable to bring herself to jog Lopakhin on, rendered dumb, perhaps, by the 'seriousness' of the situation. But by this time Lopakhin had made up his mind to go back on his promise to Lyubov.

LOPAKHIN. Where are you going now, Varvara Mikhailovna? [Addressing her formally by her name and patronymic.]

VARYA [brought out of her stupor and realising that it was all over]. Me? To the Ragulins'. I've agreed to look after their house. To be their housekeeper, I suppose.

LOPAKHIN. In Yashevo, isn't it? About fifty miles from here. (*Pause.*) [It *was* all over.] So life's come to an end in this house.

VARYA (*examining the luggage*). Where can it be? Must have put it in the trunk. [Was she really looking for anything?] Yes, life has come to an end in this house. It will never come back.

LOPAKHIN. I'm off to Kharkov now . . . by the same train. Lots to see to there. I'm leaving Yepikhodov here to keep an eye on things. I've given him the job.

VARYA [completely indifferent now to whatever he might be doing]. Have you?

LOPAKHIN. This time last year it was snowing, you remember. Today it's calm and sunny. A bit cold though. Three degrees of frost.

VARYA. I haven't looked. (*Pause.*) Anyway, our thermometer is broken. (*Pause.*)

A voice from outside through the door: 'Mr Lopakhin!'

LOPAKHIN (*as though he had long been waiting for that call*). Coming! (*Goes out quickly.*)

VARYA, *sits down on the floor, lays her head on a bundle of clothes and sobs quietly. The door opens and* LYUBOV *comes in cautiously.*

LYUBOV. Well? [It doesn't take her long to grasp the situation and realise that she has failed again.] We must go.

VARYA (*no longer crying, dries her eyes*). Yes, it's time, Mother dear. I'd like to get to the Ragulins' today. I only hope we don't miss the train.

Not a word about what happened between her and Lopakhin.

In the sudden spurt of activity, prior to their departure, only Gayev paused to discourse upon 'the feelings which now pervade my whole being', but he is shut up by his two nieces and left 'dejectedly' to pop his imaginary billiard ball into an imaginary pocket.

They all go out at last, leaving only Gayev and Lyubov behind. 'They seem to have been waiting for this moment', Chekhov's stage direction states. 'They fling their arms around each other, sobbing quietly, restraining themselves, as though afraid of being overheard.'

This stage direction fully expresses Chekhov's intention not to make this scene a scene in a tragedy. In the following brief dialogue Chekhov again makes it clear that it is not a duologue between Lyubov and Gayev, both feeling quite naturally sad at parting for good from their ancestral home, but a quartet of voices, two sad as they bid a farewell to their past, and two happy and excited as they welcome their bright future.

GAYEV (*in despair*). My sister! My sister!

LYUBOV [much more self-possessed]. Oh, my dear, my sweet, my beautiful orchard! My life, my youth, my happiness . . . Goodbye!

ANYA (*off stage, gaily, appealingly*). Mo-ther!

TROFIMOV (*off stage, gaily, excitedly*). Where are you?

LYUBOV. One last look at the windows and the walls. Mother loved to walk in this room.

GAYEV. My sister! My sister!

ANYA (*off stage*). Mo-ther!

TROFIMOV (*off stage*). Where are you?

LYUBOV [in a very matter-of-fact voice]. We're coming. (*They go out.*)

The happy, excited voices of Anya and Trofimov, heralding the coming of a new life, give no indication of what this new life will be like, but then it is their faith in a better life that matters.

The last scene of *The Cherry Orchard* consists almost entirely of sound effects which, singly and in unison, seem to take leave of the old world. This is Chekhov's stage direction:

The stage is empty. All one hears are the sounds of doors being locked and of carriages being driven off. It grows quiet. The silence is presently broken by the dull thuds of an axe on a tree, sounding sad and forlorn. Then approaching footsteps are heard. From the door on the right FIRS *appears. He is dressed as always in a jacket and a white waistcoat. He is wearing slippers. He looks ill.*

FIRS (*walking up to the door, tries the handle*). Locked. They've gone. (*Sits down on the sofa.*) Forgot all about me. Never mind. Let me sit here for a bit. Forgotten to put on his fur coat, has the young master. Gone off in his light overcoat. (*Sighs anxiously.*) I should have seen to it. . . . Oh, these youngsters. . . . (*Mutters something unintelligible.*) My life's gone just as if I'd never lived. (*Lies down.*) Let me lie down a bit. Got no strength left. Nothing left. Nothing. Oh, you—nincompoop! (*Lies motionless.*)

[At last realisation comes: it was he who was the nincompoop!]

Chekhov did not write: 'Dies', but 'Lies motionless', which, considering the usual practice of dramatists to state dramatically that one of their characters is dead, clearly shows that Chekhov did not want to kill Firs off on the stage: in none of Chekhov's indirect action plays does a character die on the stage (Konstantin shoots himself and Tusenbach is shot off stage). In a comedy like *The Cherry Orchard* Chekhov would hardly have wanted his audience to believe that Firs was dead before the fall of the final curtain. He still had a few more sound effects left and he did not want his audience to be distracted before their import – the passing of the old order – is fully understood, leaving it to them to decide whether Firs had died or whether, after his rest, he succeeded in attracting the attention of the tree-fellers in the orchard and was taken off to the hospital.

Indeed, the last two sound effects of the play have nothing whatever to do with Firs: so far as the old butler was concerned, the comedy was finished. Chekhov's last stage direction makes that quite clear: 'A distant sound is heard which seems to come from the sky, the sound of the snapping of a violin string, slowly dying away, melancholy. Silence falls, broken only by the sound of an axe striking a tree in the orchard far away.'

The first sound is a repetition of the sound that sent a shiver down Lyubov's back in the second act: a threnody for a world that is dead.

Every conscientious director of *The Cherry Orchard* will keep in mind the pace of the fourth act as Chekhov intended it. Chekhov made it quite clear that he wanted the fourth act to last twelve minutes 'at most'. Indeed, unless the action is kept at a lively speed the audience will not be able to anticipate and relish every new comic turn it takes and justice will not be done to the 'gay and lighthearted' comedy Chekhov insisted he had written.

INDEX

GEORGE ALLEN & UNWIN LTD

Head Office:
40 Museum Street, London, W.C.1
Telephone: 01–405 8577

Sales, Distribution and Accounts Departments
Park Lane, Hemel Hempstead, Herts.
Telephone: 0442 3244

Athens: 7 Stadiou Street, Athens 125
Barbados: Rockley New Road, St. Lawrence 4
Bombay: 103/5 Fort Street, Bombay
Calcutta: 285J Bepin Behari Ganguli Street, Calcutta 12
Dacca: Alico Building, 18 Montijheel, Dacca 2
Hornsby, N.S.W.: Cnr. Bridge Road and Jersey Street, 2077
Ibadan: P.O. Box 62
Johannesburg: P.O. 23134, Joubert Park
Karachi: Karachi Chambers, McLeod Road, Karachi 2
Lahore: 22 Falettis' Hotel, Egerton Road
Madras: 2/18 Mount Road, Madras 2
Manila: P.O. Box 157, Quezon City, D–502
Mexico: Serapio Rendon 125, Mexico 4, D.F.
Nairobi: P.O. Box 30583
New Delhi 4/21–22B Asaf Ali Road, New Delhi 1
Ontario: 2330 Midland Avenue, Agincourt
Singapore: 248c–9 Orchard Road, Singapore 9
Tokyo: C.P.O. Box 1728, Tokyo 100–91
Wellington: P.O. Box 1467, Wellington, New Zealand